Hollywood's Wartime Woman
Representation and Ideology

Studies in Cinema, No. 42

Diane M. Kirkpatrick, Series Editor

Professor, History of Art
The University of Michigan

Other Titles in This Series

Hollywood's Wartime Woman
Representation and Ideology

by
Michael Renov

U·M·I Research Press

Ann Arbor / London

Produced and distributed by
UMI Research Press
an imprint of
University Microfilms Inc.
Ann Arbor, Michigan 48106

Library of Congress Cataloging in Publication Data

Renov, Michael, 1950–
Hollywood wartime women.

(Studies in cinema ; no. 42)
Bibliography: p.
Includes index.
1. World War, 1939–1945—Motion pictures and the
war. 2. Women in motion pictures. 3. Moving- M o t o n
pictures—United States—History. 4. Women—
United States. I. Title. II. Series.
D743.23.R46   1988   791.43 '09 '09358   87-25546
ISBN 0-8357-1813-1 (alk. paper)

British Library CIP data is available.

For Cathy

Contents

Acknowledgments

I wish to thank Stephen Mamber for his support and sponsorship during the research and writing of this book. Further thanks are due Joseph Riddel, whose critical and editorial skills were much appreciated, and Alexander Saxton, who shared a variety of historical insights and offered invaluable suggestions. And, finally, much appreciation to Diane Kirkpatrick, whose intelligent reading of the manuscript helped to sharpen the work considerably.

To my parents, Max and Cecily Renov, a special vote of thanks for a lifetime of love and understanding. I dedicate this book to Cathy Friedman whose presence in my life has made everything possible and every day a joy.

Introduction

The eldest of three daughters is instructed by her father on the running of the family estate in his absence, with the brief explanatory remark—"You're my son." The father never returns; the girl grows up to become a mannishly dressed Barbara Stanwyck, whose vast fortune and power conflict with her desire for motherhood. A high-kicking chorus line in abbreviated satin overalls energetically dances around the body of an airplane being assembled in a factory while singing, "Overtime/That's why I'm/Doing it free/Baby's with me on the swing shift jamboree." A young woman announces her pregnancy to her dashing pilot husband who is preparing to leave on a secret bombing mission. He praises her bravery and quiet resolve before heading off to bomb Tokyo; her reply: "It's a job every girl takes on once, or maybe twice, in her life." These three dramatic situations from Hollywood films of the early forties (*The Gay Sisters,* 1942; *Star Spangled Rhythm,* 1942; *Thirty Seconds over Tokyo,* 1944) share a significant problem for the study of classical Hollywood cinema or, in fact, for any instances of popular culture. That problem revolves around the retrieval of meaning for an historical text produced in a specific cultural context whose nuances remain, for the most part, unavailable to subsequent audiences. In the following pages, I shall offer a basis for a more complete understanding of a group of American films from the World War II years, and suggest an amplified field of meaning for each of the preceding dramatic moments. To state the problem in slightly altered terms, the intent of this study is to examine the issues in the charting of historical determinancy for Hollywood films, answering the question "In what ways can a piece of popular culture be said to respond to—to shape and be shaped by —its historical moment?"

This study takes as its object of textual inquiry a body of Hollywood films from the World War II years which evidence significant interest in the representation of women. This choice of film texts results from my assessment of the degree of discontinuity achieved at this moment with regard to the manner and intensity of public address to women. By public address, I mean the communicational efforts of government appeal, advertising imagery and various forms of popular culture, ranging from the entertainment-centered to the stridently persuasive in tone and intent. It has been my purpose to examine the character of female representation within American studio production of the war years through a contingent analysis of the flux of historical conditions and of the ideological currents circulating around the notion of America's wartime woman. By examining a relatively limited historical moment (1942–43) and an even more defined stratum of popular culture within that period (female representation within Hollywood films), I shall attempt to distinguish the general patterns or tendencies of determination of context to text.

In addition, I have undertaken a further refinement of the levels of determination, historical and ideological. I examine three regions of history in an ascending order of specificity: first, a general historical survey of the period; second, a closer look at the patterns of life and work among American women; and, finally, a brief examination of the position of the wartime film industry. A section on ideology follows, offering an analysis of the mediations which intervene between social forces and flesh-and-blood people. For if the historical sections emphasize events in themselves, the ideological section looks at the relationship of events to the gridwork of social hierarchies, vested power interests and popular opinion. If, as is claimed here, ideological inquiry requires a concern for the systematic construction and deconstruction of ideas in a social formation, it is absolutely vital that major currents of belief and the systems of control over belief be examined alongside the contours of history. As a vital and historically explicit adjunct to the analysis of wartime ideological currents, a brief examination of propaganda—its defining character and its major manifestations in the wartime context—is included.

At last, I return to the films themselves. As to the explication of the complex levels of social mediation, I have constructed a series of nine categories clustered into three large groupings. The chapters containing these groupings examine a particular set of critical paradigms that have become the filter through which female representation in cinema has come to be viewed. Chapter 5 ("Unfree Agency: Women in Ideology") considers the broadest issues of ideological determination, examining several of the most frequently invoked roles available for women as cultural objects—as martyr, inspirational source, helper or stabilizer of the family. Chapter 6, "Subjectivity at a Distance," focuses upon a more film-specific discourse, namely the discussions of the limits (if not the outright impossibility) of female subjectivity as represented within Hollywood cinema. This chapter offers material support to theories regarding the fetishization of the female, her positioning within discourse as the epistemological other—always inscrutable— and the intransigence of culpability assigned to the fictive female (most familiar in the *film noir*, but discernible even in the sunniest of genres or periods). The final chapter is even more specific in its examination of the potential for filmic enunciation through the agency of the woman. "Figures in/of Enunciation" diverges from the feminist orthodoxy reinforced in the previous chapters insofar as a degree of authority, accorded to the female at the level of enunciation, is located in several film texts. Halting and provisional though this discursive potency may be, it is judged to be an effect of texts produced during a moment of cultural (as well as economic and political) eccentricity. The claim here is for the necessity of combining the theorizing and analysis of texts (with discursive figures all too frequently posited as the local or cultural manifestations of psychic drives) with study of the properly contextual: the determinants of the historical/ideological domain.

Viewed from a slightly divergent perspective, that of Marxist cultural theory, this book offers a challenge to the assumption of relative autonomy for ideological forms. No issue emerging from the work of Louis Althusser has had a greater impact upon cultural studies in Britain and the United States than his notion that the superstructural levels of politics or art production can be considered as determined by the economic or infrastructural level only in the "last instance." Kevin McDonnell and Kevin Robins, in their lengthy critique of *Screen*'s Althusserian "heresy" ("Marxist Cultural Theory: The Althusserian Smokescreen"), fault the journal for its preference throughout the seventies for a limited definition of cinema's "conditions of existence" such that larger, "external" spheres of politics and economics were subordinated if not excluded in favor of the properly discursive or "internal" domain (filtered through the conjoined regimes of Marxism, psychoanalysis and semiotics). "The question of determination within the social whole becomes a question of epistemology, as social practices are subsumed into discourse. In fact, the problems of the social context and determination of film texts is 'solved' by making it a non-problem."[1]

While there can be absolutely no doubt of the centrality of *Screen*'s role in the emergence of cinema studies as a rigorous academic discipline and intellectual pursuit on both sides of the Atlantic, it is also clear that the emphasis in *Screen* and elsewhere upon a narrowly defined problematic that appeared to bracket determinations outside discourse had significant impact upon the emergence of work that sought to frame its object of study within the larger, explicitly defined social field. That work has been taken up in earnest in the eighties—particularly in television studies—in England and the U.S. (in, among other places, the pages of *Screen*).

This book, begun in the late seventies, is the product of a moment just prior to that resurgence of interest in issues of textual determination defined in broad terms. The fundamental question asked here is, in the end, all but unanswerable: "How do films come to mean, in their social sense?" The answers—preliminary, confined in their efficacy to a particular moment of history—offer themselves as the first fruits of a project that remains a collective, if not a utopian one.

At this point, several methodological limitations of this study must be acknowledged. In theory, I seek to determine the relations of text to context in a quite specific way. One intent of the study has been to minimize the effects of authorship and eccentricity (of studio, of director, of star) by examining a broad range of films (170) from all major and most minor Hollywood studios. As a result, it has proved impossible to offer exhaustive accounts of historical/ideological determinancy for individual texts. Such an enterprise would necessitate close and progressive analyses dependent on shot-by-shot breakdowns, frame enlargements and charts of narrative patterns (the work of microanalysis so well undertaken by the exegesis of cinema-as-discourse discussed above).

The problems which emerged during the course of this work (and in my second reading of it five years later), problems resulting from the richness and contradiction of this or any historical period that defy categorization, have, at various moments, appeared insurmountable. The attempt to trace meaning from cultural framework to individual text is certainly fraught with peril. Yet it is my belief that such work repays the effort by investing texts with a range of social meanings—a field of referentiality—experienced by an audience at the time of the film's production and release. It is my interest in this region of "social meaning" and its effects upon textuality itself which motivates the pages that follow.

Part One

History and Ideology

Introduction to Part One

The historical consciousness on which Western man has prided himself since the beginnings of the nineteenth century may be little more than a theoretical basis for the ideological position from which Western civilization views its relationship . . . to cultures and civilizations preceding it . . . .

Hayden V. White, *Metahistory*

History's object, the hitherto existing, does not exist except in the modality of its current existence, as representations . . . .

The study of history is not only scientifically but also politically valueless. The object of history, the past, no matter how it is conceived, cannot affect present conditions. Historical events do not exist and can have no material effectivity in the present . . . .

Barry Hindess and Paul Q. Hirst,
Pre-Capitalist Modes of Production

Film historiography is the site of a battle being waged over the very premise of its enterprise—the writing of history. Historians outside of film have long been aware of the irreconcilable subjectivism attached to the study and narration of past events. E. H. Carr, in *What Is History?*, presages the positions of White and Hindess and Hirst: "the facts of history never come to us 'pure', since they do not and cannot exist in a pure form: they are always refracted through the mind of the recorder."[1] Others working in related fields go even further, notably Jacques Derrida, who writes of the "alterity of the sign," the unattainable otherness of the language trace which we choose to seize upon as constitutive of an absent referent. If all of signification depends upon a shared belief in the "reality" of the signifier, historical discourse is doubly suspect in that it assumes "knowledge" of objects, events and social forces through a reconstruction dependent upon the chronicles and observations of others. The most empirical data base is as surely a representation and the product of human labor as a personal diary.

Louis Althusser appears to posit an alternative to the ideological taint of historical discourse through his notion of science, which constitutes a category apart from the super-structural practices (the political, the ideological), or the economic, which in the famous last instance is determinate.[2] For scientific practice (and historical materialism is, for Althusser, *the* human science) exists outside the realm of ideology in that its proofs are generated through a self-contained production of knowledge, impervious to social relations or experiential variance. Unlike ideology, in which class interests and values deform the content of whatever "knowledge" may be produced, science has a rigorously theoretical function and can only be produced by an epistemological break with ideology. (The "Young Marx," pre-1845, is on the idealist side of the epistemological break which founded Marxist science, according to Althusser.) This formulation of science has been widely critiqued, termed in one notable instance "the final idealism,"[3] while Althusser himself has published an extensive body of auto-criticism which modifies certain theoretical positions (e.g. the science/ideology dichotomy) without altogether clarifying his shifting definition and application of terms (like science and ideology) from *For Marx* (1965) to *Reading Capital* (1970) and *Lenin and Philosophy* (1971).[4]

A problem central to the historical enterprise is thus raised by Althusser but not, by any means, satisfactorily settled—that problem being the relationship between the theoretical or logical order (advanced by science) and the "real" order. In an essay entitled "Althusser's Theory of Ideology," Gregor McLennan, Victor Molina and Roy Peters discuss Althusser's critique of empiricism/idealism in which he defines the terms as merely inverse formulations of the same theoretical humanism which (mis)places the subject as the central category of analysis.[5] Science, for Althusser, necessitates the recognition of difference between the logical order produced through science and the "real" order, which the authors describe as "natural and historical, or social."[6] Yet the question of access to the social or historical "real" by way of historical materialism is by no means an untroubled one.

Historical materialism is the science of the history of social formations. As a science it is a part of the theoretical order that can only be ascertained by its internal coherence, not through a correspondence with "reality" via the vagaries of subjectivity. To collapse the distinction—to bridge the gap between concept and reality—is to fall prey to the "empiricist temptation."[7] The result of this theorization is that historical knowledge as such is not verifiable through recourse to the "real" order. Even through the agency of science, which is itself a questionable category, there is no possibility of guaranteeing historical discourse as an accurate account of events through any process of verification or overlay of the historical with the "real". Yet without science, all is ideology, a realm founded in misrecognition.[8] For the historical materialist, the distinction between ideological discourse and the products of historical materialist practice is vital; the latter category presumes a "knowledge effect" based on the consistent application of dialectical method.

But no matter whether the system is termed scientific or ideological, historical discourse exists apart from the "real" and that separation can never be bridged.

Deprived of the safe retreat of science or of verifiable congruence with "reality," where next can the historian or analyst of social phenomena go? Barry Hindess and Paul Hirst suggest the disavowal of all such analyses as politically unsound. In the present enterprise, a variety of historically derived material (government policy, conditions of production in Hollywood, economic and demographic data, contemporary social attitudes and styles of popular imagery) will be examined and presented as constitutive elements of an historical moment within which a group of films were produced. Moreover, these film texts are, in varying degrees, overdetermined—by that I mean that they contain partially assimilated, often contradictory, material formed within the ideological currents of the time whose meaning cannot be derived through a univocal or linear reading. A contextualist strategy of analysis, rather than reconstructing a synthetic totality from the disparate elements contained within the historical period under study, expands the potential for the analysis of texts by exposing more fully the "problematic" of the text—the system of questions raised by a work, some posed, others "buried but active."[9]

The film texts, as products of ideology, are thus placed within a framework of coextensive social phenomena. Despite the problems and inconsistencies in Althusser's theoretical work, his interest in the process by which meaning can be attributed to complex products of ideology has influenced a generation of cultural critics. The critical impulse to look elsewhere, to go outside and beyond the work in order to understand it, has been encouraged by such statements as: "The meaning of . . . a particular ideology . . . depends not on its relation to a *truth* other than itself but on its relation to the existing *ideological field* and on the *social problems and social structure* which sustain the ideology and are reflected in it."[10]

Hindess and Hirst would have the Marxist critic disregard historical research altogether in order to focus on the present situation, for the pastness of prior events precludes their effectivity. History is about things past which do not exist and can have no valid claim to a "real" status. Yet, as Edward Buscombe points out in his Introduction to the "Metahistory of Film" section of *Film Reader 4,* the current situation is itself always already past owing to the nature of cognition and language. The "present" is itself a convenient fiction. The Hindess and Hirst position is a retreat from history as well as political practice since it avoids the most fundamental challenge to anyone seeking to transform the world, which is first to comprehend it.[11] To deny history access to "real knowledge" on philosophical grounds, thus rejecting further efforts of analysis is to retreat from the struggle to consciousness, a struggle which requires the positioning of oneself within a process both social and historical and which is itself a political act.

If one accepts the premise that ideological products are only comprehensible when situated within a broader ideological field and a social structure, where then does the film historian begin? A concept particularly useful for the framing of cinema within a comprehensive socio-historical matrix is that of the "institution" of cinema as developed by a variety of critics.[12] John Ellis finds that as the cinematic institution exercises a "not inconsiderable social role," it occupies an historically variable space within the social formation. This space is defined both by the "conditions of existence" of cinema and by its place in relation to other institutions of representation. The utility of Ellis's schematizing lies in the stabilizing of categories within a given social structure through a kind of social topography that fixes the key locations of ideological production.

Ellis's "conditions of existence" are defined as "those practices that are presupposed in every action of cinematic representation, right from the very first."[13] These conditions of existence, comprised of the ideological, the economic, the political and the technological, enable but do not predetermine cultural production. Any examination of a cross-section of film history, such as the World War II years, must take note of the concrete conditions and transformative shifts in each of these conditions. As a corollary, the relationship of cinema to other apparatuses of representation (e.g. journalism, the visual arts, the advertising industry) must be examined, for together these forms constitute the overlapping currents of public imagery.

At no time could an argument be successfully mounted in favor of a restrictive definition of "conditions of existence" that examined, for example, the economic and political conditions of the film industry to the exclusion of the larger pattern of social forces surrounding it. Particularly during the World War II years, the pervasive tendency toward mobilization and consolidation demands that any single industry be viewed within a broad and comprehensive context that recognizes the phenomenon of centralization—its sources and its consequences. Such a strategy requires that the broad features of American life in a wide range of manifestations (political, economic, social, cultural) be examined in order that, eventually, the specificity of film culture can be addressed.

There is also the troublesome question of separating the historical context from the ideological, particularly since the history of this period of American culture is precisely a history of ideological warfare waged at an unprecedented level of intensity. Nevertheless, it is useful to develop a sense of the general historical framework as a generative structure within which ideology and its more overt cousin propaganda were produced. Consequently, a chapter on ideology as a crucial category of production follows the historical chapters.

The historical discussion is presented in three parts, each of which progressively leads toward a comprehension of the wartime films foregrounding women. The first chapter examines the political, social and economic conditions that prevailed during World War II, tracing the fundamental currents of social life as experienced by American on the homefront alongside the headline events of politics and diplomacy which were determining the fate of nations. It is worth noting that the comprehension of films cannot be accomplished through analysis of textual operations residing entirely within the film texts. Meaning is instead an effect determined through an interaction of text and viewing subjects, and while that historical subject and that concrete viewing situation may not be recoverable, the reconstruction of meaning is advanced by an understanding of the social frame within which the film was produced and received. The World War II period was an unusually well-articulated historical moment which was universally represented as crisis, a special time, the "duration"—all the more reason for analyzing one type of cultural product within the context which produced contemporary popular consciousness.

The second chapter examines the lives of women during World War II in greater detail, with special regard for their treatment by government, industry and the mass media. A study of the shifting demographic profile of the American woman is coupled with a sense of the altered circumstances in the family, the workplace and in the self-image of women. This level of historical analysis is essential to understanding Hollywood's treatment of women when it is recalled that the American film industry has always maintained a component of contemporaneity with regard to subject matter, particularly during the first two years of World War II, and that the film audience was for the first time perceived by the industry as significantly female. While the altered percentage of women filmgoers may not provide absolute proof of studio interest in films tailored to that audience, this section offers evidence that the emergent, wage-earning female was a key ingredient in wartime advertising, official propaganda and wartime culture in general.

The third and last specifically historical chapter takes a closer look at the altered circumstances of the film community itself. At a time when every element of social life was affected by rapid changes, Hollywood was experiencing a loss of personnel and of foreign markets, an altered relationship to government and a tightening of its belt as a result of rationing and shortages of essential materials. In this chapter the most specific conditions of existence of the industry are subjected to close scrutiny, along with the response to the crisis of war. While there will be no attempt to examine each studio in great detail, an account of the salient features and characteristics of wartime Hollywood provides further insight into the range of historical determinations decipherable in the films of the period. This approach to history, then, attempts a kind of fine-tuning, moving from the general to the specific, from the social and cultural ambiance to the more specific conditions of the American woman, and finally to the state of the wartime film industry.

1

The Early Forties in Review

Prewar America

In 1939, the United States of America was still in the throes of the Great Depression. Much of the rest of the world was at arms by September 1 of that year when Hitler marched into Poland. That was in Europe. But in America, a mere 2 percent of the gross national product (GNP) was being spent in armaments. The Neutrality Acts, inaugurated by a staunchly isolationist Congress in 1935 to prevent involvement in the growing crisis of world affairs, were altered at President Roosevelt's request in November of 1939 to allow Great Britain and France to purchase arms—on a "cash and carry" basis only.[1] It was a cautious and businesslike Congress that enacted the Selective Service Act in 1940, demanding registration of men ages 21–36, with the number in training, as selected by lottery, never to exceed 900,000, each to serve a maximum of one year.[2] The act further prohibited deployment of these selectees beyond American borders.

On June 15, 1940, the United States formally refused France's appeal for assistance; the French capitulated exactly one week later. By mid-summer 1940, extensive German air raids had begun over England with a great deal of damage and loss of life sustained in civilian population centers, especially London. The British maintained air supremacy over their island by the slightest of margins. Elsewhere, the British had captured Abyssinia from the Italians, but by the end of March, 1941, Rommel had swept them back into Egypt. The Japanese had begun their invasion of Indochina in July of 1941, while in June of that year the Germans had entered into the fateful decision to invade the USSR, smashing the Soviet Non-Aggression Pact of August, 1939.

The American political scene was a divided one with a vocal faction supportive of the Allied cause as far back as the Spanish Civil War. The mood of Congress was one of considerable disgruntlement in the wake of eight New Deal years, the outspoken Isolationists being headed by Hamilton Fish in the House of Representatives and Gerald P. Nye in the Senate. Senator Nye of North Dakota was incensed by those who were leading America to the brink of war, chief among them, in his opinion, the leaders of the film industry. Just four months before

Pearl Harbor, Nye broadcast to the nation his conviction "that these movie companies have been operating as war propaganda machines almost as if they were being directed from a single central bureau."[3] Nye's opinions were echoed by a variety of public figures, including Charles Lindbergh, and received the wholehearted support of major newspapers like the *Chicago Tribune.*

Most Americans were undecided, torn between moral conviction and an unwillingness to enter what could only be a lengthy and bloody war. In the words of E. B. White, "The years between Munich and Pearl Harbor were like the time you put in in a doctor's waiting room, years of fumbling with old magazines and unconfirmed suspicions, the ante years, the time of the moist palm and the irresolution."[4] President Roosevelt continued to chip away at congressional reluctance and public indecision through the establishment of a series of agencies which were to evolve into the full-fledged wartime bureaus that dominated Washington. Organized in January 1941, the Office of Production Management (later to dissolve into the War Production Board) was a prototype of the war agency with its co-directors, union leader Sidney Hillman and industrialist William Knudsen, representing the coalition of interests that supported government efforts throughout the war. Agencies such as the Office of Production Management, the Office of Price Administration and Civilian Supply, and others were created under existing laws so that congressional approval was not required.[5]

But the gearing-up for war and the concomitant economic effects awaited Pearl Harbor. The GNP for 1940 was only half the figure of the full-throttled year 1943, while the percentage of women in the national labor force during 1940 was the same as that of 1910. Still affected by the pervasive restrictions brought on by a decade of unparalleled unemployment, many state legislatures continued to outlaw the hiring of married women who, according to the prevailing ideology, were stealing jobs from men whose natural bread-earning role was giving way to idleness and humiliation. Indeed, the legacy of the thirties was "the invisible scar" of the title of Caroline Bird's excellent study of Depression America. Uncertainty lingered in the reluctant cooperation of business and industry in the earliest mobilization efforts originating from Washington. Ironically, it was the corporate and very Republican titans of industry, perhaps the most outspoken opponents of the New Deal and its social reforms, who were now being called on to organize the massive agencies which could mobilize and consolidate the war effort in those first critical months of war.

Mobilization and Consolidation

> *Modern war was not man against man—if it had ever been. It was machine against machine. It was industry against industry. And we had the best machine. Our industry was better than their*

industry. But men had to die or be maimed to prove it. Men had
to die at the wheels or triggers of the machines.
                    James Jones, *WWII: A Chronicle of Soldiering*

The single most important word in America for three and a half years was "production" for it was the key to "victory," "peacetime," and "the return of the
boys." Never had a national economy undergone such a monumental transformation in such a short time. There is no possibility of grasping the shift of social
attitudes or public imagery without first coming to grips with the metamorphosis
of war mobilization. Economic stagnation rapidly gave way to violent expansion
fueled largely by government expenditures for armaments and related war materiel.
By 1943, a full 60 percent of the GNP was constituted by government purchase
of war goods and services. The number of Americans directly employed by
government had risen from one million to four million by 1945.[6]

Mass production in America was historically linked to warfare. It was the
War of 1812 that provided the impetus for Eli Whitney's engineering of large-
scale musket production which ushered in the era of parts standardization and,
in turn, made possible the utilization of unskilled and semi-skilled labor.[7] One
hundred forty years later, American industry was able to plug in unskilled workers,
often women with no previous factory experience, and provide minimal training
so that in a matter of months the national economy, only recently operating at
half-speed, reached 100 percent productivity. A range of altered economic conditions accompanied lightning mobilization: wage ceilings, price controls, rationing, inflation, high taxes and ceaseless war bond drives to soak up excess purchasing power and curb the inflationary spiral. All of these by-products and
regulatory measures were attributable to actions issued from Washington, the seat
of power, the site of undiminishing activity for the duration.

A brand of unabashed corporatism prevailed in America. While the "miracle
of production" was attested to by the changing tide of war in the Pacific by
mid-1942, thanks to the ever-more productive industrial complex (for example,
cargo ships by 1944 were being built in seventeen days, while the man-hours
required to build a bomber were reduced from 200,000 to 13,000), the little man
was taking it on the chin. In these years of expansion, more than half a million
small businesses failed, while the top ten corporations received 30 percent of total
federal funds (the top one hundred received 75 percent).[8] The idea was that, with
the stakes so high, it made the best sense to entrust major contracts to the largest,
most experienced corporations. Firms scrambled for these contracts because of
the favorable conditions attached to them which virtually insured profits with no
risk. Payment was based upon cost-plus-a-fixed-fee while low-interest loans and
outright subsidies financed whatever physical conversion was necessary. The
government allowed five-year amortization of war plant improvements and the

firms were promised the opportunity to purchase war production facilities at bargain basement prices after the war.[9] President Roosevelt boasted that the war had created seventeen million new jobs for his threadbare constituents. It had also more than doubled corporate profits after taxes.[10]

Conversion of industrial facilities turned soft drink bottlers into explosives manufacturers, bedspread tycoons into mosquito netting executives and mechanical pencil makers into experts on bomb parts and precision instruments. Activities once considered monopolistic or in restraint of trade were winked at as the anti-trust specialists in the Justice Department were silenced until the outcome of the war was insured. Patent pooling, once outlawed, was common practice, particularly in the dynamic aeronautical industry which expanded tenfold during the war years. Reluctantly, Attorney General Francis Biddle and anti-trust specialist Thurman Arnold deferred to pressures from the newly strengthened government–big business alliance, effectively suspending operations. Not until August of 1944 did President Roosevelt authorize a renewal of litigation and then only against international cartels composed of such giants as Du Pont and I. G. Farben, a German-based firm. While many factions in and out of government objected to the laissez-faire attitude adopted, the results were undeniable. By 1944, United States war production was doubling the combined output of the three Axis powers.

Another effect of all-out industrial productivity was the shift of population from rural to urban centers where relatively high-paying jobs were available. Farm population fell by 17 percent while fewer and fewer farmers generated greater and greater profits (cash income quadrupled from 1940 to 1945).[11] American agribusiness as we know it today was born during this period of rapid mechanization and consolidation. Between five and six million farming Americans headed for the boom towns, among them Detroit, Norfolk, Mobile and San Diego. The state of California registered a population increase of two million; Mobile, Alabama grew by 61 percent. Those that left the land were joined by others who sought better jobs or wished to remain close to husbands and fathers stationed at distant bases. In all, some 15.3 million civilians moved across county lines during the war years, causing a strain upon community services, housing and transportation in the urban centers while contributing to the growing concern about juvenile delinquency and crumbling family values.

Lest it seem that the early forties were a time of singular gains for big business, it must be acknowledged that labor—big labor—strengthened its grip as a key power broker within the state. What's more, statistics indicate that a modest leveling of income occurred (due to higher taxes and increased overtime by war workers) such that the share of national income held by the wealthiest 5 percent fell from 23.7 percent to 16.8 percent.[12] Despite this upbeat figure, one-fourth of the manufacturing work force earned less than sixty cents an hour in 1944. The labor movement made dramatic gains: membership grew from 10.5 million to 14.75 million between 1941 and 1945.[13] Labor's ascendancy was connected to its membership in the wartime coalition forged by Roosevelt. A no-strike pledge was agreed upon in the early weeks of the war guaranteeing top priority to the maintenance of maximum productivity with the understanding that the National War Labor Board, with equal representation from business, labor and the public, would fairly settle any dispute. John L. Lewis was violently opposed to the abandonment of labor's crucial weapon and proved this by calling out the nation's coal miners for a protracted strike in 1943. With coal miners scandalously low paid and underprotected, Lewis was unwilling to abide by the War Labor Board's Little Steel formula which allowed wages to rise only 15 percent over January, 1941, levels. His old foe Roosevelt seriously considered sponsoring legislation to draft strikers.

While the War Labor Board had adopted a "maintenance of membership" policy in the summer of 1942, which authorized a fifteen-day escape period during which a newly-hired worker could resign from the union (thus tacitly endorsing a "closed shop"), a growing backlash against labor was developing in Congress. The Smith-Connally Act evidenced distrust of unions by its provisos: authorization of seizure of strike-bound plants "useful" to the war; mandatory supervision of strike votes; fines and imprisonment for those instigating strikes in war plants; registration of unions; the filing of data on union finances; and the prohibition of union contributions to political parties. This last stipulation was particularly galling to the president, whose veto was promptly overridden. [14]

In spite of the antilabor sentiments in Congress, the earning power of the American working person rose dramatically during the war years, particularly for those employed in vital industries such as munitions, for which a forty-eight hour work week had been decreed. A variety of fringe benefits were achieved through arbitration, many of which were to be effective after the war. Although much was made of the wildcat strikes and protracted grievances that afflicted the mining industry and others, less than one percent of the total working days lost during the war were attributable to strikes or lockouts. [15] Although opinion polls among the military overseas indicated a decided hostility toward the "unpatriotic" worker more concerned with wages than winning the war, labor leaders publicly claimed at war's end that no strike had caused a shortage of materiel on any war front. [16] Many complained of antagonistic coverage of the American labor scene by the media, which encouraged the GI's distrust. The rationale for labor's efforts, these leaders reminded the returning soldier, had been to contribute their wholehearted efforts to maximum production while maintaining their hard-won freedoms and standard of living "so that you might come home to a better country than the one you left." [17]

Most histories of this period speak of the alphabet soup of federal agencies usually headed by "dollar-a-year" men who chose to abandon their executive positions and high salaries in order to help prosecute the business of war. These men were not the New Dealers of the previous Roosevelt years with their zeal for social reforms; the country was now being run by no-nonsense, efficiency-minded businessmen. Rather than attempting to list and describe the vast array of agencies, we will survey here only a number of the most influential bureaus, in order to provide a sense of their structure and operation. The Office of War Information was established in June of 1942 to supplant the Office of Facts and Figures, thus inheriting that office's charge "to disseminate . . . factual information on the defense effort and to facilitate a widespread understanding of the status and progress of that effort." The word propaganda was studiously avoided by the Office of War Information, preferring instead to adopt a "strategy of truth." That strategy was sorely tested during the first year of war, called by historian Allan Nevins "the most discouraging (year) in American memory—as dark as the first year of the Civil War in the North."[18] The province of the OWI was broad, with both domestic and overseas branches. Its chief, Elmer Davis, expressed the guiding principle of the bureau, a principle in constant opposition to the War and Navy Departments, "that the American people have a right to know everything that is known to the enemy. . . . We believe that the better the American people understand what the war is about, the harder they will work and fight to win it. We are not press agents for the government."[19]

The Office of War Information was constantly at war within itself over the appropriate level of promotional appeals. One faction, characterized as "liberal intellectual," had a fundamental belief in the ability of the public to make subtle distinctions and to think clearly and independently. The writing produced by this group was literate and dramatic while the copy issuing from the rival clique dominated by advertising executives was more plainly pitched towards selling the war to Americans. In the spring of 1943, many of the writers resigned, delivering the agency into the hands of the ad men, a circumstance to be addressed at greater length in the discussion of the role of advertising in the shaping of popular wartime culture.

An OWI section particularly relevant to the present purpose was the Bureau of Motion Pictures, which produced short informational films and maintained an official liaison with the film industry in Hollywood. Yet another area within OWI was the Bureau of Intelligence which, for a time, evaluated the content of Hollywood films in order to judge the industry's contribution to an understanding of war issues and to evaluate the images of America projected on the screens of the Allies and the Latin American nations. While the Bureau's activities and observations will be fully considered in the section on ideology, it is important to establish the pervasive and unprecedented power of the state in the private sector at this time. Nevertheless, two factors mitigated against the power of the OWI. First, unlike its World War I counterpart the Committee on Public Information, the OWI had no jurisdiction over censorship. Second, the domestic branch of the agency was decimated by Congress in June of 1943, after only one year of operation; its budget for film production and script evaluation was altogether rescinded. The OWI, in the eyes of the new Congressional majority of Republicans and southern Democrats, was a mouthpiece for the President and was far too concerned with promoting the goals and achievements of the Administration. Congress thus returned the entire field of domestic propaganda to the media and advertisers.

Another key agency was the War Production Board, whose job was to "exercise general responsibility" over the economy, particularly all aspects of production. From its inception in January 1942, the War Production Board clashed with the War and Navy Departments over the appropriate allocation levels for the military and the most desirable allotment strategy for major contracts. The military favored fewer, bigger contracts with major industrialists like Henry Kaiser, architect of the prefabricated cargo vessels called Liberty ships. The head of the WPB, Donald Nelson, a former Sears and Roebuck executive, along with number-two man, Charles E. Wilson, formerly the president of General Electric Company, waged an unceasing battle against the warlords in the Pentagon while attempting to referee the scramble for scarce commodities such as steel, copper and aluminum. Nelson's agency exercised controls of other sorts as well, as evidenced by their edict of March 1942, which forbade the manufacture of men's suits with an extra pair of trousers, a vest, patch pockets or cuffs. The new "victory suit" would be single-breasted with shorter jackets and narrower lapels. The new policy, intended to ease the shortage of wool supplies, had the opposite effect—men rushed to purchase the suits at three times the normal rate.[20]

The female counterparts of the "victory suit" were the fashions legislated in compliance with the general "no fabric over fabric" rule—no pleats, patch pockets or full skirts, with limited use of lace or embroidery. There were only six shoe colors authorized for the duration. Girdles were scarce due to the rubber shortage, but the War Production Board ruled that the cosmetic mainstays—face powder, lipstick, rouge and deodorants—were of crucial importance for civilian morale and their manufacture continued. A WPB spokesman offered the following rationale for allowing free rein to the American woman's cosmetic needs: "Her resultant vivacious spirit, self-confidence and geniality, being infectious, are transmitted directly to the male members of the family."

Freed from competition with continental fashion centers, Hollywood became the unchallenged source of female fashion. With regard to hair styles, an interesting relationship appears to have developed between war sacrifice and the complexity of the coiffure, with Hollywood in the lead. David Chierichetti has noted that, with more money and fewer consumer goods for purchase, American women turned to their beauty parlors for diversion and recreation. The longer the war lasted, the higher, wider and more cleverly padded grew the hairstyles. With elaborate pompadours the established Hollywood fashion, the hairdresser often became the star's best friend. Barbara Stanwyck's hairdresser doubled as her secretary, while Marlene Dietrich's hair stylist invariably took a leave of absence from the studio to follow Dietrich when she was "loaned" elsewhere. Public demand for elaborate hairdos indicated this rise to power of the hairdresser. A key promotional element of any new film was the release of the star's special hairstyle for that role. Olivia de Havilland recalled the emphasis on hair fashion: "After we finished shooting the movie, we'd go to the portrait gallery and spend several days shooting portraits. We would repeat all the hairstyles used in the film, but then my hairdresser and I would have to come up with some others. The more important fan magazines would insist that we give them an exclusive hairdo, dress and background for the cover that no other magazine could have."[21]

During the war years, a woman's hairstyle was a signifier of her social position and an indication of her desire for glamour. In the 1943 MGM release *Slightly Dangerous*, Lana Turner played Peggy Evans, a drugstore clerk from Hotchkiss Falls who goes to New York to start a new life. Having decided to change her name, Evans spends her last hundred dollars at a ritzy Manhattan salon. The clearest contrast in her appearance, before and after, is her hairdo. As Peggy Evans, her hair falls softly around her shoulders in a youthful bob, but the new woman who emerges from the salon has a masterfully up-swept, intricately designed hairstyle that testifies to her changed fortunes. Within a handful of scenes, she becomes Carol Burden, long-lost daughter of an eccentric millionaire, and yet another Hollywood fairy tale comes true.

Chierichetti has called VJ Day the death knell for the pompadour. With women returning to full-time domestic chores and child-rearing in ever-increasing numbers, the extravagant and time-consuming hairdos were no longer practical. Hollywood soon followed suit with shorter, simpler styles. The trend was apotheosized by Orson Welles' public clipping of Rita Hayworth's auburn tresses for her role in *The Lady from Shanghai* in 1947. The wartime pompadour phenomenon suggests several hypotheses. First, the penury of rationed living literally "went to the head" of the American female, with elaborate hairdos a compensation for loneliness and lack of consumer outlet. Second, the relationship between Hollywood and audience is complex and reciprocal, the stars providing the leadership in a mode of fashion that ultimately responds to the patterns of popular consumption. Wartime fashion in Hollywood, particularly hairstyles, became more and more extreme as the average American woman grew less and less able to indulge herself in stylish adornments.

The Office of Price Administration was responsible for the rationing of scarce commodities on the homefront. In April 1942, OPA chief Leon Henderson instituted a program known as General Max (General Maximum Price Regulation) which froze retail prices at their highest level during March, 1942. This was a particularly unpopular measure that encouraged the growth of a black market. Although General Max was abandoned, further wage and price controls were enacted by Congress in October. For the average American in 1942, Henderson's agency was noteworthy for its coordination of ten major rationing programs with coupons distributed for such staple items as meat, shoes and coffee, not to mention gasoline and automobile tires. Roosevelt, ever the canny politician, postponed full-scale rationing until several weeks after the elections of 1942. In January 1943 a ban, later relaxed to a restriction, was levelled on all pleasure driving. Political controversies engulfed the agency to the extent that Henderson pronounced the Office of Price Administration "the special target of every 'producer' pressure group in the country."[23] Henderson, the personal target for much criticism, resigned toward the end of 1942, but not before John Q. Citizen was able to state that "Rockefeller and I can now buy exactly the same amount of sugar, gasoline and tires."

Yet another superagency (one that will receive extensive treatment in the section on women's history) was the War Manpower Commission, whose membership represented the interests of the War Labor Board, the War Production Board and the Selective Service System. Paul V. McNutt, formerly the governor of Indiana, was chosen to head the agency, whose charge was to predict the future manpower needs and to allocate these human resources among the military, war industry, agriculture and other essential civilian industries. McNutt's job was made more difficult by the characteristic lack of power for enforcement of manpower decisions. The President, concerned that morale might suffer under a policy of coercion, preferred the notion of "voluntary cooperation." While McNutt's preference was to draft fathers before men employed in vital industries, Congress ruled otherwise. One senator voiced both his own opposition to the proposal and the general hostility felt for many wartime agencies when he suggested that "slackers in the government bureaus" should be inducted "before American homes are broken up, before children are driven into the streets."[24]

A brief survey of the climate of American politics in 1942 and 1943 indicates a marked conservative backlash and widespread criticism of President Roosevelt, Vice President Henry Wallace (soon to be dumped as vice-presidential running mate) and of the various agency heads. The war news was bad from Corregidor, Bataan and Guadalcanal while word of successes at the Battle of Midway and in North Africa were classified. Thus, the administration's management of the war was vulnerable to the criticism of a shell-shocked public unaccustomed to military defeat.[25] The capitulation of General Wainwright and his force of 11,000 at Corregidor was the first such action since Appomattox. The 1942 elections resulted in a gain of Republican representation in Congress: forty-seven additional seats in the House, ten in the Senate. Given the number of staunchly conservative Democrats from the South and elsewhere, the ten-year old New Deal coalition was at low ebb. The chairman of the Democratic National Committee explained the crisis of public faith as a result of the "politics of resentment"—

resentment of bureaucracy, resentment of the conduct of the war, resentment of the Office of Price Administration, resentment of the labor policy, and resentment towards farmers. By the summer of 1943, Congress had overruled a presidential veto en route to passage of the Smith-Connally Strike Limitation Bill, ravaged the domestic branch of the Office of War Information, abolished the National Youth Administration, lifted the $25,000 net ceiling on salaries favored by Roosevelt, and cut back appropriations to the enforcement division of the Office of Price Administration.[26]

Racism Goes to War

A study of American wartime culture might well begin with an assessment of racial attitudes since all wars generate a surplus of jingoism and xenophobia. The case of World War II, however, is a peculiar one. There was little antipathy evidenced toward German and Italian-Americans who were well assimilated by 1941, though a persistent strain of anti-Semitism remained in evidence during these years. Wartime public opinion studies disclosed that Americans distrusted Jews more than any other European people except Italians.[27] The official refusal to proposals for the ransom of European Jews scheduled for annihilation was described by a strategy summed up in the upbeat phrase "rescue through victory."

The most virulent expressions of racism were aimed at the Japanese-American population. It was the Governor of Idaho who proposed a homegrown "final solution" for these first- and second-generation Americans: "A good solution to the Jap problem would be to send them all back to Japan, then sink the island. They live like rats, breed like rats and act like rats."[28] The official policy was slightly more pragmatic: 110,000 people, two-thirds of whom were American citizens, were forced from their homes and businesses in the three West Coast states and sent to desolate locations far inland. The underlying cause of this mass relocation was profoundly racist in that American officials felt incapable of judging the loyalty of a population living at the very site of what many feared to be an imminent Japanese invasion. Rumors of espionage were common. J. Earl Warren, then the Attorney General of the State of California, expressed the rationale for relocation succinctly: "We believe that when we are dealing with the Caucasian race we have methods that will test the loyalty of them. . . . But when we deal with the Japanese we are in an entirely different field and we cannot form an opinion that we believe to be sound."[29]

Of equal importance was the lack of political power of this group (unlike the German, Italian and Jewish populations) and their employment in fields that were not vital to national defense: four out of ten Japanese-Americans were small farmers, many others were small businessmen or were engaged in service occupations. They were insular, had maintained their language and customs and were highly visible. In addition, there were small but vocal groups, such as the

Native Sons of the Golden West, who had long been anxious to find cause for the elimination of the Japanese population. The small businessmen and agricultural interests of the area stood to gain from the removal of Japanese competition; most Japanese residents were forced to sell their holdings for a fraction of their true market value. While property losses pale in comparison to the deep psychological and emotional harm done to these people, the financial losses suffered have been estimated at $350 million.

The loss of civil rights was profound and widespread as six states passed laws to limit the Japanese-Americans' right to vote, own land or obtain commercial licenses. These measures were intended to dissuade the unwanted from emigrating to Texas, Arkansas, Utah, Wyoming, Arizona or California. *Los Angeles Examiner* columnist Henry McLemore vented his hatred in public: "Herd 'em up, pack 'em off. . . . Let 'em be pinched, hurt, hungry and dead up against it. . . . I hate the Japanese." The words of General John L. DeWitt, head of the West Coast Defense Command, are equally clear in their expression of unbridled racism: "A Jap's a Jap. . . . It makes no difference whether he [sic] is an American citizen or not. . . . I don't want any of them. . . . There is no way to determine their loyalty."[30] When, in early 1945, President Roosevelt decided to release those interned in the camps dotting western America, only half of the evacuees returned to their West Coast homes. The Native Sons of the Golden West and the racism masquerading as nativism which they propagated had, for the moment at least, prevailed.

The response of the first-generation (Issei) and second-generation (Nisei) Japanese-Americans to their internment ranged from rage and rebellion (evidenced by the riots at the Manzanar camp in December 1942) to melancholic acceptance among many of the older internees. By early 1943, Secretary Stimson decided that the young male Nisei should be given an opportunity to prove their loyalty by officially forswearing allegiance to the Japanese emperor and by taking up arms to defend the country that had imprisoned them. In the face of months of brutal disregard for their human rights, 28 percent of the draftable young men refused to take the oath. Many of those who chose to fight did so with a lust for combat that made the 442nd Regimental Combat Team—the "Go-for-Broke" regiment—the most highly decorated unit in United States military history. The regiment was a segregated unit recruited from among young internees. In one near-suicidal operation, the "Go-for-Broke" regiment rescued the 2nd Battalion, 141st Infantry of the all-Texan 36th Division from behind German lines, sustaining 800 casualties, to free the 275 members of what came to be called the "Lost Battalion." During a 1980 reunion among members of both units, many of the Japanese-Americans publicly expressed their emotions for the first time, among them Henry Nakada: "There were a lot of ironies in those years. There were seven of us brothers in the service. In 1945 my mother was selected as the service mother of the year. She was in a concentration camp at the time. You should have seen all those gold stars for sons killed in action on the doors of the barracks in those concentration camps."[31]

Perhaps the most visible racial problem of these years was a wholly internal one centering around the black community. In 1941, A. Philip Randolph organized a massive March on Washington from which he was dissuaded by an anxious President. The black community had for years been critical of the Administration's unwillingness to implement the social programs that had anchored New Deal support. While Eleanor Roosevelt continued to lend her moral support to civil rights causes across the nation, implementation of substantive reforms failed to materialize; the patience of blacks was growing thin. Randolph's march was intended to rally the attention of the world to the inequities of the American social system, emphasizing in particular the racism of the military establishment. In addition to practicing staunch racial segregation, the armed forces commissioned no black combat officers. War Secretary Stimson himself had made the policy—and the rationale—clear: "Leadership is not imbedded in the Negro race yet and to try to make commissioned officers to lead men into battle—colored men—is only to work a disaster to both."[32] In addition, discriminatory employment policies within most war-related industries ruled out the possibility of black participation in the defense effort, which was heating up by the summer of 1941. Randolph's plans to mobilize ten to fifty thousand black Americans to march on Washington was viewed as disastrous public relations by Roosevelt, who swiftly dispatched Eleanor and New York's Mayor Fiorello La Guardia to appease the agitators. It was action that Randolph demanded and action he received in the presidential appointment of a Fair Employment Practices Committee to "receive and investigate complaints of discrimination" and take "appropriate steps to redress grievances."[33] The outbreak of war brought less than vigorous enforcement of "appropriate redress" as the priority of the Administration remained full production in a tranquil nation. As late as 1945, only 8 percent of war workers were black. The continuing inability of black Americans to break the AF of L separatist stranglehold on the skilled craft positions was exacerbated by the firm coalition of government, big business and organized labor which insured the maintenance of the status quo.

The anger and resentment of black Americans was tragically expressed in three days of violence in Detroit in June 1943. In the years since war production had begun, some sixty thousand blacks had moved to Detroit where substandard housing, tuberculosis and high infant mortality rates within the black community were appalling facts of life. One hot Sunday evening, fighting broke out between black and white teenagers which was fueled by rumors of rape and murder. The violence became a pitched battle in which twenty-five blacks and nine whites were killed, seven hundred injured.[34] The governor reluctantly dispatched six thousand soldiers to patrol the streets when it became clear the local police were unwilling and unable to enforce the peace. Other such incidents occurred that summer, notably in Harlem where Mayor La Guardia's personal diplomacy and even-handedness minimized the severity of the outbreak. Despite the Mayor's best efforts—he deputized many black volunteers, teaming white and black patrolmen—three hundred were injured. Most Americans remained unwilling to examine the conditions which produced the summer's violence; Martin Dies' House Un-American Activities Committee investigation of the Detroit riots blamed the conflagration on "communist influence" in the black community.[35]

Carey McWilliams has noted that the prejudices expressed during World War II were directed primarily at our own racial minorities rather than, as in world War I, against enemy aliens and naturalized citizens of German descent.[36] The degree of racial paranoia was attested to by the widespread myth of the "Eleanor Clubs", which were said to have been organized by Mrs. Roosevelt among black domestics with the intention of getting "a white woman in every kitchen by 1943."[37] The truth of the matter was that the grossly underpaid (often two dollars a week) black domestics were beginning to profit from the manpower shortage and were finding better-paid war jobs.

An equally intense outbreak of racial violence occurred in Los Angeles with the so-called "zoot-suit" riots early in June 1943. There some three thousand attackers (mostly servicemen, with military and civilian police looking on) preyed upon Chicano teenagers, crashing into movie houses, stripping the youths of their zoot-suits (double breasted with pleated trousers, draped at the knees, pegged at the cuffs), cutting their hair (often long, greased and ducktailed) and beating them up. The rampage was retaliation against alleged attacks on sailors by these street-wise Chicano gang members, known as pachucos. The response of local government characterized the inept solutions for racial unrest throughout these years—an ordinance was passed forbidding the wearing of zoot-suits within the city limits of Los Angeles.[38]

The stability of the American family structure was shaken by the dislocations of these years. The combined effects of twelve million men inducted into the armed forces, fifteen million civilians relocating (creating a great strain on community services in the mushrooming industrial centers) and the rise of women workers, 5.5 million of whom had children under fourteen in 1943, produced the widespread awareness of a social malaise shared by all Americans, rich and poor. Several new expressions entered the lexicon such as "latchkey children," referring to those youngsters who returned from school each day to an empty house. The term "teenager" came into popular usage as this segment of the population grew increasingly visible due to a tripling of teenaged workers. Child labor laws were slackened for the duration in order to meet pressing manpower needs. A related phrase was "juvenile delinquency" which was the new label for the increasing incidence of "antisocial" behavior among the young. Although crime rates in general fell during the war, juvenile arrests rose by twenty percent in 1943, the most frequent offenses being vandalism among boys and "sex delinquency" among girls.[39]

The specter of sexual promiscuity lingered throughout the war years, usually connected to the "khaki-whacky" teenaged girls, sometimes called "V-girls," whose characteristic attire was the Sloppy Joe sweater, hair ribbon, bobby sox and saddle shoes along with heavy makeup and bright red lipstick. A double standard flourished whereby the GI was considered to be a lonely and pitiable figure (many advocated legalized prostitution near military bases) while his young female counterpart was disparaged and condemned for her casual sexual liaisons. Not all parents pitied the soldier; many enforced a strict "hands off" policy with regards to their daughters.

The marriage rate underwent understandable fluctuation. It rose from 1940 until 1942, when the boys began to ship out, and skyrocketed again in 1945. A particularly telling statistic indicates a fourfold increase of households with married women at their head, due in large measure to the drafting of "pre-Pearl Harbor" fathers, deferred until 1943. Service wives were given a minimum allotment of $50, a practice which gave rise to the phenomenon of the "Allotment Annie." These were women who married any number of soldiers in order to cash in on multiple allotments, with some particularly hard-hearted "Annies" specializing in aviators in the hopes of collecting on their $10,000 life insurance policies.[40] At least one film, *Allotment Wives,* was based upon this phenomenon, although it may not be entirely unwarranted to assume that the notoriety of allotment abuse fed more upon the absent soldier's suspicions and sexual fears than upon the prevalence of the crime.

Popular Culture

Despite the fact that the intent of this study is the analysis of a portion of wartime film culture, it is essential that attention be given to the co-existing forms of American popular culture.[41] Every form of entertainment or communication was touched by the war and the rapid alterations of social patterns. Popular songs were, as ever, a kind of barometer of contemporary experience with the favorite tunes offering a rough chronology of the emotional tides of the day—the sorrow of parting ("I'll Wait for You," "I'll Never Smile Again"), the giddiness of rapid change ("Boogie-Woogie Bugle Boy," "GI Jive"), the blend of nostalgia and postwar optimism ("White Christmas"). But unlike World War I, with its rousing anthem "Over There," tunesmiths were unable to galvanize the emotions of the days after Pearl Harbor into a single, rallying song, although they did their best with such forgettable efforts as "Goodbye, Momma, I'm Off to Yokohama," "Slap the Jap Right off the Map" and "To Be Specific, It's Our Pacific."[42]

Many songs, written under the aegis of the Songwriters' War Committee, expressed clearly propagandistic aims. "Fighting on the Home Front *WINS*" was tagged as the "official war song of the American housewife."[43] Other female-oriented tunes were "The Woman behind the Man behind the Gun," "We're the Janes Who Make the Planes," "We Build 'em, You Sail 'em" and "Rosie the Riveter." While many a bawdy ditty celebrated the soldier's romantic exploits ("Dirtie Gertie from Bizerte"), the girl he left behind was left holding the double standard. It was rare that a song suggested her infidelity except in the most humorous vein ("You Can't Say No to a Soldier," "I'm Doin' It for Defense"). More likely she was depicted as the loyal and lonely girl of the GI's dream, as in "Don't Get around Much Anymore" and "Saturday Night Is the Loneliest Night of the Week." These songs, although aimed at the largely female home front audience, express the male wish and point-of-view, thus constituting one example among many of the manner in which the ideological regime (in this case, identifiably patriarchal) shapes and produces popular culture.

The war created an insatiable demand for news coverage; the newspaper industry responded with aggressive coverage on every front. The newspaper business underwent the same kind of consolidation and growth evidenced elsewhere in the economy: fewer newspapers survived the war, while overall circulation rose dramatically.[44] The sheer volume of reportage was unprecedented, with four-hundred and fifty newspaper correspondents covering the landing on Normandy Beach on D-Day.[45]

While many of the most celebrated writers of fiction lay down the pen for more active war participation (Theodore Dreiser's comment is indicative of the trend: "Only a slacker would set about writing a novel when there were so many cartridges to be milled and ditches to be dug"),[46] the purveyors of the comic art were not similarly inclined. It was estimated that forty million readers each day followed the exploits of a blond prizefighter name Joe Palooka as he enlisted into the service. Most of the other top-rated strips ("Blondie," "Li'l Abner," "Li'l Orphan Annie") chose to avoid direct participation in the war with the philosophy (based upon their mailbags) that the GIs wanted to maintain a connection to home and to peacetime. Several of the women's strips took a different tack. Although "Dixie Dugan" (the source of a war-oriented 20th Century-Fox comedy in 1942) remained a hare-brained heroine, "Winnie Winkle" married a soldier and "Tillie the Toiler" joined the WAC.

The literary fortunes of war generally favored nonfiction over fiction, with first-person accounts of war remaining popular. The nonfictional bestsellers, although diverse in tone and intention, shared a common interest in the world beyond our borders: William L. Shirer's *Berlin Diary,* ex-Soviet Ambassador Joseph Davies' *Mission to Moscow* (later to become a Warner Brothers production), Private Marion Hargrove's overnight comic bestseller *See Here, Private Hargrove* (also sold to Hollywood) and the surprise hit by 1940s Republican presidential candidate, Wendell Wilkie, *One World,* which was the top-selling book in America for sixteen consecutive weeks in 1943. A major trend in popular fiction was the religious epic, as exemplified by Lloyd Douglas's *The Robe* and Franz Werfel's *The Song of Bernadette.* John Steinbeck was the only major novelist to write a bona fide war novel, *The Moon Is Down,* which, like its film adaptation, was received with mixed reviews owing to its unwillingness to portray its major German character as a full-fledged villain. John Hersey emerged as a promising young writer with three war novels, the last of which, *A Bell for Adano,* was awarded the Pulitzer Prize. There were several popular novels authored by women, among them Pearl Buck's *Dragon Seed,* Betty Smith's *A Tree Grows in Brooklyn,* and Kathleen Winsor's *Forever Amber.*

But the real wartime story of women's literature was the emergence of a new genre of writing based upon first-hand experiences in war factories or observations on the burgeoning opportunities and responsibilities of the American woman. Many were humorous: Constance Bowman's *Slacks and Callouses,* Nell Giles' *Punch In, Susie!: A Woman's War Factory Diary,* or Elizabeth Hawes's *Why Women Cry or Wenches with Wrenches.* Others took a more serious but equally personal approach often adopting a first-person narrative style, e.g., Mable Gerken's *Ladies in Pants: A Home Front Diary,* Augusta H. Clawson's *Shipyard Diary of a Woman Welder,* and Margaret Buell Wilder's *Since You Went Away . . . Letters to a Soldier from His Wife* (quickly bought and adapted to the screen by David O. Selznick). A related cycle of books appeared which were guides to the bewildering new world of war jobs and were more directly informational: *Women in War Industry: The Complete Guide to a War Factory Job,* by Laura Nelson Baker; *Arms and the Girl: A Guide to Personal Adjustment in War Work and War Marriage,* by Gulielma Fell Alsop and Mary F. McBride; and Evelyn M. Steele's *Wartime Opportunities for Women.* This flood of women's literature was one manifestation of the exhilaration and creative energy which the war years helped unleash in the American female population.

The war was a boom period for the magazine industry. With the War Production Board's mandated allotment of 75 percent of prewar paper tonnage, it become increasingly difficult to find copies of the most popular magazines. This was the heyday of photojournalism with the pages of *Life* and *Look* bringing the war theaters to the home front each week. The most popular American magazines began to be exported worldwide and joined the motion pictures as major purveyors of the American way of life to the world. A change in the women's magazine market paralleled the rise of women's fiction. With women a growing percentage of the reading audience, several magazines were founded which were aimed at the younger, newly affluent readership: *Mademoiselle, Glamour* and *Seventeen,* all of which remained fixtures of the industry.[47] Clearly, the altered profile of the American woman was having a profound effect upon marketing strategies within the publishing industry.

World War II was the golden period of radio. Broadcast income rose 125 percent from 1942 to 1944.[48] The higher rates of taxation convinced many corporations to advertise rather than turn over huge amounts of their capital to Uncle Sam. This fact, coupled with newsprint shortages which resulted in a lack of advertising space, made radio the windfall recipient of extensive sponsorship. Businesses and major corporations stood in line to sponsor prime-time programming. The major formats were detective/mystery dramas, which often involved war themes, comedy/variety shows, and, of course, news programs. The medium was deeply involved in the war effort. The Office of War Information allocated pertinent subjects to be discussed during serious curtain talks on each comedy show. Many comics including Bob Hope took their shows on the road, broadcasting from military bases and hospitals around the world. And, of course, radio stars such as Hope, Fred Allen, Eddie Cantor and Edgar Bergen played an active role in the series of war bond campaigns that were helping to finance the war.

As for radio advertising, early evidence of bad taste was particularly apparent by its juxtaposition with serious war coverage. A broadcast from a war zone was likely to be interrupted by a message from a sponsor saying, "Here is a late important news bulletin. Use Smith Brothers Cough Drops," or "Use Gillette Blades which last longer, and thereby conserve steel for national defense."[49] Stations and even networks began to ban this kind of crass and exploitive commercialism.

As was the case with the newspaper industry, the backbone of radio during this period was hard news; CBS estimated that war coverage comprised more than one-third of its total program hours from Pearl Harbor to V-E Day.[50] Many news personalities who were to achieve prominence in the yet-to-be-born television industry captured public attention through their on-the-scenes broadcasts from the war fronts. Edward R. Murrow gave listeners a first-hand description of the bombing of Berlin in a radio first. Eric Sevareid bailed out over the Burmese jungle and lived to tell Americans about it.

The major radio networks donated time and costs for the broadcast of a wartime morale series, "This Is War," which was carried simultaneously by 550 stations.[51] In a manner similar to the motion picture industry, the radio networks donated countless hours of commercial programming for broadcast by the Armed Forces Radio Service. The single biggest radio event of the war years was the coverage of the death of FDR, who had been the first president to include radio correspondents in White House press conferences and had used the medium most cannily in his Fireside Chats; Roosevelt's death was broadcast to the nation one minute after it was announced at the White House on April 12, 1945. For the next three days all commercial advertising was cancelled during the coverage of the funeral procession from Warm Springs, Georgia to Washington to Hyde Park.

The last facet of popular culture to be discussed, while rarely considered to be an area of artistic production, played a particularly crucial role during the war years. The American advertising industry provided much of the leadership in the mounting of government strategy for the management of the war on the home front. From the outset of hostilities, it was clear that the newly appointed agency heads in Washington, most coming directly from business and industry, favored the promotion of governmental programs through campaigns modeled on commercial advertising techniques. Furthermore, the mass media—newspapers, magazines, radio and motion pictures—were instantly recognized as the key instruments of state policy. Early in the war a group of advertising executives formed the War Advertising Council (the WAC acronym was exceedingly popular, designating at once a female branch of the armed services, the film industry's War Activities Committee, and the Women's Advisory Committee to the War Manpower Commission), which helped to coordinate the various campaigns from Washington while persuading thousands of firms and individuals to donate advertising space, time, and talent.

Within government agencies there was a decided split between those favoring the talents of writers and journalists in the promotion of war programs (scrap drives, man- and womanpower campaigns, bond drives) versus those who supported the use of more commercially oriented writers, the "soap salesmen" as they were called. The rift and its eventual outcome are represented by the transformation that occurred within the Office of Facts and Figures. Established in October 1941, the agency was headed by Archibald MacLeish, poet and Librarian of Congress, whose sensibility and political concerns rendered him an early and eloquent opponent of Fascism. MacLeish was a believer in the power of the American people to act wisely when given adequate information and a little gentle guidance. "A democratic government," said MacLeish, "is more concerned with the provision of information to the people than it is with the communication of dreams and aspirations. . . . The duty of government is to provide a basis for judgment, and when it goes beyond that, it goes beyond the prime scope of its duty."[52]

But a rising tide of opinion favored the view espoused by Harvard psychologist Gordon Alport: "Public relations, advertising and public opinion work are war industries and ought to be mobilized."[53] An executive order in June of 1942 established the Office of War Information from the ashes of the Office of Facts and Figures and was the occasion for MacLeish's departure in favor of Elmer Davis, a newspaperman and radio broadcaster whose straightforward manner and media experience were more appropriate to the new policies of the agency. A key component of the new operation was the utilization and manipulation of the very "dreams and aspirations" eschewed by MacLeish. The door was opened to the dream-peddlers of Madison Avenue, and the OWI, along with other major government agencies, was soon "selling" its ideas to the American public. The outcome of this internal struggle is crucial to an understanding of the tenor of state involvement in the evolution of American wartime culture.

The full cooperation of the advertising industry was chiefly facilitated by a bargain struck with the Treasury Department which, early on, announced that advertising in "reasonable" amounts constituted a legitimate wartime business expense and was therefore tax deductible at a time when soaring tax rates were causing corporate America great distress. With the livelihood of its members insured for the duration, in 1942 the War Advertising Council embarked on a series of energetic campaigns for eight different government agencies, with that number doubling in 1943 and again in 1944.[54] Under the tutelage of the War Advertising Council, American businesses donated over a billion dollars in print space and broadcast time to promote war aims and government-sponsored drives.

The symbiotic relationship between government and the private sector was nowhere more apparent than in the ad campaigns of the many companies whose plants had been converted to the manufacture of war products. With profits and taxes sky-high and a generous advertising budget sound business practice, it was nonetheless impossible for these businesses to promote the familiar peacetime consumer items. Yet it was imperative that these firms maintain high product visibility in preparation for the post-war boom of consumerism that lay ahead. The government, lobbying for the donation of "war advertising" by private industry, defined as advertising that "which induces people, through information, understanding, and persuasion to take certain actions necessary to the winning of the war."[55] Many of the major manufacturers, disenfranchised by conversion to war production, chose to attach their names or logos to unvarnished promotional pitches for some government-sponsored program or other—a bond or scrap drive, a rationing reminder—thus avowing their patriotism and generosity while keeping themselves in the public eye. As a result of such strategies, advertising volume in dollars rose dramatically during the war years despite the 25 percent reduction in available paper for publishing. Other commodity-producing concerns adopted a creative approach to war advertising exemplified by a war slogan that sold hats: "Keep It under Your Stetson" (a warning to beware of loose talk that could betray the secrecy of war operations). The campaign thus enabled the Stetson Hat Company to enhance the prestige of its commercial operation while promoting a war aim. A particularly noteworthy advertising strategy involved negative incentives for commodity consumption under the pretext of patriotism and public interest. Firms such as B. F. Goodrich invested in campaigns to encourage the conservation of rubber since "Hitler smiles when you waste miles."[56] Long term goals were being served with the philosophy that such copy would maintain brand name preferences and help to create postwar demand. Whatever the strategy, advertising continued to play a key role in the shaping of the communal beliefs which fueled the fighting on the home front. The tangibles of the American way of life were the cars, the appliances, the homes that the soldiers were defending and to which they hoped to return. The linkage of consumerism and patriotism, although temporarily reversed ("the good citizen learns to conserve"), was preparing the way for new levels of peacetime business prosperity that would wipe out the memory of the depression years.

2

(Her)story: Women at War

The historical analysis of American life during World War II and the Hollywood cinema produced concurrently requires careful consideration of the unprecedented rate of change in the public images of women during the years of war. Leila J. Rupp, in her excellent study *Mobilizing Women for War,* makes the distinction between public or popular images, which are representations manufactured en masse for popular consumption, and sex roles, which are deeply rooted in the beliefs which a culture shares toward the appropriate functions and positions of its men and women. Rupp's thesis is that public images may undergo rapid changes while sex roles are far more intransigent and resistant to change. Viewed as a "chiseler" who stole jobs from family men only a few years previously, the American working woman was heralded as the "glamour girl of 1942" on magazine covers and in advertising copy across the land. Yet by late 1944, the internal memoranda of government agencies show that the female work force was being termed "excess labor" and efforts were being made to induce voluntary withdrawal,[1] an attitude even then being transmitted from the editorial pages of major newspapers, magazines and through other public opinion forums. These three stages of representation—"chiseler" to "glamour girl" to "excess labor"— provide a sense of the altering tides of popular opinion with regard to the working woman during this volatile period. In chapter 4 an in-depth examination of the currents of thought will trace the development of attitudes toward contemporary women. Here, a preliminary task is essayed: to outline the development of events which shaped the fortunes of the American woman as well as the social and demographic patterns discernible among the female populace. Only then is it possible to determine the relationship between cultural products, the Hollywood film, and the historical subjects they portray, the American woman.

Womanpower: The Appropriation of Female Labor

At the outset, it is worth considering several historical conditions which influenced the course of events in wartime America. Unlike Germany, the United States had not developed a policy of all-out production prior to hostilities. Despite attempts by the Roosevelt administration to encourage industrial conversion for the purpose of war preparation, the United States was largely unprepared for its role as producer. The manpower drain created by military conscription could not be alleviated by foreign labor sources as, for example, the conquered peoples who manned German factories. The only solution lay in the indigenous population, primarily the women who either could not or had chosen not to work during the previous years. It was this human resource which had to be tapped in order to achieve the "miracle of production."

A *Fortune* poll in February 1942 indicated that many employers viewed the hiring of women as the lesser of evils.[2] The other possibilities included hiring minorities (blacks in particular) or encouraging radical population shifts to bring new workers into industrial areas from other locales. Such a program promised to create severe strains on community services of the sort that occurred in many boom areas from Detroit to Mobile, often resulting in social tensions and class or race warfare. Prospective women workers were a far less threatening prospect; they needed only to be cajoled and encouraged by the proper authorities and through peer pressure, a task requiring both delicacy and forcefulness. Judging from a sampling of the slogans employed to this end, womanpower promotionals were more likely to opt for forcefulness over delicacy. While the chief Office of War Information slogan—"America at War Needs Women at Work"—adopted a moderate approach, many other one-liners were considerably less restrained in tone. "You, too, are fighting this war, Mrs. America,"[3] reminded the Eureka Vacuum Cleaner Company in a 1943 ad, while Margaret Hickey, chairperson of the Women's Advisory Committee to the War Manpower Commission, was even more direct in her oft-quoted statement, "The day of the lady loafer is almost over." Another public figure, Susan B. Anthony II, stressed the immediacy of the challenge to the American woman: "Housekeeping as usual ended in America on the day of Pearl Harbor."[4] To understand the full impact of such proclamations it is necessary to place these womanpower campaigns within the context of the social forces that shaped the destiny of America's female populace from the years just prior to war through the return of the servicemen after VJ Day.

Many of the women employed during this boom period had been barred from jobs the decade before. One of FDR's first pieces of legislation had been the Economy Act of 1933, which denied government employment to two family members. While the statute did not specify the manner of implementation, the law as enforced was sexually discriminatory since the woman—daughter or wife—was invariably the expendable family member.[5] The law forced the resignation or early retirement of many working women within the public sector while establishing a trend of legislative actions aimed at curbing the employment of married women in an effort to "solve" soaring unemployment. Such solutions, originally affecting government employees only, soon spread to the private sector. These measures were not perceived as discriminatory because of deeply ingrained attitudes toward sex roles which relegated women to the care and sponsorship of men—fathers or husbands. The bachelor woman, a socially aberrant and often pitied female, was allowed to support herself because she had no man to support her.

In tracing the significant trends within the wartime female population, the most dramatic developments pertain to the mobilization efforts leveled at previously unemployed women, primarily through government policy as it impacted upon the availability of jobs, the equitability of pay standards and improved conditions, including organized childcare. It has been estimated that some three million women took jobs during the war years who would otherwise have remained at home.[6] Such estimates depend upon the results of public opinion polls sponsored by magazines, newspapers and government agencies. The popularity of such polls was matched by their level of mutual contradiction. One can corroborate any number of positions with the use of these surveys often aimed at determining such conditionals as how many women would or would not have chosen to stay at their jobs after the war had they been given the chance. Predictably, the results produce a broad range of response. In addition, another million young women between the ages of fourteen and eighteen worked part- or full-time during the period rather than continue their education. Two other categories of women must be considered, however: those who had been employed before Pearl Harbor and these who provided the volunteer work force of Civilian Defense, the Red Cross and other vital service organizations. Moreover, the women of all these categories comprised the homemakers of America to whom were pitched the duties and responsibilities of home front patriotism, e.g., rationing, conservation and collection of vital materials. An analysis of the wartime American woman must recognize this multiplicity of her historical persona, for an understanding of her representations depends upon this plural and often overlapping status.

During the years between the world wars, the basic public image of the American woman had been as wife and mother.[7] A woman's entrance into the labor force was essentially viewed as a stopgap measure, an interim period between girlhood and marriage. The combining of marriage and career provided "selfish gratification" in that employment diverted the best energy of the wife/mother away from her central tasks in the home. At best, working provided "pin money" for the overly ambitious.[8] While it is clear that attitudes of this sort were perpetuated by male-dominated institutions (Congress itself enshrined motherhood in 1914 by creating an official Mother's Day), it is equally necessary to note the complicity of the most respected women in the reification of female characteristics. The noted feminist author Charlotte Perkins Gilman wrote about the brave new world that could result "from a new sense of the duty of women to the world as mothers—mothers not merely of their own physical children, but

world mothers in the sense in which we speak of city fathers, only with their duties more nobly apprehended and more practically fulfilled."[9] Some years prior to Gilman, Jane Addams had promoted a similar ethos by which a "mother class" composed of concerned and compassionate women could begin to clean up and resuscitate American cities. The notion that motherhood was the intrinsic female function, capable of extension for the public good, served to reinforce the accepted notions of "human nature" which defined the character of woman and the behavior appropriate to her.

These accepted beliefs were to be challenged by wartime necessity. Yet less than three months before the attack on Pearl Harbor, *Life* magazine ran an eight-page spread entitled "Occupation: Housewife" which featured a prototypical American housewife from Kankakee, Illinois, a "woman who keeps her figure, her husband, her makeup and her humor no matter how tough the going."[10] Several components of this public image are notable: first, that the model wife celebrated in the media excluded non-white, non-Americanized, poor or even working women. Second, as durable as this image seemed, bolstered by movies, magazines and billboards, it was susceptible to rapid and unexpected transformation. Not even *Life* magazine could scoop the sudden turn of events created by war mobilization.

The struggle to attract women workers in sufficient number to meet the demands of the war effort was viewed as a formidable task by government officials, particularly those directly involved in the womanpower campaigns—the War Manpower Commission and the Office of War Information. Eleanor Straub, whose analysis of government policy toward women during World War II is a seminal work in the field of women's studies, suggests that the recruitment efforts involved an ideological intervention of unprecedented magnitude: "From Pearl Harbor until VJ Day, convincing women to enter paid war work was a program entirely dependent upon publicity, special promotions and public relations techniques."[11] At first, direct enrollment drives were undertaken within the vicinity of war production centers. While the August 1942 drive in Detroit was cited as a great success, the technique was not practical on a national level due to the volume of volunteers required for the canvassing process, either by mail or door-to-door. Ernest Kanzler, the regional director of the War Production Board and a major architect of the direct enrollment program, explained that the drive would "make it more attractive for the women to seek work, make it a little more—well, shall we say, stylish or the vogue."[12] Significantly, the efforts in Detroit were planned without the participation of a single woman. The government, intending to lure women to the shops and factories by glamorizing employment outside the home, was confident that it could appeal to the female imagination without the guidance of women themselves. This tendency to avoid female participation in the design of programs and policies related to women's affairs remained evident throughout the war years and helps to define the concrete character of patriarchy during the period.

One possible solution to the shortage of womanpower was universal conscription, a concept hotly debated in Congress from 1943 until 1945. Such a plan would have provided for the registration of all men between the ages of eighteen and sixty-five and all women ages eighteen through fifty. Originally unsympathetic to the proposal, President Roosevelt began to support it in 1944, perhaps as a result of his growing impatience with escalating labor unrest. Indeed, unions strongly opposed the bill as it would have allowed government to relocate civilians at will in the interest of utmost efficiency and would quite likely have been used as a strike-breaking weapon. While the supporters of this National Service Act felt that it would ensure "equality of sacrifice," its critics saw in it a dangerous extension of the powers of government. From all accounts, the inclusion of women in the proposal did not generate much congressional discussion pro or con. In fact, the Women's Advisory Committee to the War Manpower Commission was never even allowed to voice its support of the bill which ran counter to the official WMC position. While universal conscription had been adopted in Great Britain, the USSR and Germany, it is interesting to note that in the U.S. the only organized female dissent was launched by the Crusading Mothers of Pennsylvania, who decried the attempt to "Sovietize America."[13] In fact, the measure died a quiet death in committee late in 1944.

The relationship of women to political power at this time was largely phenomenal. While the Women's Advisory Committee had been formed in August, 1942, only four months after the War Manpower Commission was established with Paul V. McNutt at its head, it had neither power nor influence and was allowed representation on the Management-Labor Policy Committee, the agency's decision-making body, only as an observer. With no chance of implementing its policy positions despite the many hours of debate and deliberation by these highly competent and concerned leaders of the women's community, the WAC was the quintessential women's organization—locked out of power at a time when pressure groups and vested interests of every kind were exerting control over all aspects of government policy. As feminist historians have pointed out, women were unable to organize themselves or be perceived as an effective power bloc, which ruled out their participation at the decision-making level. The Women's Bureau of the Labor Department exercised a similarly ineffectual function as decision after decision was steamrolled over its protests.

The Women's Advisory Committee had four priorities which it was unable to promote within the War Manpower Commission in a forceful manner. (The WMC itself was handcuffed vis-à-vis enforcement of its policies, so that the WAC was at least two removes from effectivity.) The priorities were the need to protect labor standards despite the open floodgate of new labor power, open training for women, aggressive enforcement of equal pay for equal work, and immediate inventory of women available for war work. But unlike Great Britain, whose policies toward women were a matter of legislation, United States government policy for women was, according to Eleanor Straub, "a mosaic of half-measures, makeshifts, and temporary expedients . . . the induction of six million women into America's war production machine occurred as a response to an urgent, immediate situation, with slight notice given to its long-range consequences."[14] In addition to the organizational difficulties, the WMC was hindered by its condescension toward the public, particularly the female population which it felt could be hoodwinked without the need to solicit its participation. In the words of a WMC pamphlet, "Simplicity is all-important because of the limited receptivity and limited understanding of the great majority of the people whom we must reach."[15] Mary Anderson, director of the Women's Bureau, writing a decade later noted that there had been a "great tendency among government officials . . . to speak about 'the people' as a whole, but when they spoke of 'the people' they meant the men."[16]

The Office of War Information became deeply involved in the womanpower issue, utilizing a kind of media blitzkrieg which became the model for wartime appeals. The agency's "strategy of truth" did not rule out hearty participation in whatever campaigns were deemed necessary for furthering war aims. By September 1942, canvassing techniques for female job recruitment were supplanted by slick package promotions, the first of which was launched in Baltimore. The technique involved saturation of public awareness through radio, press, movies, public speeches and newspaper ads. In this case, the support of various women's organizations was enlisted, invariably brought in after the planning stage, to endorse and publicize the government efforts. The strategy proved successful as one thousand job referrals were made monthly at a specially created women's recruitment center. September was an important month for the War Manpower Commission campaign: it had been targeted as the month that major magazines were to dedicate their covers to the theme of the new working woman. A special competition for these magazine covers was sponsored with a public exhibition of the entrants' handiwork displayed at New York's Museum of Modern Art.

In the early months of this all-out publicity campaign, surveys showed that fully one-half of the media attention to war work focused on the woman worker, who comprised but one-quarter of the total work force.[17] Government entreaty spawned such campaigns as the one sponsored by *Woman's Home Companion* in which four women war workers were taken to Hollywood to be outfitted, made up and photographed—proof of the certifiable glamour of the new American female.[18] Various beauty products began to use the industrial worker as their models, as was the case with Pond's skin cream which heralded one Hilda Holder, "adorably pretty, adorably in earnest about her war job."[19]

Recruiting efforts were sufficiently strident to convince most Americans that the female worker was largely a product of the war crisis. A little known fact was that, even at the very height of the war, nearly two-thirds of the women employed began working well before the Pearl Harbor watershed. Moreover, government surveys indicated that a majority of these workers hoped to remain on the job at war's end.[20] Such inclinations were overwhelmed in the post-war period by popular opinion, expressed in numerous polls and surveys by men and women alike, that women were best kept off the tightened job market, particularly if they were married. When asked by the American Institute of Public Opinion in 1945 to approve or disapprove of a married woman holding a job when her husband was able to support her, 86 percent disapproved as against an 82 percent disapproval rate in a similar poll taken in 1937. The war did little to dislodge deep-seated attitudes toward the proper social roles for men and women.[21]

If wartime Americans viewed Rosie the Riveter as a "new" worker, they also visualized her in a war factory, welding, riveting or assembling "victory" ships, fighter planes or bombsights. These were the elite jobs which, while physically demanding, paid well above the national average and brought with them a glamour and status absent from the majority of tedious and/or poorly paid jobs available to women as teachers, nurses, dieticians and restaurant workers, laundry workers, childcare supervisors, clerks and stenographers. These were the jobs that the War Manpower Commission stressed were "as vital to the war as work in an aircraft plant, shipyard, or munitions factory." There were also many openings for women as replacements in traditionally male jobs outside the factory: as bus and cab drivers, baggage clerks, telegraph messengers, street car conductors, blacksmiths, stevedores and agricultural workers. While most of these positions were low-paid, government propaganda heralded such work as the utmost in patriotic service. In fact, the National Labor Relations Board implicitly discouraged the widespread acquisition of high-salaried posts for women workers out of fear for the dangerously spiralling inflation rate. In virtually every in-house memorandum, the War Manpower Commission cautioned its regional personnel to downplay high wages as incentives for women's entry into the job market. It was far preferable to promote female employment within a context of volunteerism and noble sacrifice which was, after all, quite familiar to women and fiscally responsible as well. Finally, in terms of sheer numbers, three industries have remained the bulwarks of female employment throughout this century: the textile, garment and electrical industries. Despite the attention to Rosie the Riveter, many more women found jobs in these three industries than in shipyards or aircraft factories.

Concrete Achievement/Dashed Dreams

In spite of the disparity between government propaganda and actuality, tangible gains were achieved by women during the period, marking it as a key phase of development for the emergent American woman. More than six million women took jobs during the war, increasing the female labor force by over fifty percent.[22] The number of married women who worked doubled so that, by war's end, the average woman worker was, for the first time, married and thirty-five or over.[23] Four times as many women belonged to unions as a result of wartime employment gains. William H. Chafe, whose work on the changing economic status of women is preeminent, sees the World War II years as crucial ones: "The war marked a watershed in the history of women at work, and, temporarily at least, caused a greater change in women's economic status than half a century of feminist rhetoric and agitation had been able to achieve."[24]

There is no denying the concrete benefits of the glamour jobs in aviation, shipbuilding and munitions with their forty-eight hour weeks and pay scales forty percent above the average factory levels (which were, in turn, higher than those of white collar and traditionally female occupations). Female participation in the aircraft industry rose from one percent in December 1941, to thirty-nine percent two years later, while women comprised fifteen percent of the work force in the previously all-male shipbuilding industry.[25] At the height of war production, these industries had the highest percentages of women workers: communications equipment, small arms ammunition, electrical equipment, professional and scientific equipment, rubber products and weapons under twenty millimeters.[26] Despite the growth in the number and status of white collar workers, increasingly the bastion of the American middle class, factory workers consistently outearned them. One result of war and greater variety of job opportunity was a ten percent drop in the number of women employed in the lowest paying positions: domestic, personal and recreational services. Thousands of domestic workers found greater remuneration on the assembly line while their employers took up their own housekeeping chores for the duration.

Women went to work in government at a record pace; there were one million female civil servants hired during the war at a rate four times greater than men.[27] Many traditional women's colleges began to respond to the changed conditions and new opportunities for women. Barnard offered courses in auto repair, map-reading and airplane-spotting. Mount Holyoke gave credit to students working part-time in munitions factories.[28] And yet, despite the undeniable gains, the down-side of the employment statistics was inescapable: women were clustered in the least skilled, lowest paying jobs, while advancement and upgrading was slow. Investigations show that women were being used in skilled and supervisory positions while still classified as "helpers." In their in-depth study of the effects of war on one small midwestern town, *The Social History of a War-Boom Community,* Havighurst and Morgan note that while many women received training as welders through an experimental program at the local high school, very few women were ever promoted to "mechanic" status at the shipyard; they were usually assigned as helpers to men.[29] Opposition to women's promotions to supervisory positions was strong among shop foremen, management personnel and labor unions alike, their one shared characteristic being their maleness. The ideological position was often elevated to dictum in the literature of management, e.g., "Women, as a rule, make poor bosses in a factory or office." This cliché was comparable to the standard line on black leadership in the military; discriminatory practices were supported by smug aphorisms.

Pay differentials for women were often based on heavy/light classifications (women's jobs were invariably placed in the "light" category regardless of the job's duties) rather than on male/female distinctions which had been outlawed. The government was slow to prosecute such inequities. The root of the problem was that women's work was intrinsically *valued* less in the marketplace, in accordance with the common belief "if a woman can do it, it must be worth less." This deeply held conviction lingers today in what are currently deemed "female" jobs—secretarial, teaching, nursing.

While it was true that union membership increased dramatically during the war, the benefits of unionization were not equally dramatic. In fact, in the words of Women's Bureau head Mary Anderson (in a letter to a friend): "Labor unions are the outstanding opponents to the employment of women."[30] The male leadership stubbornly guarded its hard-fought perquisites and seniority lists for its absent male membership; women were usually placed on separate seniority lists, the better to oust them at war's end. Certain "brotherhoods" were more outspoken in their opposition to women than others. The Teamsters won the label as the toughest opponents by withholding sickness and death benefits from women members, while stipulating that every woman member sign a statement recognizing the union's right to withdraw her membership "whenever in their [the union's] judgment the emergency ceases.[31] Women were consistently denied a voice in union activities, while being accused of an unwillingness to participate and provide leadership. When allowed to serve on union committees, Women's Bureau investigations showed that women were typically relegated to recreational and social affairs. The situation was historically rooted in that women had not participated (or been allowed to participate) in the slow but steady gains achieved by organized labor over the decades. What was required, but rarely implemented, were organized educational programs which only a few unions with large female memberships, like the United Electrical Workers and the United Auto Workers, chose to undertake.

While female industrial workers struggled for equality, professional women fared no better. Very few professional or executive positions were available to women despite the apparent shortage of personnel. Despite an urgent need for qualified physicians, the Army refused to commission women doctors until 1943, and then only on the strength of Congressional dictate. As was the case with the frustrated attempts at leadership among the Women's Advisory Committee and the Women's Bureau, female civil servants were generally excluded from policy-making positions. A list supplied by the Office of War Information, entitled "Outstanding Women in the Federal Government Engaged in Defense Activities," indicates that most high-ranking women were engaged in traditionally female areas: consumer affairs, children's and family affairs, nutrition and home economics, education, nursing and volunteer services. Even the most vocal women in leadership positions—Frances Perkins, Secretary of Labor; Mary Anderson, Director of the Women's Bureau; Margaret Hickey, Director of the Women's Advisory Committee to the War Manpower Commission—were unable to develop an identifiable "women's position" which could actively influence policy. One statistic serves as a summation of feminist frustrations: despite lobbying and legislation, women employed in manufacture earned sixty-five percent of the salaries earned by men.[32]

Quite a different set of questions surrounded the problems of absenteeism among women workers, roughly twice that of their male counterparts. The difficulties arose from the double duties of all female workers; besides their jobs, they were expected to perform domestic and childcare duties. Three-quarters of the newly hired women were married and many were mothers, so a child's illness or cleaning and shopping responsibilities often resulted in lost work days.[33] Typically, women were given the least favorable work shifts due to their lack of seniority—swing or graveyard shifts—so that few groceries, department stores or banks were open during their free hours. Unlike the British merchants who tended to cooperate with the female workforce by extending retail hours, American businesses never adequately responded to government prodding for such adjustments. Another cause of absenteeism was inadequate provision for transportation to and from war plants (often located on the edge of major population centers). Tire and gasoline rationing, a scarcity of mass transit, odd working hours, and worksite locations that threatened personal safety combined to cause an inflated rate of absenteeism among women workers.

The childcare question was another major stumbling block to all-out female participation in the war effort. The circumstances surrounding this problem illustrate the complex tangle of ideology that often caused women to reject the very measures which could benefit them most. Bureaucratically, federally sponsored daycare was a disaster, but the real source of difficulty remained the reluctance of most women to leave their children in a public facility. To mothers who had experienced the years of depression and government relief, such programs smacked of charity. With the closest antecedent to government-sponsored day care being a nursery school project begun in 1933 for underprivileged children by the Works Project Administration, a social stigma clung to new attempts to organize daycare available to women workers of all economic strata. The majority of women preferred to leave their children with friends or family, but the dislocations of war isolated many families from friends and relatives. Indeed, a Gallup Poll showed that fifty-six percent of the mothers interviewed said they would not take a job even if free childcare were available. It was a classic double bind in which women were being propagandized to take jobs, while their social conditioning taught them that motherhood was paramount. For most women, the guilt of public childcare was stronger than the appeal for patriotism and self-sacrifice. Moreover, public officials were utterly confused as to the propriety of the working mother who was, after all, a statistical inevitability. Their uneasiness was somewhat assuaged by continual pronouncements that mothers should be the last to take jobs.

The War Manpower Commission estimated that two million children were in need of some form of childcare arrangement due to the employment of their mothers. Some few private companies sponsored supervision of their employees' children. One particularly enterprising Kaiser plant in Portland financed a twenty-four-hour community school for children aged eighteen months to six years.[34] While such on-site facilities were occasionally organized, the locations of most war plants, often in heavy industrial or warehouse districts, ruled out widespread participation. To whatever degree organized day care succeeded during these years, it was the federal government which bore primary responsibility. Government sponsored childcare centers were, in the words of Eleanor Straub, "the most significant social experiment of the war years."[35] Yet the significance lay more in concept than in scope of execution, as only 100,000 to 120,000 children, less than ten percent of those in need, ever benefited from federal sponsorship. The Lanham Act, basis for federally funded childcare, was an ironic choice of vehicles for sponsorship since Texas Congressman Fritz Lanham never intended that his bill include such measures. One Washington observer noted that Lanham's legislation was "pulled" into child care "by the heels."[36] Far from supporting a new type of social reform, Congress viewed child care as a business proposition and was adamant that public funds should not be used except as a means to release women for war jobs.

But it was the jumble of government bureaucracies that most hampered the effectiveness of the Lanham Act. Although the concepts were originally developed by representatives of the Children's Bureau, the Office of Education, the Women's Bureau and the Office of Defense Health and Welfare Services with advice from the Works Project Administration, funding was to be administered through the Federal Works Agency which was concerned with housing construction. The plan called for financing beyond the original construction costs to be raised at the local level by participating parents and community sources. As a result of the unwillingness of local communities to undertake financial responsibility, the Federal Works Agency agreed to underwrite half and eventually all operating expenses with only the cost of meals to be covered locally. Coupled with reluctant community support, the internecine squabbles among the agencies involved and the endless red tape required for implementation destroyed any chance for a successful and fully available child care resource. Further legislation which might have simplified the administration of public funds was bogged down in prolonged controversy, with virtually every concerned interest group adopting a different position. Some agencies favored continuation of the old program, others advocated a new proposal, while the Women's Advisory Committee chose to remain neutral. President Roosevelt was variously claimed to support both sides.

The newly proposed bill died in the summer of 1943. Both the Lanham Act and its failed replacement emphasized the temporary nature of their child care programs; these were strictly war emergency measures which were to be curtailed within six months of the war's end. The administrative director of the day care program under the Lanham Act, Florence Kerr, stated the position of her agency: "Whenever possible, mothers should be at home. We have what amounts to a national policy, that the best service a mother can do is rear her children in her home. . . . We look upon child care as a war manpower problem, not a social welfare problem."[37] Indeed, federally supported day care was terminated within six months of the armistice despite the protests of many subscribing communities. Thus, the noble social experiment which was never acknowledged as such was statistical failure for a variety of reasons: the widespread reluctance of mothers to participate due to the residual stigma of day care as charity; bureaucratic mismanagement and hampered administrative effectiveness resulting from overlapping jurisdictions; the marked ambivalence of public opinion leaders (including child care officials themselves) toward the utilization of the facilities by those for whom they were intended—working mothers who could ill afford to stay home out of guilt over inadequate mothering; and the limitations of a "day care" system for women who often worked at night or who worked odd hours (graveyard or swing shifts). Estimates of utilization of the available child care resources were as low as thirty-seven percent of capacity.

The strength of ideologically rooted opposition to the notion of public support for child care is evidenced by the urgings of the Office of Education to avoid the very terms "day care" or "child care" in favor of "extended school services."[38] Feminist historian J. E. Trey has interpreted the intervention into the child care arena as a key to government policy toward women: "Providing or not providing child care is one of the most clever (and most effective) ways a society can manipulate its female labor reserve."[39] Rescinding organized support for day care facilities contributed in a large way to the postwar rate of attrition among women workers, many of whom wished to remain on the job.

Volunteerism on the Home Front

Unlike the much-heralded and glamorized work of the female factory worker, the volunteer work performed by American women was consistent with accepted patterns of social conduct. The temptation to focus solely on Rosie the Riveter, encouraged by the media attention garnered by the iconoclastic industrial worker, ought not obscure the role of the many thousands of women whose home front chores were unpaid. Although it was the uprooted, newly-enlisted working population that captured the attention of citizen and historian alike, it was the volunteer workers of each community, largely women, who insured the maintenance of public services for the newcomers, workers as well as servicemen. Across the land, thousands participated in their local Civil Defense Councils, the U.S.O., the Red Cross and the American Women's Voluntary Services. The air raid wardens, recreation leaders, bandage-rollers and canteen hostesses constituted a vital, unsalaried labor supply. Some twenty-nine thousand Americans joined the Women's Land Army to harvest crops, heeding the government's pleas to "Take a Fruit Furlough."[40] Under the guidance of Eleanor Roosevelt, the Office of Civilian Defense coordinated the eclectic assortment of women's groups that sprang up after Pearl Harbor. In zealous commitment to duty, such organizations as the Green Guards of America, the Women's Ambulance and Defense Cadet Corps of America, the National Legion of Mothers of America and the Women's Army for National Defense were founded.[41] Well over half the membership of the Office of Civilian Defense were women.

Volunteer work extended into the home; "home mobilization" was a term coined to dramatize the importance of conservation, rationing and collection for the war effort. James M. Landis, formerly a Harvard dean, named to succeed Fiorello La Guardia as the director of the Office of Civilian Defense, expressed his view on the importance of the homemaker to the war effort in an address in July 1943:

> War is not always a battle line, war is a housewife pouring fat into a container, preserving vegetables grown in her own garden, buying foods with understanding and knowledge, accepting uncomplainingly the necessities of rationing. War is women working at canteens, listing housing facilities available in their neighborhoods, assisting with the many tedious clerical tasks that new wartime agencies have to have done. War is delivering a message door by door, organizing for their schools and their homes the collection of tin cans, scrap iron and old rubber . . . to the degree that a community organizes itself to make known these responsibilities, and provides volunteers to undertake them, to that degree is that community at war.[42]

Other agencies enlisted the active support of the American housewife, among them the National Defense Advisory Commission whose consumer advisor devised the Consumers' Victory Pledge, in which a housewife promised to buy carefully, take care of what she had and waste nothing.[43] The Office of War Information organized a "housewives panel" to provide the agency with monthly reports on the problems and difficulties faced by consumers.

In this light, it is interesting to consider the 1943 MGM film *The Heavenly Body* in which Fay Bainter's astrological predictions to young wife Hedy Lamarr are anathema to husband William Powell, a noted astronomer. Science and superstition are aligned beneath a male/female distinction: the observatory is an all-male preserve, while Bainter's readings are accompanied by doilies and afternoon tea. The work of the film is to reestablish Powell's hold on his male prerogatives while playfully challenging his stiff male superiority, all in true screwball fashion. Powell begins to become jealous, less concerned with his work and zanily obsessed with reclaiming his taken-for-granted spouse ("There's still time to show me I'm your wife, not just a pretty woman you like when you're not working," says Lamarr). While the film is eager to destroy Powell's smug and humorless facade, Bainter's too-certain powers of female intuition are also equally discredited. This is accomplished by the disclosure that she has been hoarding a vast supply of canned goods in a secret vault. While this admission is played as a comic one-liner ("I won't need a canned good until 1987"), it finalizes the defeat of the challenge of the female order represented by a chain of terms headed by "astrology," "intuition," and "blind romance." Powell's male domain is insured by his willingness to admit a degree of emotional vulnerability so that wife Lamarr can at last feel needed ("You've always been a bachelor"). The historically determinate crime committed by Bainter, while not responsible for the resolution of narrative conflict, serves to tie off one troublesome thread of the exposition by discrediting an alternative and woman-centered epistemology.

The war bonds program became aware early on of the importance of aiming their drives at the female population. Each state had a chairwoman of the defense savings program; a "Women's War Bond Week" was held in November 1942.[44] Various ploys were attempted to sustain interest in the successive bond drives such as the creation of seven different stamp corsages or "warsages" by name designers.[45] Other more specialized appeals leveled at the female community included the launching of the "Grandmothers' War Bond League" by Mrs. Roosevelt and Mrs. George C. Marshall, as well as a "Pin Money Bonds" project aimed at low-income women. The Treasury Department commended women's efforts in the bond sales, proclaiming that they "established a record, an achievement which has no parallel in the history of our country."[46]

The Roots of Postwar Backlash

This commendation, delivered near the end of the war, was counter-balanced by a steady current of ill will directed at working women. An Office of War Information survey of newspaper editorials during February and March 1944, found "half-veiled antagonism toward the entrance of women into industrial or military service," mostly stemming from fear of the economic consequences.[47] This climate of animosity, functioning as a negation of female achievement, was never entirely absent during the war years and was preserved within the minds and hearts of women themselves. The moral ambivalence and double binds which confronted the newly recruited female worker, the wives and girlfriends of absent GIs, the school-age girls who took jobs and the mothers who were fated to absenteeism either at home or on the job instilled the shards of self-doubt and fostered the neuroses which animate the bleak moral landscapes of *Double Indemnity*, *The Postman Always Rings Twice*, *Mildred Pierce* and *The Woman in the Window*.

While some critics have contended that the key to the rising pessimism of female characterization in the middle and late forties was the anxiety and sexual jealousy of the absent men, it seems clear that women were feeling acutely vulnerable to allegations of moral turpitude by the end of the war. The Catholic Church, to name one powerful social institution, remained a vocal opponent of the working woman and a vigorous adversary of organized child care.[48] In a *Fortune* magazine poll in 1946, only one-quarter of the women surveyed agreed that all women deserved an equal chance for a job regardless of their economic need to work; less than one-half of the sample felt that even those women forced to support themselves were entitled to equal opportunity.[49]

There was a great deal of sexual tension generated by the altered ratio of unmarried men and women: single men outnumbered single women three to two in 1940, but by 1944 there were two and one-half times more single women than men living in America.[50] During the same four-year span, divorce rates nearly doubled.[51] Such statistics suggest that sexual dynamics were in radical flux with greater female competition for available men and greater dissatisfaction among mates (although the divorce rate reflects the results of speedy GI marriages, disillusionment in the marital bond was no less a by-product). If women were willing to internalize their discontent and the confusion bred by the departure from behavioral normalcy, the male-dominated institutions proved more than willing to promote these self-doubts in editorial pages, through job layoffs, and in "black widow" characterizations in popular culture. This postwar backlash, particularly in a popular, box office-oriented medium such as motion pictures, is simply not comprehensible without understanding the ideological complicity of women which was forged in the social tumult of the war years.

The answer to the question "Are we women going to be thrown out of work now that the war is over and the men are returning to their jobs?" was, in many cases, a resounding "yes." Within one month of the war's end, 600,000 women lost their jobs. From the high-water mark in the summer of 1944 (over nineteen million women employed), more than two million women were out of work by November 1946. Some estimates ranged as high as four million fewer women workers by 1946.[52] In many cases, employers had chosen to hire the wives of their ex-employees, the better to justify their layoffs when the men returned home. In certain industries, including the aircraft industry, cutbacks began as early as August 1944. Many women who remained at work were transferred to "women's jobs" which resulted in wage rollbacks. Unemployment compensation was even denied to some women who were unwilling to accept less than their wartime wages in a new job.[53] Although many women continued to work or returned to jobs after interims of unemployment, they were, for the most part, forced out of the industrial sector of the economy and into lower-paying, traditionally female areas such as the clerical, teaching, and service fields. It is a distressing revelation that, in terms of stature of job classification and equity of pay scales, the contemporary working woman has yet to equal the achievements of her wartime predecessor.

3

Hollywood Embattled

Supervision or Censorship?

The World War II period was a time during which external forces exerted unprecedented influence on the development of the motion picture industry. This was consistent with the fates of other American industries, all of which relied upon the government to extend favorable conditions through allocations of materials, production priorities, and contracts. The film industry was particularly vulnerable to attack as the source of an expendable commodity, an industry whose vast resources could be put to more efficient use elsewhere. Such fears were allayed by President Roosevelt's statement made in the immediate aftermath of the Pearl Harbor attack. Its tone was reminiscent of Lenin's official pronouncement on the cinema during revolutionary times ("Of all the arts, for us the cinema is the most important"): "The American motion picture is one of our most effective mediums in informing and entertaining our citizens. . . . The motion picture must remain free insofar as national security will permit. I want no censorship of the motion picture."[1]

While outright censorship was publicly eschewed, government supervision became a fact of life. Lowell Mellett, as the appointed Coordinator of the Motion Picture Bureau of the Office of War Information, was charged with the responsibility for producing and distributing informational films for civilian audiences while advising and consulting the industry as to its proper role in the war effort. Mellett was conciliatory in the tone of his initial statements to the Hollywood moguls: "We are hoping that most of you and your fellow workers will stay right here in Hollywood and keep on doing what you're doing because your motion pictures are a vital contribution to the total defense effort."[2]

Characteristically, the film industry foresaw the possibility of infringement upon its prerogatives and had taken preventative measures. Hollywood executives had banded together in mid-1940 to form the Motion Picture Committee Cooperating for National Defense, a group that was to distribute, transport and exhibit government-made films dealing with national defense. The Committee insisted on maintaining its own version of quality control born of its aversion to educational films, inciting Arch Mercey to write to his superior Mellett: "The Committee is exercising a censorial power over the government at the moment."[3] The state of war speedily reversed these roles. The specter of governmental scrutiny by the legislative and judicial branches was the source of further anxiety in Hollywood.

The industry had begun to come under investigation in the Senate in the summer of 1941 as a result of the efforts of Isolationist elements headed by Senators Burton K. Wheeler of Montana and North Dakota's Gerald F. Nye, who accused Hollywood of bringing America "to the verge of war." The scent of anti-Semitism was apparent in their attacks upon the producers and directors whose "national and racial emotions" had "run riot." They feared for the control of "this mighty engine of propaganda" which was in the hands of men "who are naturally susceptible to these emotions."[4] The hearings, held for two weeks in October, were recessed and ultimately discontinued after Pearl Harbor.

Criticism of movie content was launched by interventionist factions as well, as evidenced by the *Nation's* angry editorial of September 1941 against the film industry, which "far from being too vigorously anti-Nazi . . . avoided making any films that might endanger their markets in Germany and Italy. Business was their first consideration."[5] Other critics attacked the Hollywood community for its eagerness to please the administration at a time when antitrust actions posed a real threat to business as usual. On 20 November 1940, the Justice Department and the five major studios became parties to a consent decree which prevailed until 1944, when the government undertook more vigorous litigation. The interim agreement insured that no attempts would be made to press for divorcement of the affiliated theaters from their production-distribution companies. In exchange, the industry agreed to modify or eliminate certain practices: blind selling was prevented by the introduction of trade screenings (which independent exhibitors were soon to decry as inconvenient and inadequate); block booking was limited to five features; the forced purchase of short films was prohibited; and the use of unreasonable clearance was abolished.[6] Clearly, the wartime status quo was favorable to the producer-distributors whose cooperation with the administration was the more evident feature of a symbiotic relationship. The *Paramount* case, as the 1944 landmark antimonopoly suit came to be called, reached the Supreme Court in 1948, with shattering effect for the composition of the industry. Yet, it should be recalled that the anti-trust division of the Justice Department remained dormant throughout the war years despite forceful opposition from various quarters; the rapprochement was by no means confined to the motion picture industry. Nevertheless, the enthusiastic and highly publicized Hollywood war effort occurred within a context of impending litigation and diverse, often critical, public opinion as to the industry's motivations and intentions.

Shrinking Markets/Rising Profits

At least one attack on the motion picture industry, the charge of soft-pedaling the anti-Fascist line for fear of curtailing foreign markets, was vastly overstated. In fact, foreign markets began shrinking as early as 1936 in Spain, 1938 in Japan and Italy, and in France as of July 1940.[7] While the industry's timidity in the face of worldwide conflagration was unquestionable, European markets had all but vanished by the time of publication of the *Nation's* accusatory remarks of September 1941. Germany began to phase out American imports by 1936, and in August 1940, an official ban was declared for all annexed territories. This loss of European markets accounted for a 30 percent share of all foreign profits in the U.S. movie industry.[8]

For a time, even the British market (which constituted 60 percent of all foreign business) was lost when, in 1939, all 5000 English theaters were closed down amidst massive air attacks. The reopening of 90 percent of these theaters at the end of the summer in 1940 was cause for jubilation as film attendance skyrocketed (gross box office receipts tripled from 1939 to 1945). For a time, the studios were unable to benefit from this upward turn as currency restrictions prevented them from retrieving their profits. According to an impassioned letter from United Artists' Vice President Arthur Kelly to Britain's Chancellor of the Exchequer in July of 1942, American producers had already lost 16 percent of world grosses from occupied territories and were now facing a loss of half of all earned revenues in other countries as a result of currency restrictions. The monetary restrictions were lifted in Britain in 1943, although the harm to United Artists proved to be irreparable.[9]

In fact, United Artists was the only company to show a deficit ($311,000 in 1944) during the war years. In general, Hollywood's fortunes of war were exceedingly favorable, as evidenced by the following tables which indicate a steady and profitable trend during the period. Increased profits were attributable to a combination of factors including gas and tire rationing, an increase in entertainment dollars resulting from higher salaries and taxes, and the closing down of many nightclubs and racetracks. The neighborhood theaters appear to have been the primary beneficiaries of these unique conditions.

Studio Net Income[10]

Studio	1939	1946
Paramount	$4,000,000	$44,000,000
Twentieth Century-Fox	4,000,000	22,000,000
Warner Brothers	1,700,000	19,000,000
Columbia	2,000	3,000,000
United Artists	445,000	409,000

Industry-Wide Pre-Tax Profits[11]

1940	$ 52,000,000
1941	79,000,000
1942	156,000,000
1943	255,000,000
1944	261,000,000
1945	239,000,000
1946	316,000,000

While 1946 was the peak industry year of all time, profits had risen steadily prior to that highwater mark (with the exception of the slight 1945 downturn). The significant leap in the figures for 1946 can be attributed in large measure to the renewal of foreign and domestic markets at the war's end. In this regard, it is worth noting that the GIs, whose movie-going habits were indulged gratis by the industry, had begun to pay for their entertainment.

As foreign markets became increasingly unavailable, the American film industry began to turn to Latin America, where Hollywood had enjoyed a near-monopoly without fully exploiting the market potential. In the immediate prewar years, the share of American films shown in Brazil, Venezuela and Argentina was 86 percent, 70 percent and 66 percent, respectively.[12] Brazil and Argentina each had over 1000 theaters, which represented more than two-thirds of the total outlets in all of Latin America. Indigenous film production at this time was minimal. Nevertheless, the Latin American market remained less developed than the Hollywood studios wished, thus failing to compensate for the loss of major foreign markets for several reasons: 1) shipping remained erratic due to the German naval presence; 2) war subjects, so timely for domestic audiences, offered considerably less appeal for Latin American audiences; and 3) national film production had at last begun to exercise a strong influence on the Spanish-speaking market, particularly in Argentina and Mexico (with the latter beginning to export its product by 1943).[13]

In addition, American films continued to play to a predominately urban audience in these countries as exemplified by these 1943 figures for Argentina. In the 600 urban theaters, the Hollywood product accounted for 65 percent of the films shown while in the 500 cinemas of the interior the American percentage was only 29. This differential was related to the high rate of rural illiteracy. Subtitled prints were thus unusable, while dubbed versions were perceived as foreign-sounding since the Spanish language editions of Hollywood features invariably used a neutral-sounding Castilian dialect.[14] The net result of these developments in overseas markets was summed up by one film industry historian: "By the time America entered the war, it was apparent to the industry that it would have to rely on the domestic market."[15]

Box office figures indicate that American filmgoers constituted a very reliable market indeed, with weekly attendance hovering around the 85 million mark. The combination of strong attendance and fewer releases (involving less overhead) resulted in the soaring profits previously chronicled. Studio budgets were dramatically reduced by the government's January 1943 policy of raw film stock allotment which mandated a 25 percent across-the-board cutback and the War Production Board's $5,000 per picture limit on new materials. Producers had shrewdly anticipated such conditions and had begun hoarding stock and shelving completed features months before. At the inception of raw stock rationing it was estimated that producers held over 100 unreleased films.[16]

Feature Motion Pictures Released[17]

Date	Majors	% Majors	Independents	% Independents	Total
1940	363	54	310	46	673
1941	379	63	219	37	598
1942	358	67	175	33	533
1943	289	68	138	32	427
1944	270	61	172	39	442
1945	234	62	143	38	377
1946	252	54	215	46	467

There is some dispute on the effects of the war upon the level of independent production. The table of motion pictures released indicates that the percentage of independent releases during the 1941–45 period remained seven to fourteen percentage points below the 1940 and 1946 levels. The usual explanation given for the drop-off in independent production describes the difficulties of procurement outside of the major studios, whose standing sets and contract players allowed speedier production schedules and reduced overhead. But the pattern was contradicted at United Artists where a growing percentage of independent producers became contractually bound to the studio, the number rising from "only a handful" before the war to forty by 1946.[18] Tino Balio's account of this period at United Artists suggests that wartime conditions rendered independent ventures far less risky in that demand was on the rise while output was on the wane—the odds were simply better. Another reason given for the increased output of the independents at UA was the altered structure of taxation during the war. By operating one's own production company, a producer, director or actor in the top tax bracket could reduce the rate of taxation from 90 to 60 percent, with profits taxed as capital gains at a greatly reduced level.[19] Yet another explanation has been offered for increased independent production. In accordance with the 1940 Consent Decree, which modified industry-wide distribution practices, the majors agreed to discontinue package selling procedures whereby independent exhibitors were compelled to screen shorts, re-issues, serial westerns and newsreels with their main features. Independent producers hurled their product into the breach, for a newly competitive market existed for second-billed features and fillers.[20]

The question of ''A'' and ''B'' pictures and their respective rates of production is also a matter of dispute. Garth Jowett claims that ''B'' pictures were considered more expendable and, at a time of limited resources, were produced with far less frequency during the war. Just the opposite is claimed by Frank Capra and William Wyler, two major directors who left Hollywood for several years of military service. Both claim that ''B'' pictures comprised 80 percent of feature production at this time, a relatively high figure and one that may well reflect the filmmakers' personal disdain and sense of frustration more accurately than the state of the film industry. According to producer William Dozier, in an address to the Writers' Congress organized by the Hollywood Writers' Mobilization, the range of production costs for a wartime feature was $400,000 to $1,000,000, but he makes no mention of the relative distribution of films within that range. The entire question of ''A'' and ''B'' production is clouded by the loss of male personnel within the studios, which necessitated a greater frequency of pictures starring women, children and animals. The unfamiliar faces of young actors whose 4-F draft classification constituted their greatest asset makes many a first-grade production appear otherwise in retrospect. At no other time could Sonny Tufts have become the leading male star on the Paramount lot.

Scrutinizing the Hollywood Product

While the number of films released may have diminished, the Hollywood product was scrutinized as never before. President Roosevelt, in his State of the Union address delivered one month after Pearl Harbor, defined the categories within which the informational war was to be waged. The six topics—the issues of the war; the nature of the enemy; the United Nations and peoples; work and production; the home front; and the fighting forces—were adopted by the Office of War Information and its Motion Picture Bureau in their dissemination and analysis of war data. In this regard, the motion picture was but one of many modes of war data which had great potential to aid Americans in the understanding of the war. With interest in the fiction film as an instructional tool at an all-time high, it is not surprising that aesthetic (or perhaps, more correctly, entertainment) values were largely ignored by government analysts in their rush to count and categorize the Hollywood product.

Communications research and propaganda analysis had become areas of significant scholarly concern in the late thirties and into the forties, with New York the center of activity through the Institute of Social Research and Columbia University's Bureau of Applied Social Research. Such notables as Max Horkheimer, T. W. Adorno, Paul Lazarsfeld, Harold D. Lasswell and C. Wright

Mills were involved in these studies. The first major publication examining film research, *Hollywood Looks at Its Audience: A Report of Film Audience Research* by Leo A. Handel, was published in 1950, although George Gallup's Audience Research, Incorporated, began to provide motion picture studios with research data as early as 1940. Handel's own Motion Picture Research Bureau existed concurrently, although after 1942 MGM was its sole client. In addition to the activities of all other wartime intelligence agencies, the Research Branch of the War Department undertook the study of the effects of orientation films on service audiences. In 1946, a permanent Department of Research was established within the Motion Picture Association of America, evidence of the producers' full acceptance of the efficacy of social research for the industry.[21]

Chief among the counters and categorizers of the wartime Hollywood product was Dorothy B. Jones who, as head of the Film Reviewing and Analysis Section of the Hollywood office of the Office of War Information, personally screened or read in final script form two-thirds of the 1,300 features released from 1942 through 1944. The prognosis was poor. In an article published in October 1945, Ms. Jones concluded that out of the 1,300 films, "there were forty-five or fifty which aided significantly, both at home and abroad, in increasing understanding of the conflict. This means that approximately 4 percent of the film output of these three years, or about one out of every ten war pictures, made such a contribution."[22]

In a piece entitled "Hollywood Goes to War" (*Nation,* 27 January 1945), Ms. Jones discussed the major tendencies among each year's group of releases. She found that while more than one-quarter of all releases in 1942 dealt primarily with the war, some 65 percent of them were spy pictures, comedies or musicals about camp life with the result that "the bulk of Hollywood's 1942 product gave foreign audiences a poor picture of America's understanding of the war and must have caused much resentment."[23] The section discussing the 1943 product was subtitled "More and Better War Pictures." After noting that twice as many films addressed the "issues of war" and three times as many were concerned with the United Nations, Jones concluded that "the number of films of value to the war effort increased. . . . 1943 as a whole was distinguished by a more realistic and more seriously intentioned screen treatment of the war."[24] The following year was described as exhibiting a marked decline in interest in war themes, although a large backlog of films were steadily released with the result that the statistics appear to deny this trend. The prospect of a victorious end to the hostilities began to redirect the thematic focus of many films toward the problems that lay ahead: "Hollywood groped uneasily for post-war themes. Uncertain where to find them, it swung back to known pre-war formulas, and scores of light musicals, murder mysteries and other escapist films unrelated to present events were put into production. On the whole, there were fewer films of value and significance to the war effort than in the preceding year."[25] The bias of such an evaluative process becomes clearer when the praiseworthy films are listed: *Mrs. Miniver, Wilson* and *Mission to Moscow*. With the exception of *Mrs. Miniver*, which appeared early in 1942 and offered audiences a tearful but entertaining view of our heroic British allies, these films were neither well-received in box office terms nor were they pleasantly remembered by the industry when political tides began to turn.

In fact, the attitudes of government officials toward the motion picture industry were inconsistent if not schizophrenic. On one hand, Lowell Mellett assured producers that "our operation is largely one of keeping producers informed of wartime problems and conscious of possible implications of proposed pictures or details of pictures. . . . There is a clear understanding on the part of the producers that they are completely free to disregard any of our views or suggestions."[26] Mellett's statement came on the heels of a request that all motion picture scripts be sent to him before production started, and that all films be shown to him in long version, before cutting. But the fond dreams shared by most intelligence officials called for a loftier purpose for wartime cinema, as in the words of OWI's deputy director Leo Rosten, himself a former member of the Hollywood community:

> The movies can give public information. But they can do more than that; they can give the public understanding. They can clarify problems that are complex and confusing. They can focus attention upon key problems which the people must decide . . . the basic choices which the people must make. They can make clear and intelligible the enormous complexities of global geography, military tactics, economic dilemmas, political disputes, and psychological warfare. The singularly illuminating tools of the screen can be used to give the people a clear, continuous, and comprehensible picture of the total pattern of total war.[27]

It is impossible to know what effect such utopian thinking may have had on a film industry anxious to sustain soaring profits while bolstering its public image and maintaining favorable government relations. The industry was clearly perceived as a crucial source of public influence with its 16,000 theaters and 11,000,000 seating capacity (with an additional 7,000 on-base movie houses servicing the military population). For nearly a year (until funds were cut off by a suspicious Congress), it was the duty of the Bureau of Intelligence, Office of War Information, to produce weekly reports on the "politically and socially significant content" of feature motion pictures released in the United States.

Although the Bureau of Intelligence was primarily a data collection agency that gathered information to be turned over to the Motion Picture Bureau, it was also intent on assessing the effects of motion picture content upon audiences. Its grandiose intentions were never achieved due to cessation of funding, but during the months of its existence it did manage to produce hundreds of film summaries complete with ratings of the promotional effects of each release in three areas: portrayal of the United States; portrayal of Latin America; and treatment of war-related matter.[28] Regarding the first area, the Bureau judged each picture as "objectionable," "neutral," "promotional," or "none" based upon its presen-

Hollywood War Films, 1942–1944[29]

Category of Information	1942	%	1943	%	1944	%
Films telling why we fought— films dealing with issues of war	10	7.9	20	15.0	13	11.3
Films about the enemy, including examinations of ideology	64	50.8	27	20.3	16	13.9
Films about the Allies—the "United Nations" theme	14	11.1	30	22.6	24	20.9
Films on American production—the war effort and production front	5	4.0	9	6.8	7	6.1
Films about the home front— problems at home	4	3.2	15	11.3	21	18.3
Films about the fighting forces— the fighting man, his training, combat and adventures on leave	29	23.0	32	24.1	34	25.4
Total number of war films	126		133		115	
Percent of total releases	25.9%		33.2%		28.5%	

tation of "American life, institutions and ideals." The same categories of evaluation were used for assessing a film's portrayal of Latin America, given "our interest in not offending Latin American audiences by an unfavorable portrayal of their countries and people." The example of objectionable material offered is the "characterization of Latin American men as being solely devoted to flirtation and the rhumba." The promotional counterexample is the "representation of the courage and idealism of leaders, as 'Juarez.'"

The final area of evaluation, "Treatment of war-related matter," concerns the presentation of material related to "the issues, the enemy, our allies, our foreign and domestic policies, the character of our armed forces, our prospects of victory, and so on—*and our concern with picturing the conflict to foreign audiences in a way favorable to our side.*" A particularly enlightening statement appears in the example given for a "neutral" evaluation for this category: "For instance: a picture touching on the war only in wisecracks and jokes about the rubber and gasoline shortages and restrictions." Simply stated, the Bureau of Intelligence's weekly reports were aimed solely at overt ideological content with little attention given to the subtleties of expression found in humor or formal variation. Indeed, there is no indication in any Bureau of Intelligence correspondence of an awareness at any level of the materiality of the medium—its use of image, sound and often the contradiction of one by the other. In attempting to produce an exhaustive assessment of feature film production, the Bureau reduced their study objects to propaganda tracts and judged them as so many "reports to the troops."

If the Bureau of Intelligence's evaluations appear humorless and over-literal, it is worth noting that content analysis was but one of four sections of the Bureau's overall plan as outlined in an 15 August 1942, memorandum. The official goal was an "inter-related series of operations keeping in close contact with pictures of all types from their beginnings to their viewing and appraisal by audiences." The end result of the process was the propagandist's dream: the perfect propaganda film. Stage one, which was never fully realized, consisted of pre-production analysis of the Hollywood product which would analyze the initial stages of film preparation, following the script from treatment to scenario. Even at this early stage, various government agencies could be apprised of forthcoming story material as a guide to developing their own campaigns, e.g., the Office of the Coordinator of Inter-American Affairs' Latin American program whose informational short subjects could then be thematically linked to a feature release. Section two was the program of content analysis already discussed.

The Bureau's film analysts worked in the isolation of the Film Library of New York's Museum of Modern Art. The reviews read as though they were the product of some alien intelligence never before exposed to moving pictures. This may well have been a conscious by-product of their strenuous attempts at objectivity. Witness the review of Paramount's *Star Spangled Rhythm*, released in March 1943. Under the heading "War Material," subheading "Armed Forces," the following observation is made: "One scene shows the sailors, an army sergeant, a girl, and one of the sailor's father going for a ride in a jeep. It is a strange use of Army equipment." At times, the clinical tone of the analysis gives way to judgments of a more aesthetic nature as in the comment that "Paramount shows all of its stars. The performances are not all good." Under "Characterizations: American," there is some brief discussion of several of the dramatic roles with no attention given to the actors who play these roles: "The switchboard girl (Betty Hutton) is a very violent person whose lovemaking is vulgar. She has a loud voice, a big heart, and exhaustless energy."[30] A more correct nomenclature for the bureau's assessment would have been "Characterization: Betty Hutton," since no self-respecting filmgoer would have confused the energetic blonde for the typical working girl.

It is possible that the Bureau of Intelligence was reserving its best efforts for its audience research section, certainly its most ambitious project. The bureau intended to produce data in five categories.

1. Audience size and composition broken down by geographic area, sex, age and economic status for every feature.
2. Special Group Campaign Data which would determine the type of audience for "each theater in the country." Such data would facilitate the targeting of information to specific segments of the population—"Negroes, foreign-born, etc."

3. Audience Reaction to Films Already Released, which would assess the public's reaction to films as a whole, to specific parts of films and even to "technical aspects of the production (length, sound, etc.)."
4. Pretesting of Proposed Film Continuities would actually provide advance testing of audience receptivity toward specific story material.
5. General Opinions about Motion Pictures would secure hard data on public preferences for various types of pictures, perhaps even genres.[31]

The scope of the bureau's projected programs is staggering. The motion picture industry had itself been engaged for years in a variety of evaluative processes sponsored by individual studios and trade organizations. The results were painstakingly slow and difficult to verify. The underlying motivation for the government's zeal was a fundamental distrust of the Hollywood approach to substantive issues which was felt to lack intellectual and ideological force. Too often, conflicts of principle were decided by a stiff uppercut to the jaw. In the words of a Bureau of Intelligence official, not one film "represented the conflict as one, which if ending in defeat for us, would mean an end to our cherished and fundamental institutions."[32] The dearth of pictures "correctly researched and correctly emphasized" led OWI's Archibald MacLeish to label the American motion picture "escapist and delusive." The difficulties arose, as usual, with the enthusiastic public endorsement of the industry, as measured at the box office. Indeed, the top-rated box office attraction of 1943, as chosen by the nation's film exhibitors, was Betty Grable (the first woman to be so honored by the exhibitors), the very prototype of the "escapist and delusive." It was the Grable of such entertainments as *Pin-Up Girl, Coney Island* and *Song of the Islands*, the unrivalled pin-up girl of the war, who attracted the moviegoers in largest number. Perhaps at the end of all the pre-testing, composition data and audience sampling, the government's answer to the perfect propaganda vehicle was "Betty Grable."

If the Hollywood community was at all amused at the best efforts of the Bureau of Intelligence, there were no signs of anything short of whole-hearted cooperation in the first stages of the war. A letter from MGM's Ray Bell to Arch Mercey, administrative assistant to Motion Picture Bureau Coordinator, Lowell Mellett, evidences the energetic solicitation of an industry eager to please. In praising its recently completed feature, *Joe Smith, American*, MGM was anxious to convey a sense of dual purpose—entertainment and message—in peaceful harmony. The film cast Robert Young as a defense plant worker who refuses to divulge industrial secrets to a gang of fifth-columnists, even under mental and physical duress. Much of the film is composed of flashbacks to Joe's wife (Marsha Hunt) and son (Darryl Hickman), who represent the way of life which Joe's silence is protecting. The film created some impact, due in part to its timely release in January 1942. Bell's letter to Motion Picture Bureau headquarters in Washington, dated 23 December 1941, indicates how carefully tailored studio productions tended to be in the first grim months of war:

> It is a film which preaches a most potent message, yet does not lose its qualities of being a most absorbing entertainment; a very acceptable sort of "whodunit" story. I realize that various pictures have been made which either "sell" Americanism or defense, but this is the first film made which endeavors to bring him (sic) a truism without being branded as puerile propaganda. I feel that it is the very kind picture (sic) which the Administration would wish to make, should it seek to emphasize the very theme this film does . . . I strongly urge that, in spite of today's obvious pressure and time limitations, that Mr. Mellett see this feature. I believe he will become a convert to its message as have we minions of Metro.[33]

Wartime Contributions

The status of the Hollywood film industry was by no means a secure or stable one at the outbreak of the war. Not until the 8 February 1942 announcement by General Lewis Hershey, director of the Selective Service System, classifying the industry as an "essential" one did the studio heads begin to breathe easily. The "essential industry" rating allowed employers to apply for deferments for "irreplaceable" workers.[34] But the relief felt by studio executives was short-lived in the light of ensuing developments. Industry employees responded that they wished no favored status. By October 1942, 2,700 men and women from the industry (12 percent of the total number employed that year) entered the armed forces.[35] A 1945 report estimated that one-fourth of the male employees within the industry went into uniform by the end of the war.[36] Yet another source claimed that 40,000 of the 240,000 persons engaged in the manufacture, distribution, and exhibition of films entered the service.[37] A quick listing of some of the most newsworthy recruits offers some idea of the potential effects of such a mass exodus:

Actors	Clark Gable, Tyrone Power, Jimmy Stewart, Henry Fonda, David Niven, Mickey Rooney, Robert Montgomery, Bob Cummings, Douglas Fairbanks, Jr. (most of these recruits served with special distinction and much fanfare).
Writers	Carl Foreman, Eric Knight, Tony Veiller, Garson Kanin.
Cinematographers	Joe Biroc, Joe Valentine.

Directors	Frank Capra, William Wyler, John Huston, John Ford, Anatole Litvak, George Stevens.
Producers and studio executives	Darryl Zanuck, Sam Briskin, Kenneth Macgowan, Manny Cohn.

Many of the Hollywood enlistees worked with the Signal Corps, among them Darryl Zanuck, whose promotion to full colonel in January 1942 accompanied his assignment to London by Chief of Staff George C. Marshall. Zanuck was chosen to coordinate all training films for the U.S. Army and later to film military action in the Aleutians, over Europe and in North Africa. Other recruits were assigned to Special Services where Frank Capra was placed in charge of production for a special group of documentaries, the *Why We Fight* series, again commissioned directly by General Marshall. (Many a Hollywood autobiography includes a fond passage or two describing the special relationship of the filmmaker to such wartime notables as Marshall or Roosevelt.) Capra's documentary series was intended to explain the principles for which Americans were willing to risk their lives. Other documentary films intended exclusively for American or military audiences were commissioned under Capra's tutelage, including *The Negro Soldier*. Few of the film personnel had ever been involved with the documentary form but had been chosen on the basis of enormous commercial success in feature film production (in this regard, the Hollywood recruits functioned in a similar capacity to the dollar-a-year men in Washington whose professional expertise was tapped for the duration).

A great deal of the production activity took place in Washington under the watchful eye of the military bureaucracy, but much of the footage was, of necessity, shot on location, very dangerous locations at that (Zanuck's *Tunis Expedition,* Ford's *Battle of Midway,* Huston's *Battle of San Pietro* and *Report from the Aleutians,* Wyler's *Memphis Belle,* from which experience Wyler sustained permanent hearing loss). Other projects were completed in Hollywood in previously abandoned studio space, refurbished for the purpose. An old Twentieth Century-Fox studio on Western Avenue was the temporary home of Capra's film section and for Armed Forces Radio.

Other studio personnel contributed out of uniform by volunteering their time and talents as narrators, writers or composers for informational films. The list includes Walter Huston, Lloyd Nolan, Robert Flaherty, James Hilton, Dimitri Tiomkin and Alfred Newman. The services of entire departments of studios such as Fox, Paramount and MGM were made available for the sound, music and dubbing of these films. Walt Disney provided the talents of his animators for the maps and graphics of countless government-sponsored films, often under round-the-clock time constraints.[38] Under the auspices of the Office of the Coordinator of Inter-American Affairs, Disney also produced several films (including the much-praised *Saludos Amigos*) which were the result of an unprecedented amount of on-the-spot research in Latin American countries. The audiences in these countries had long begun to resent the stereotyped characterizations of themselves in American films. (If Fox wished to stimulate its Latin audience, it merely cast Carmen Miranda complete with turban and accent.) At a time when relations with these nations were particularly critical, the State Department was anxious to encourage a new bond with our southern neighbors by means of a newly sympathetic Donald Duck and other recognizable characters.

The industry was quick to promote itself as a tireless resource in the war effort. A group known as the Motion Picture Committee Cooperating for National Defense was formed a year before Pearl Harbor, renamed simply the War Activities Committee, Motion Picture Industry, upon American entry into the war. Self-aggrandizement surged forth from various studio sources, e.g., Louella Parsons' "Hollywood Meets the War Challenge" in a March 1942 *Photoplay-Movie Mirror,* or Walter Winchell's "Keep 'em Rolling Hollywood" ("Hollywood values an Academy Award but thinks even more of the Congressional Medal of Honor").[39] Perhaps the most truthful insight was offered in the pages of *Film News* in February 1942, when it announced that "Hollywood, through voluntary organization in the War Activities Committee, has escaped government regulations."[40] The strategy of protection through self-regulation was certainly a familiar one for the film industry, dating back to the efforts to avert external censorship from church and community pressure groups via the creation of the Hays Office and the Production Code Administration in the 1920s and early 1930s. The strategy was reactivated during the blacklisting era and through the inception of the motion picture rating system of Jack Valenti in 1968 (a man whose experience in Washington as an aide to Lyndon Johnson made him the perfect heir to the throne of Will Hays, formerly Harding's Postmaster General). In each case, the formula for avoiding the threat of intervention from government or pressure groups was to anticipate these efforts and replicate them internally. Such was the motivation for the WAC, in tandem with the patriotic fervor of the moment.

Soon that fervor was translated into terms far more familiar to the minions of the entertainment industry: the balance sheets of production. In a report by the WAC entitled "The Industry at War," in the Twelfth Anniversary issue of *The Hollywood Reporter,* it is noted that within sixty days of the war declaration the studios had presented 1,200 16mm prints of current features and short subjects in 90-minute programs to the War Department for free showings to American combat soldiers. Reports of the miles traveled by entertainers, the assorted personal sacrifices, the dollars raised for various charities and war bond drives were legion.

A book entitled *Movie Lot to Beachhead,* published by *Look* magazine in 1945, is a 300-page paean to the energy and magnanimity of the Hollywood community. Among the many photographs is a candid pose of comedienne Carole Lombard who was one of the first casualties in the film community (her plane crashed on its return from a midwest bond tour). A chapter on the role of the newsreel as chronicle of international events from the Philippines to Addis Ababa is followed by a section on training films which, it is claimed, reduced the training time of servicemen by as much as 40 percent.[41] Further praise is given the Research Council of the Academy of Motion Picture Sciences which produced over 150 training films for the U.S. Army Signal Corps at cost.[42] Included in the training film category are the orientation films such as Capra's *Why We Fight* series, "nuts and bolts" films which demonstrated mechanical techniques or elements of warfare, and morale films, including those intended to help ease the awkwardness of the GI's reentry into civilian life. The chapter concludes with a quotation from the army officer in charge of instructional film production, that "the production of informational and combat films constituted one of the most important developments of the war."[43]

Movie Lot to Beachhead contains several biographical closeups of film personalities such as Jimmy Stewart and Joe E. Brown, each chosen as outstanding examples of Hollywood personalities who were selflessly dedicated to the war effort (the overage Brown covered more than 150,000 miles in less than two years while entertaining troops). The USO circuits are memorialized in word and picture, including the standard, de-glamorizing shots of actresses playing cards with wounded GIs, signing autographs and dancing in canteens. All four USO circuits, under the coordination of an organization called the Hollywood Victory Committee, are described in some detail, particularly the Foxhole Circuit which brought entertainers to the frontline troops around the world. Another chapter of *Movie Lot,* entitled "Beachhead Bijou," documents the massive outpouring of celluloid to itinerant servicemen, estimating that, on any given day, more than 1,150,000 GIs attended more than 3,000 film showings.[44] The films at theater outposts were selected by a board of six Army and Navy officers and two civilians who chose 156 features yearly, chiefly musicals, comedies, mysteries and romantic dramas. The claim is made here, as elsewhere, that real fighting men were disdainful of war films, preferring newsreel footage of actual engagements to the make-believe kind. According to this account, the most popular films (referred to as "two-hour furloughs") were those that depicted home: street scenes, sweethearts, life as normal. The monumental efforts toward scrap collection, Red Cross and March of Dimes campaigns and bond drives on the part of the motion picture exhibitors were touted at great length, with the conclusion that "the industry did all this for no reward—except its self-respect and public goodwill."[45]

The industry's concern for public relations was no doubt spurred by the presence of the Motion Picture Bureau's 142-member staff and 1.3 million dollar budget which, though a paltry sum, did in fact constitute a publicly funded, rival film-producing institution. Hollywood never tired of heralding its achievements in such house organs as the Public Information Committee of the Motion Picture Industry's *Motion Picture Letter* and the WAC's annual *Movies at War*. Witness the October, 1945 estimate of the film industry's total "gift" to the U.S. government: $45,000,000 for 204 weeks of service, 1042 different features and 1051 short subjects. Moreover, it was revealed that studio employees had traveled five million miles to "keep the boys happy" and that theater audiences had contributed $35,582,826.33 to charity drives (with perhaps the loudest applause due the book-keepers).[46] Another remarkable statistic was offered by Bosley Crowther, in his assessment of the film industry during wartime, that 11 percent of all E-bond sales were consummated in movie theaters.[47]

All of this was accomplished despite the material afflictions caused by government restrictions on raw stock, location shooting and general expenditures. Studios began to share expensive movable sets, and one studio technician even invented a device which picked up stray nails to be sorted and straightened. Hairpins were checked in and out of dressing rooms due to a two-pound-per-month limit.[48] While location shooting on the West Coast was initially discontinued by cautious authorities during the first months of the war (there was talk of a Japanese invasion), studios later opt for more location shooting as a cost deterrent as well as for more rehearsals, to avoid wasting film.[49]

The frugality of the day affected even the image-makers, the studio publicists who kept the stars in the public eye. An October 1944 *Daily Variety* described the modified techniques of a wartime star buildup:

> No longer are actresses pictured as leisurely, luxury-loving dolls. Today's femme star or player is as virile as the men—shown washing dishes in canteens, sweeping, hefting five-gallon coffee cans, doing hundreds of other things to prove she can take it, that she's doing her share in the war effort. Jewels, clothes, luxury are out—screenlady today is war conscious . . . minimize theatrical qualities, magnify human attributes. Factual publicity comes into its own.[50]

A great deal of attention was given the Hollywood Canteen, founded by Bette Davis, which entertained thousands of servicemen lucky enough to dance with stars like Joan Crawford, Ann Sheridan or Barbara Stanwyck, while a Humphrey Bogart or a Jack Benny washed dishes and waited on tables. Warner Brothers released a film (*Hollywood Canteen*, 1944) which, like its 1943 predecessor *Stage Door Canteen* (a Sol Lesser production), dramatized the humble exploits of the glamorous and their dedication to the American fighting men.

Quite a contrasting response to the war crisis was evidenced by the Hollywood Writers' Mobilization, a group which included many of the left-leaning, intellectually inclined writers of the film community. Under the aegis of the Mobilization, a Writers' Congress was held in October 1943 at the University of California, Los Angeles, in an effort to examine the range of contributions which a concerned motion picture industry could make toward world peace and understanding. The proceedings of the Writers' Congress, published in 1944, contains over six hundred pages of speeches, panel discussions and addresses from industry personnel, politicians (including Wendell Wilkie and Henry Wallace), foreign dignitaries (among them Mikhail Kalatosov, Soviet film administrator), social scientists and military officials. A number of imponderables were discussed: the true role of the American motion picture industry in the world struggle, the particular task of the writer, the ideal and most effective forms of propaganda (director Edward Dmytryk speaks of the audience's "dislike for philosophical or ideological chatter from the screen") and the need for international cooperation in the arts as a guide to diplomacy. The tone of the addresses is serious, the intent of the colloquium far removed from the self-promotion exhibited elsewhere. Yet the analyses are characteristically idealist, couched in the optimism of "One World," of popular fronts, and of ideological coalition.

At the same time, the majority of the writers were firmly rooted in the practical necessities of a multi-million dollar industry. In discussing propaganda trends in motion pictures, screenwriter Ben Barzman acknowledges the need to equate potency of propaganda with box office clout: "These pictures must be evaluated in terms of their effective propaganda content; that is, box office success, expressed public opinion, and expressed critical opinion. I have felt, therefore, that pictures which have attained the greatest success could be offered as best indicating the most important propaganda trends in the motion picture."[51] The congress straddled, at times uncomfortably, the impulse towards contemporary social concerns and world peace through the cinema and an awareness of the economic realities of the filmmaking craft. At times the Pollyanna component predominated, as in the pronouncement of professional film analysts Virginia Wright and David Hanna: "A survey of the Hollywood product leads to a hopeful and encouraging conclusion. One becomes vividly aware of the fact that the motion picture has made tremendous strides in the five short years it has been allowed to develop a social and political conscience."[52] The Writers' Congress was an impassioned expression of the ideals and aspirations of the most progressive elements in the industry. The texts of the proceedings are relevant to an understanding of the post-war purges visited against many of the participants (Dalton Trumbo, Edward Dmytryk, John Howard Lawson, Robert Rossen, Ben Barzman, Hans Eisler) as internationalism gave way to the strictures of Cold War politics.

Hollywood remained concerned with external controls even after the dismemberment of the Motion Picture Bureau by a penurious Congress in the spring of 1943, most pointedly with regard to the Office of Censorship, that agency responsible for allocating export licenses. In an effort to exorcise thematic material considered unsuitable for export, the Office of Censorship banned the following subject matter: gangsterism, which reflected poorly on the law-abiding nature of the American people; racial discrimination; luxurious or lavish lifestyles of

Americans who were unconcerned with the lot of their fellowmen; single-handed heroism by American fighting men or the suggestion of nationalistic superiority; imperialist tendencies by any Allied nation or any discreditation of the war effort by the Allies; and, obliviousness towards the war and its conditions by Americans or towards the efforts of any Allied nation.[53] These taboos were unevenly interpreted and enforced, but the scrutiny of this agency created yet another source of pressure upon film producers. Insight into Hollywood's strategies for self-preservation is provided by the historical footnote that the Director of Censorship, Byron Price, was chosen Vice-President of the Motion Picture Association of America just after the war (in line with the Hollywood tendency to hire the opposition).

The motion picture industry no doubt felt over-regulated despite its public disavowals. The published statement of one producer evidenced only casual concern: "At the suggestion of Lowell Mellett, the industry is including in its regular product special scenes, dialogue and background material which in no way impairs the entertainment qualities of the films, but which further the war effort."[54] Such claims for painless propaganda remain difficult to accept at face value. By the end of 1945, five major federal departments were working with the industry to "insure maximum development of overseas markets": the State Department, the Department of Commerce, the Office of War Information, the Office of the Coordinator of Inter-American Affairs (an agency that maintained a representative among the members of the Production Code Administration),[55] and the Justice Department.[56]

Despite concerted efforts to inform Americans about the issues of war, the role of the Allies, and the nature of the enemy and its rival ideologies while presenting believable but positive images of America to audiences abroad, Hollywood was ceaselessly scourged for its failure on all fronts. In the words of Dorothy Jones, "It is beyond question that Hollywood failed deplorably in its responsibility to portray and interpret the role of management and labor in the winning of the war."[57] Decades later, historians and critics continue to attack the film industry for its perceived inadequacy in the face of war. One questions the validity of such sweeping critiques as that of historian Charles Alexander, in the introductory essay to *Hollywood at War: The American Motion Picture and World War II:* "War films absorbed and diffused the experience of war, but received little inspiration from it. Just as Hollywood had eluded most of the realities of Depression America, so it refused to deal honestly with the realities of America at war."[58]

The conflict between the call to "emotionalize" the viewing public on the one hand and on the other to "clarify and inform" Americans about complex issues was irresolvable, particularly for an industry whose first principle was profits. All the criticisms and content analyses could not alter the entertainment orientation, the basis of the Hollywood film. Although one observer admonished

Return on Invested Capital (Percent)[59]

Fiscal Years	Paramount	20th Century-Fox	Warner	Loew's	RKO
1939	4.7%	8.7%	4.0%	8.6%	4.8%
1940	7.9	4.2	4.4	9.2	0.8
1941	11.6	9.4	6.7	10.1	3.0
1942	15.4	13.2	8.2	10.0	3.3
1943	16.5	13.6	10.4	10.8	16.5
1944	13.7	16.1	9.6	11.7	11.2
1945	12.8	15.2	8.1	10.5	12.1
1946	25.6	20.7	14.7	11.6	16.9

the industry to "keep the blondes out of the bomb racks," such a request proved impossible to grant, given the generic, formal and thematic conventions of the medium (in the form of both studio policy and audience expectation). The various contributions (the distribution of informational films, the volunteering of studio time and personnel, the fund-raising campaigns) successfully deflected efforts to alter the standards and intentions of studio filmmaking. In terms of design and execution of product, the war era was remarkably unchanged from adjacent periods of production. The industry emerged from the war in excellent health, with little thought or preparation given to the grim years that lay ahead.

4

Ideology Becomes Propaganda

In the introduction to *Working Papers in Cultural Studies 10—On Ideology,* an issue of a British journal devoted to the examination of various questions of Marxist theory in the field of cultural studies, a particularly revelatory statement is made. One of the opening statements, despite the exhaustive nature of the nine essays and 250 pages of copy that follow, is that "there is at present no wholly satisfactory theory of ideology."[1] Far from being a pro forma disclaimer, the assertion is reinforced by any survey of the literature. For although there have been numerous books and articles written in many traditions—the Marxist, the social scientific, the philosophical, the semiotic—the notion of ideology as a fixed and workable concept remains elusive. Perhaps no key term in these respective fields remains so frequently analyzed and so seldom agreed upon. For the present purposes, ideology is viewed as a level of mediation between history and texts. There are substantial grounds for such a structuring beyond that of practical methodological clarity. Terry Eagleton has remarked that the notion of a direct, spontaneous relation between text and history "belongs to a naive empiricism which is to be discarded. For what would it mean to claim that a text was *directly* related to its history? The text can no more be conceived as directly denoting a real history than the meaning of a word can be imagined as an object correlated with it."[2] For Eagleton, the critic's task is the analysis of a text's insertion into an ensemble of ideologies (general ideology, authorial ideology, aesthetic ideology). In his aptly titled volume *Criticism and Ideology,* Eagleton posits a schema of constituent elements, a hierarchy of levels, out of which a Marxist theory of literature can be constructed: (i) General Mode of Production (GMP), (ii) Literary Mode of Production (LMP), (iii) General Ideology (GI), (iv) Authorial Ideology (AuI), (v) Aesthetic Ideology (AI), and (vi) Text. For Eagleton, the task of the literary critic is the analysis of the complex historical articulations of these structures which are said to produce the text.

While an identical itinerary would not suffice for film studies (the question of authorial ideology alone is enough to sabotage the model), the idea that texts cannot be examined as though they were unmediated reflections of reality (even a concrete, historical reality) prepares the way for the necessity of a theory of ideology. For all cultural products exist as discourse, products of an inescapable mode of exchange between human subjects existing within the domain of beliefs, images, representations of every sort that are accepted and shared. It is to ideology that the critic must look in order to comprehend the full range of determination within a text, the pressures and limits exerted toward an effect of meaning for an audience. But how best to conceptualize this notion of ideology and insert this theoretical enigma into a discussion of World War II culture and the films produced in and for that culture? First, I shall sketch out an historical context for the ideology problematic, thus establishing a working definition for the present purposes. Then I shall examine the allied region of propaganda as a pertinent and definable category of analysis. A section follows in which I shall analyze the specific strategies of government mobilization efforts towards women and those of the private sector via advertising. A further subject of inquiry is the role of such entertainment forms as *Life* magazine for its composite character as purveyor of instruction and diversion, a close ideological counterpart to the motion picture. Then, I shall examine the film industry itself as a cultural institution bearing a significant relationship to state power and authority. The final portion of this chapter is a compilation of the significant strains of ideology with regard to women during this period, presented as a heterogeneous, often contradictory ensemble of ideas-as-experienced, shaped into a pattern of ideological elements for critical purposes.

Theories of Ideology

Although numerous historical antecedents for the concept of ideology can be found, among them Machiavelli, Descartes and Bacon, the usual attribution of the term's origin is to Antoine Destutt de Tracy, a French philosopher of the late eighteenth century who used the word to describe a ''science of ideas'' that would analyze the origins, nature and social functions of ideas. Influenced by the Enlightenment belief in reason as the source of liberation from error and delusion, Destutt de Tracy held that the rational study of prejudice and false belief could effect a ''purifying of the mind'' which could in turn prepare the way for a restructuring of the social order. Napoleon, initially sympathetic to the project, eventually denounced the ''ideologues'' as ''vile metaphysicians'' when his personal ambitions required the appropriation of such traditional belief systems as Catholicism in order to foster allegiance among Frenchmen. Following Napoleon, the term ideology assumed a pejorative connotation that it has never entirely lost.[3]

But it was Karl Marx who developed and refined the notion of ideology in several early works, notably *The German Ideology* (1845–46) and the 1859 Preface to *A Contribution to the Critique of Political Economy*. Marx's use of the term, however, was far from unequivocal with the result that a variety of positions have been argued as the ''correct'' interpretation of the Marxian concept of ideology.

Unfortunately, the passages invariably quoted are inconclusive and overbroad, many exegetes believing that Marx intended to return to the ideological problematic at a later point in his life. The 1859 Preface provides the basis for most base/superstructure arguments in that it proposes a key distinction between the economic foundation of a society and the related forms of consciousness which accompany productive relations, all or some of which comprise ideology:

> The changes in the economic foundation lead sooner or later to the transformation of the whole immense superstructure. In studying such transformation it is always necessary to distinguish between the material transformation of the economic conditions of production, which can be determined with the precision of natural science, and the legal, political, religious, artistic or philosophic—in short, ideological forms in which men become conscious of this conflict and fight it out. Just as one does not judge an individual by what he thinks about himself, so one cannot judge such a period of transformation by its consciousness, but, on the contrary, this consciousness must be explained from the contradictions of material life, from the conflict existing between the social forces of production and the relations of production.[4]

Although a clear mandate for a materialist approach to the study of culture is proposed in the passage, an ongoing debate as to the degree of determinancy of the economic foundation has led to the division of the "vulgar economists" from those who grant a greater autonomy to the ideological forms. Others have been disturbed over the broad scope of social processes and institutions deemed "ideological" in the passage, contending that not all products of consciousness are properly termed ideological.

For many analysts of ideology in the Marxist tradition, the term requires a stricter functional definition whereby ideological forms are those representations that conceal contradictions produced within a society. For these critics, it is the Marx of *The German Ideology* with an emphasis on class conflict and the role of ideology in maintaining a pattern of hierarchy within society who is most frequently quoted:

> The ideas of the ruling class are in every epoch the ruling ideas, i.e., the class which is the ruling material force of society, is at the same time its ruling intellectual force. The class which has the means of material production at its disposal, has control at the same time over the means of mental production, so that thereby, generally speaking, the ideas of those who lack the means of mental production are subject to it. The ruling ideas are nothing more than the ideal expression of the dominant material relationships, the dominant material relationships grasped as ideas; hence of the relationships which make the one class the ruling one, therefore, the ideas of its dominance. . . . For each new class which puts itself in the place of one ruling before it, is compelled, merely in order to carry through its aim, to represent its interest as the common interest of all the members of society, that is, expressed in ideal form: it has to give its ideas the form of universality, and represent them as the only rational, universally valid ones.[5]

For one faction of critical thinkers, ideology, in the modern western context, is bourgeois ideology and is a fictive construct that deceives the dominated and is directly attributable to the ruling class. Such a position, however, hardly explains the active participation of oppressed groups in the promulgation of beliefs that contribute to their oppression. Why, for example, did the Women's Bureau during World War II help promote the idea that women were naturally suited to precise, often monotonous tasks eschewed by men? The notion of ruling class ideology is inadequate to the subtlety and complexity of real, historical conditions. In like manner, the strict interpretation of ideology as a form of consciousness that conceals contradiction begins to assume a monolithic character for the ruling class, difficult to justify during a crisis or ruptural unity in which a coalition of class factions dictate policy. This definition is particularly confining in the case of cultural products whose efficacy as concealer of contradiction may be far less significant than the subtlety of its elaboration of values or attitudes. The art object is no less ideological for its resistance to the stamp of class appellation.

And yet, it is clear that the domain of ideology is pertinent to the present account of American culture and the analysis of socially determined and determining institutions ranging from the family to the church, the educational system, the military and the various cultural institutions. In all cases, the conditions of war recast the internal dynamics of these institutions while unifying them towards a single goal: the preservation of the nation. All areas participated in the promotion of specific values which were intended to mobilize the citizenry; all appear to be linked by a shared function which will here be termed ideological. In order to establish a more efficient basis for this analysis, and a relatively fixed meaning for ideology, a series of questions will have to be posed. To a degree, these questions are oriented toward a greater precision of theoretical terms, but the aim is increased clarity of concrete analysis.

In the first place, is ideology the opposite of science? Louis Althusser's infamous concern with Marx's "epistemological break" was founded in his belief that historical materialism is constituted as a science with a verifiable method and a knowable object. As such it is to be differentiated from the pre-scientific theorizing of the young, idealist Marx. Just where that break can be located depended upon the critical perception of the analyst; Althusser deemed *The German Ideology* as the textual site of the break. Other critics, notably Norman Geras and Paul Q. Hirst, attack this clearcut distinction as idealist since the conditions within which scientific knowledge is generated are social and historical, not hermetically sealed from contamination with ideological forms. Althusser's claims are based upon the supposition that science, unlike ideology, designates an existing reality *and* provides us with a means of knowing it. Historical materialism is the science of social formations and their history with a precise methodology evidenced in *Capital* and other works of the mature Marx. But it is unclear whether there is any qualitative distinction to be made between historical materialism and mathematical or physical science. Are they to be considered as nonideological, utterly independent of the social formation? Is science a neutral pursuit or is Marxist science the lone instance of self-contained and uncontaminated knowledge? Althusser's subsequent auto-critiques suggest that ideology is not definable as the opposite of science and that other questions need to be asked. The adherents of the science/ideology distinction wish to establish an ineradicable split between a detailed and connected knowledge, which is positive and scientific, and the assumptions, concepts and points of view which distort that knowledge. The distinction is, in itself, an idealist assumption, hence ideological, and of limited use for constructing a working definition of ideology.

Yet another question has dogged the continuing discussion around the problematics of ideology: is ideology a "true" or "false" consciousness? It was Lenin's belief that a postrevolutionary society would produce social relations and an ideological nexus freed of the obfuscation characteristic of the capitalist mode of production. Unlike the "false" ideology of prerevolutionary societies which misrepresented social relations in order to advance the interests of the dominant order, proletarian ideology—no longer the product of the bourgeoisie—was a true form of consciousness which had no need to conceal contradiction. After all, Marx's analysis in *Capital* explained the genesis of such phenomenal forms as surplus-value or the wage form whose inner structure, based upon the exploitation of labor power, remains invisible. Ideology, in turn, fetishizes appearances, separates them from their real connections and perpetuates the self-deception of the dominant class and the mystification of the dominated. Lenin's belief that postrevolutionary ideology would no longer function as a misrepresentation, as "false" knowledge, is based upon a strict reading of the base/superstructure relationship whereby consciousness is an emanation or reflection of the economic mode. The developments in several postrevolutionary states (the USSR, China and Cuba, to name a few) suggest that Lenin's true/false distinction based solely upon the economic and class relations within a social formation is untenable.

A more sophisticated but equally optimistic version of "true," revolutionary ideology is presented in Roland Barthes' key essay "Myth Today." Barthes' use of the term "myth" in the book *Mythologies* (for which "Myth Today" serves as a final, methodologically explicit summation) is roughly equivalent to "ideology" in that it indicates a speech act that has been emptied of history, eternalized and "naturalized"; that is, made to appear inevitable, the result of human nature. The focus of Barthes' analysis is language, although he stresses the class origins and connections for every speech act. The bourgeoisie removes its name from the language that helps to maintain its domination not through denial but by a process of purification and eternal justification which, in lieu of explanation, states facts. Myth is depoliticized speech, "the most appropriate instrument for the ideological inversion which defines . . . society."[6] But Barthes holds out one hope for the abolition of myth: revolutionary language, "the language of man as a producer." There is some connection here to the Leninist vision, although

Barthes' formulation, idealist as it may be, achieves a higher degree of specificity due to its linguistic focus.

> Revolution is defined as a cathartic act meant to reveal the political load of the world: it *makes* the world; and its language, all of it, is functionally absorbed in this making. It is because it generates speech which is *fully,* that is to say initially and finally, political, and not, like myth, speech which is initially political and finally natural, that Revolution excludes myth. . . . The bourgeoisie hides the fact that it is the bourgeoisie and thereby produces myth; revolution announces itself openly as revolution and thereby abolishes myth.[7]

The link that exists between the Leninist position and that of Barthes is based upon a shared belief in the "end" of ideology as false knowledge or myth through revolutionary activity. Other critics have taken an opposite view of the historical character of ideology.

With the question of the truth or falsity of ideology another question occurs: is ideology historical or ahistorical? The two areas are closely connected in the work of French philosopher Louis Althusser, whose theoretical formulations have been deeply influenced by the rereading of Freud advanced by Jacques Lacan. For Althusser, the notions of "truth" or "falsity" are intertwined in his definition of the term: ideology is a "representation" of the imaginary relationship of individuals to their real conditions of existence. The representations are described as material in that they are constituted by concrete practices (religious rituals, magazine advertisements, political slogans) and the ideas, values and social relations which constitute ideology are real because they are experienced by men and women in their daily lives. It is the *relationship* of the individual to these lived conditions that is imaginary, that is, based upon a principle of misrecognition. The concept of misrecognition is founded in Althusser's assertion that all ideology has the function (which defines it) of constituting concrete individuals as subjects. Just as Lacan wrote about the "mirror phase" of infantile development when, between the ages of six and eighteen months, the child gazes upon the mirrored image of his/her body and sees there a unified being despite the undeveloped motor functions and pre-linguistic capability, Althusser posits a function for ideology as extending that construction of the subject by hailing or interpellating concrete individuals as concrete subjects. For subjecthood places the individual at the center of discourse, as the locus of understanding, the *place* from which an act of communication becomes comprehensible. Ideology transforms individuals into subjects by the hailing process, typified by the expression "Hey, you there!" so that the object of address is convinced that "it was really him (her) who was hailed and not someone else."[8] By this process of interpellation, ideology ensnares the individual into a willing, if unconscious, participation while at the same time effectively negating its presence. For Althusser, ideology addresses itself first and foremost to the individual rather than to a class or a social grouping. Because the processes of ideology via interpellation begin with the earliest experiences of childhood, ideology is rendered invisible and eternalized. Individuals are *always already* subjects. Therefore, it is because the interpellative process, hence ideology, addresses itself to the unconscious that Althusser can make the statement that "ideology has no history."[9] For while ideology always operates within a determinate historical context, as a process it is defined, like the Freudian proposition of an eternal unconscious, as "omnipresent, trans-historical and therefore immutable in form throughout the extent of history."[10]

In answer to the true/false distinction, the Althusserian response is yes/no in that ideology is deemed to incorporate apparent opposites within it—imaginary and real, recognition and misrecognition, historical and ahistorical. Indeed the ideological process is *defined* by the interpenetration of these seeming opposites. Ideology works through its adherence to *real*, lived relations which are *recognized* as consistent with the *historical* conditions at any given moment. But because ideology functions through an appeal to the unconscious within individuals, it is simultaneously imaginary, founded in a misrecognized connection between subject and discourse, hence a part of psychic processes which operate outside a temporal frame. Although the Althusserian version of ideology cannot be accepted without a thoroughgoing critique (in which he himself has participated), this formulation accounts for the enduring presence of ideological elements within post-revolutionary societies. It also offers a useful framework within which to analyze cultural products and a high level of explanatory power in the analysis of concrete instances of ideology. One final aspect of Althusser's theory relates to the meaning of the term "subject" which contains a double meaning. On the one hand, the subject as constituted by ideology is the source of mastery, the locus of meaning. Conversely, the individual is "subjected" to a hierarchy of meaning through ideology which effectively fixes him/her within a regime of knowledge. If ideology required the sense of concealment of contradiction for one faction of Marxists, for Althusser the term requires this doubling of subjecthood which simultaneously erects the individual as sovereign origin of meaning and fixes that same individual in a position of subjection or domination.

Yet another pertinent question with regard to ideology is whether it is a reflection of material processes or itself a material process, hence the question of effectivity, wholly determined or determining? The notion of consciousness and its products as entirely dependent on the economic base, as ineluctably superstructural, is the result of an overzealous application of the base/superstructure model described earlier. It becomes clear through the examination of World War II culture and the mobilization campaigns and ideological onslaughts practiced everywhere that so-called superstructural forms exercised a significant degree of determination upon economic decision-making, that is, upon the productive forces and relations usually considered to be infrastructural. The two-part spatial model of social formations must give way to a theory of reciprocal determination in which forms of consciousness are viewed as material processes with their own conditions of existence. Raymond Williams has propounded a position based on a working theory of "cultural materialism" in which cultural and ideological forms are viewed as primary processes, social and material, based upon the primacy of language and cognition for all human action. With the exorcism of cultural forms as secondary emanations of the strictly economic mode, the idea of mutual determination becomes more tenable. Moreover, Williams bases his argument on elements of the Marxist canon—specifically, the notion of "imagination" in the labor process—usually overlooked in favor of the famous synonyms for consciousness used by Marx in various tracts, for example, "reflexes," "echoes," "phantoms," and "sublimates":

> For "consciousness and its products" are always, though in variable forms, parts of the material social process itself: whether as what Marx called the necessary element of "imagination" in the labour process; or as the necessary conditions of associated labour, in language and in practical ideas of relationship . . . "thinking" and "imagining" are from the beginning social processes (of course including that capacity for "internalization" which is a necessary part of any social process between actual individuals) and . . . they become accessible only in unarguably physical and material ways: in voices, in sounds made by instruments, in penned and printed writing, in arranged pigments on canvas or plaster, in worked marble or stone.[11]

By removing cultural forms from their secondary relationship to economic (allegedly infrastructural) forces, Williams provides a conceptual basis for comprehending the effectivity of ideology upon the productive activities of men and women. For Williams, determination is nothing more nor less than the exertion of pressures and the setting of limits which one social component exercises over another. If ideological forms produce pressures and limits upon social process—a film is alleged to increase the number of Marine Corps recruits or production quotas are met for the first time in the wake of a full-scale advertising campaign— one can then begin to speak of the *determination* of material life by cultural forms.

But if indeed the ideological realm is held responsible for transforming and reorganizing the mode of production in the World War II instance, the question of ruling class intentions arises. Is ideology dictated by a ruling bloc or is it the product of all classes? If the latter case is true, how can this be theorized? The notion of dominant or ruling class ideology has remained a convenient fiction in the Marxist tradition, but within it are concealed the complex connections between class and social meanings that go beyond the simple couplet dominant/dominated. In order to comprehend the participation of the ruled—the vast majority in any social order—it becomes critical to employ the concept of hegemony as articulated by Gramsci. For Gramsci, ideological domination and subordination are not understood in isolation but as one dialectical term operating on many levels at once—economic, political, cultural, and ideological. Hegemony involves the organization of "spontaneous" consent which can be won, for example, by the ruling block making economic concessions that "yet do not touch its essential interests.''[12] It is through hegemony that the social bloc is cemented and unified in the interest of "spontaneous consent." Because the pressures and limits of a given form of domination are experienced and, in fact, internalized, the whole question of class rule is transformed.

For within the Gramscian formulation, hegemony is always contested, that is, it is defined by its subtle interplay of coercion and consent, domination and direction. But a war crisis, in producing a kind of ruptural unity, reduces the level of contestation to an all-time low, so that the interests of capital appear to coincide with the interests of the people—to preserve democratic principles, to insure the continued existence of the state, and, in so doing, to lift itself from the Depression. In fact, that wartime consensus is sandwiched by bitter labor strife: the militancy of the Flint, Michigan outbreaks in 1937 and the protracted labor disputes of 1946 and 1947. The war years were characterized by a community of interest, a consensus that can best be understood in terms of the hegemonic: coercion overtaken by consent, domination actively perceived as direction.

The discussion of the film industry in chapter 3 illustrated the complex interactions characteristic of the hegemonic order, intensified in wartime. The distinctions between compliance and contribution become blurred as do donations of private resources and their allocation by the state. The litany of unique conditions for the film industry—censorship and unprecedented supervision, loss of personnel through military enlistment and rampant volunteerism, priority assessments, high taxation, impassioned fundraising—suggests the meshing of normally oppositional categories—public and private, labor and capital, legislated and volunteered—which typifies the hegemonic.

The questions asked about ideology begin to reveal the complex and controversial character of the term. Although commonly placed in opposition to science, ideology cannot be sealed off from any form of human endeavor requiring imagination, conceptualization or verbal articulation. Marxist science (historical materialism) can no more be held exempt from the effects of ideology than the physical sciences. As for the truth or falsity of ideological discourse, the most acceptable account of the phenomenon recognizes the play of recognition/misrecognition so that *real* conditions and social relations, as lived and experienced, are represented in an *imaginary* relationship to a given individual who is the *subject* (and apparent master) of ideological discourse while being subjected to the hierarchy of meaning and social positioning it enforces. Moreover, ideology gains access to the psychic processes of the individual by means of interpellation or hailing. Although a product of consciousness, ideology is no mere reflection of material processes but a constitutive and even determining social process in its own right. Finally, the ruling class does not dictate the terms of domination to the ruled majority in an uncontested, unitary manner. Rather, a hegemonic domain exists within which always contested ideological forces act to cement and unify all factions, classes and interest groups. It is through the category of ideology

that the analyst gains access to cultural objects or texts which are reworkings
of the world within recognizable form, hence, products produced within ideology.
For ideology is experienced as common sense, the way things are, the internalized voice of social authority which inhabits one's dreams, hopes, fantasies and
reason.[13] As Terry Eagleton has noted, ideology seen from within has no outside. Within the hegemonic context, ideology exhibits binding powers over traditional social rifts or distinctions, those of class, religion, gender, ethnicity, race,
or age.

Propaganda: Ideology's "Special Case"

There is a special category within ideology of particular significance for a study
of the World War II period, that special case being propaganda. The boundary
between ideology in general and propaganda is not a clear one; yet it is important
in the present instance to establish working definitions for both terms in order
to suggest certain rhetorical and semantic distinctions between them. A usable
notion of propaganda is vital to the illumination of the conditions of wartime
cultural production. Throughout the thirties and forties, social scientists wrestled
with a definition of propaganda that could set apart one type of social communication (ranging from the mildly didactic to outright brainwashing) from forms more
properly termed "education," "patriotic reiteration," or even art. Harold D.
Lasswell, the first American social scientist to study propaganda systematically,
proposed the following definition: Propaganda is the deliberate attempt to influence
mass attitudes on controversial subjects by the use of symbols rather than force.
While ideology-in-general serves a practical-instrumental function in orienting
people toward the dominant beliefs and practices and is generally experienced
as unintentional, even unconscious, propaganda displays a more focused attention to "mass" effectivity. While ideological discourse is characterized by a
steady, almost imperceptible, accretion of practical knowledge, propaganda
unleashes a greater urgency in its transmission. The intentions of the propagandist are certainly perceived by the analyst as overt, but this singular line of analysis
is hindered in a crisis context which is universally experienced as a moment of
heightened historical awareness and self-consciousness, a time of mobilized social
values (patriotism, chauvinism, nationalism), the sense of the "duration." So
all ideological production is stamped with a stronger sense of purpose or intentionality, visible in cultural products ranging from songs to magazine ads to films.

Analysts have long been aware of the variability of propaganda as a perceived phenomenon. The notion of "controversial" subject matter (one of the
defining elements of the term) may well change from one viewing audience or
situation to another, depending on the specific context. An American film's treatment of patriotic values is non-controversial in the United States particularly during
wartime (as typified by the response of baseball fans during the national anthem—

unconscious unanimity), but may be viewed as sheer propaganda in a non-aligned country like Argentina. The same can be said of seeing a 1942 film in 1987 when public attitudes and popular imagery may have altered. Viewing conditions affect the status of the text as ideological discourse. The awareness of manipulation by the viewer is yet another essential ingredient, an awareness which will vary according to levels of exposure, training or general inclination. A television commercial for blue jeans or for a political candidate assumes the guise of propaganda when the viewer becomes cognizant of overzealous salesmanship.

The intentionality factor is the source of great confusion in the definition since all advertising, for example, is deliberate (it addresses mass audiences via symbols rather than force). The element of controversiality is also cloudy. Two categories of near-propaganda are "education" and "patriotic reiteration" which share a similar function: the transmission of noncontroversial subject matter. Patriotic reiteration, exemplified by pageants, poems and patriotic reenactments, dramatizes accepted political values. Here one encounters the limitations of traditional accounts of propaganda, which tend to undervalue the materiality and the specificity of the medium of transmission, including the rhetoric of its mode of representation. In the first place, patriotic values are generally noncontroversial; flagwaving, like Mom and apple pie, is an accepted element of the American vernacular. But the intrusion of patriotic values into the personal agenda renders these values highly controversial. The emphasis shifts to the individual *response* to these values rather than their mere elaboration or description: "What are *you* willing to do about *your* beliefs?" In this sense, the shared truisms of quieter times become the propaganda of crisis times. "Uncle Sam Wants You" and he indicates this with an outstretched finger. Herein lies the significance of the rhetorical syntax of propaganda in which the interpellation of the ideological process becomes intensified. A factor that could be called "interpellative urgency" intercedes so that the impersonal third-person forms of address of peacetime are transformed into the immediacy of first and second persons ("I joined," says the beaming WAC, "what about you?"). Interpellative urgency, then, functions as an indicator of the relative "pressure of address" within rhetorical utterance. As in the WAC recruitment poster, a subject is hailed with an intensity expressed by the "I/you" structure (rather than the impersonal third person construction), an intensity rooted in the historical conditions of wartime crisis. Even slogans that suppress the "I/you" verge upon the imperative voice with its understood subject "you" ("A slip of the lip sinks a ship" elides the "you" only slightly).

The degree of interpellative urgency of a transmitted message, if accurately ascertained, can spell the difference between the conventional (albeit ideologically charged) communication and the propaganda piece. Some media produce a greater effect of immediacy than others, as witnessed by the divergent levels of censorship and public outcry visited upon television compared to the print medium, for example. In like manner, Wendell Wilkie, representing the film industry during the Congressional hearings in the fall of 1941, decried the hypocrisy of attack against filmed versions of anti-Fascist material that had never been judged offensive in their original book form. Clearly, the character of filmic representation garners greater audience identification (constructing an imaginary or subjective position for the viewer) while simultaneously *subjecting* that viewer far more strenuously to its regime of meaning as an active process that controls the duration of its unfolding. The reversible, self-generated process of reading a book, poem or poster allows, at times requires, a more energetic participation of the subject, thereby affording a greater freedom from the "pull" of the imaginary processes. The visual media have a heightened dramatic effect for the spectator created by processes of identification and voyeuristic fetishism. As these processes are hidden within the spatio-temporal unity of the narrative, the film gains an intensified power of recruitment over the viewer. The cinema is thus relatively more likely to be perceived as propagandistic due in part to the nature of its expressive or formal conditions.

For the cinema "hails" the individual as subject from among the throng of spectators in the darkened hall. Certain films of the World War II period contain particular moments in which a direct address is made to the audience by fictional characters with a war message to punch across. In Paramount's 1942 musical, *Priorities on Parade,* a key female character turns her gaze directly upon the camera as she says, "But it's getting to be the smart thing to do for girls to get in there and pitch too, whatever way they can." Although the speech is addressed to an inscribed audience within the diegesis, the pronouncement is intended as a plea to the viewing audience as well. Here, propaganda overtakes ideology due to the altered interpellative urgency of this privileged moment. A new level of intentionality is momentarily discernible and a formally encoded invitation is made to the spectator in a manner that diverges from the rest of the film, as from most films. (One strongly encoded element of the classical cinema concerns the denial of the apparatus. It is rare that the imaged character directs his/her gaze at the camera, with the notable exception of the comedy film from Chaplin and Keaton to Jerry Lewis and Woody Allen. At Paramount during this period, Bob Hope was making a career of his asides to the camera.) In this instance, it is possible to isolate a point of rupture within the text in which the noncontroversial, the unintentional and the "invisible" characteristics of ideological discourse give way to the more obtrusive mode of propaganda.

Several major difficulties in the determination of propaganda arise in Lasswell's (or any other) definition of the term. First of all, intentionality is empirically unavailable to the analyst (even avowals of purpose by authors or directors are to be regarded as discursively separate from the meaning-creation of the original text), so that the degree of "deliberateness" of a represented attitude remains the subject of conjecture rather than concrete analysis. Beyond that, the controversial nature of a "symbol" (which can be an icon, a gesture, a word or a color, in short, any vehicle of meaning) is based in part on its specific social-historical context. What appears to be jingoistic rhetoric or imagery to a 1980s eye may well have been perceived as a nearly invisible element of the mise-en-scène in the fevered months of 1942 when the Stars and Stripes were everywhere apparent, even in the sale of cowboy hats and baby food.

But most wartime propaganda was willing to be acknowledged as such due to the unanimity of purpose which generated it. While the regions of entertainment and propaganda are by no means antithetical, much wartime propaganda exuded a no-nonsense attitude towards its subject matter that stood as a mark of pride. In any case, purity of definition in the ideology/propaganda problematic is an idealist conception, despite the best efforts of social scientists such as Lasswell, Paul Lazarsfeld and others. Most propaganda contains an entertainment component while "patriotic reiterations," intended as a non-propaganda category, never set out to leave the audience unchanged. During a crisis period, many forms of social address evidence nuances of the transformative impulse which reaffirms the contemporary relevance of accepted values in order to reactivate and rededicate the audience.

The Hollywood Writers' Mobilization subscribed to a particularly broad definition of propaganda growing out of their concern for the social effects of their craft. "Every film or radio program which is dramatic or creative, that is, which involves in any degree selection, emphasis or arrangement of materials, should be regarded as a propaganda document. This is true whether or not such arrangements are consciously designed as propaganda."[14] This definition of propaganda hinges on the potential for influence, thus encompassing any instance of ideological discourse. The broadness of the Mobilization's definition may well have been part of an attempt to deflect public attention from the passionate handiwork of a vocal faction of its membership, commonly branded left-wing. If conscious design was removed as a criterion for propaganda, then all who participated in the creative process were equally culpable, even the most unconscious laborer in the film factories.

Mobilization and Advertising: The Merger of Public and Private Spheres

Most government propaganda evidenced more than a nuance of the transformative impulse; it was clearly dedicated to redirecting the energies and productive capacities of the state and its resources. One type of propaganda, the most direct form of presentation was the government pamphlet, which aimed at providing answers to inquisitive citizens. Such a format, although clearly promotional, did not exhibit any marked powers of recruitment over the unsuspecting and thus occupies a position on the ideology/propaganda spectrum far removed from a Hollywood fiction film like *Priorities on Parade*. An example of the approach of the government publication is provided by *Women at Work in Wartime,* a public affairs pamphlet authored by Katherine Glover. Much of its information was available in much smaller doses in advertising copy, billboards and newsreels. Here the emphasis is on answering most of the major questions a prospective woman worker might have and allaying doubts as to the availability of war work. One indication of the pamphlet's ideological mission is the liberty it takes with its descriptions of prevailing conditions which take the form of wish rather than fact: "But many new precedents are riding in on the tide of war production. And old ones are riding out. The distinction between 'man's work' and 'woman's work' has certainly gone with the winds of war. So has the distinction between white-collar and blue-collar jobs."[15] The pamphlet contains several full-page graphs and illustrations of key points, the better to secure speedy comprehension and persuasion, including "Women for War Work," which breaks down the female population into categories of workers or potential workers; "What America's Women Are Doing," which includes the homemaker as its largest grouping; and "How to Start a Child Care Program," which simplifies a process never successfully mastered by the federal government.

But the most significant insights into the pamphlet's ideological agenda are provided by two statements near the end of the pamphlet. In writing of the "Farm Front," Glover reiterates the Women's Bureau warning "that it is unsound policy for women out of patriotic fervor to work on farms for little or no wages. That would depress the wages of regular farm workers who are dependent upon farm work for a living."[16] And two pages later, it is stated that "the greatest care will have to be taken to keep women's wages at the same level as men's. For if their wages are lower, men may have great difficulty competing with them."[17] In both instances, the point of view of the pamphlet is clearly that of the state, impersonally regarding the play of market forces, not that of a woman dedicated to educating and building the morale of her sisters. These statements disregard the welfare of the recruited females or the notion of "equal pay for equal work," a slogan rarely enforced by government. Instead, the emphasis is on avoiding any imbalance of standard work relations by what is clearly viewed as "temporary labor," the women who are shuttled into the fields and factories to replace absent male workers. The patriarchal perspective, which was a dominant ideological factor in all mobilization efforts, breaks through the surface of a pamphlet which appears to be the product of a dedicated female activist, Katherine Glover.

One of the previously mentioned characteristics of propaganda is its intentionality. The Glover pamphlet and the other government-sponsored and -influenced war messages were the product of a concerted and much-researched effort to reshape public opinion concerning the nature and social function of the American woman. The Office of War Information's Owen Lattimore made no excuses for government propaganda efforts in one public statement:

We were forced into propaganda warfare exactly as were forced into the war as a whole, when we were caught unprepared at Pearl Harbor. Propaganda warfare is something that was imposed on us by ruthless and efficient enemies who themselves use propaganda with great skill. We can no more afford to do without it than we can afford to do without tanks.[18]

Countless internal memoranda within the government agencies overseeing the mobilization campaigns testify to the strenuous efforts and preparation required to insure the most effective methods and yield the greatest results in terms of recruitment of paid and volunteer female workers. One memorandum from 4 August 1942, to George Pettee, a ranking official within the Office for Emergency Management (a temporary agency working in close contact with the President) was a capsule summary entitled "Government Statements on Women." For seven pages, an OWI employee summarized the various, often contradictory, statements and statistics on women made by the President, the Bureau of Commerce, the War Manpower Commission and various private citizens in an attempt to stabilize the official profile on a controversial issue. Rather than evaluating the various citations, the memo calmly notes the rhetorical discrepancies, as with the projected figures for needed womanpower which varied from one official source to another by as much as three million (the War Manpower Commission predicted two million more women would be needed while the Women's Bureau and the Department of Commerce produced a figure of five million the same year).[19]

The memo to Pettee is much like another Bureau of Intelligence communique to the Office for Emergency Management on 5 August 1942, which summarizes "Statements of Private Thought Leaders on Women and the War." At this early stage of the war effort, strenuous efforts were being made to monitor the public pronouncements of the state and of the private citizenry in order to enhance the aura of cohesion and consistency which could boost morale. It was the purpose of government ideologues to eradicate apparent contradictions within the official line, to dispel the dissonance which threatened the manufactured unity of state utterances. As social scientists Paul Lazarsfeld and Robert Merton concluded in "The Psychological Analysis of Propaganda": "Propaganda is no substitute for social policy and social action. But it can strengthen them in the understanding of the people."[20] The power of ideological and propaganda campaigns lay in their presumed ability to alter the public perception of government action and even of world events.

The task of polling and ultimately harnessing the contemporary currents of thought on women was a difficult one in that it involved the manipulation of many deeply engrained prejudices. The intent of the intelligence research was the construction of a solid front of facts and figures that suppressed many strains of thought determined to be counterproductive; for example, the statement of one "private thought leader," a sociologist from Goucher, who publicly suggested that "the present war might jar the middle class wife out of her present life of parasitic ease.''[21] This process of ideological streamlining was not without its opponents in government, many of whom realized that the consistent promotional themes of war mobilization were inadequate representations of complex conditions with a Madison Avenue veneer. One such objection was raised by Mary Brewster White in an OWI inter-office memo on 13 August 1943. Ms. White criticized the "definite tendency to reduce all women's recruiting programs, insofar as the listener or reader is concerned, to the 'buy bonds—save fats' level. . . . If you will take a look at much of the copy written for war bond campaigns, for salvage programs, and for women's recruiting programs, you will find an appalling similarity among them, and I'll bet a reference to 'keep guns, tanks, and planes coming,' 'sacrifices' and 'boys in fox holes' is included in every one of them. It is little wonder that our exhortations to women to turn their lives upside down fall on deaf ears. . . . As I see it, our job is to *explain* and *reassure*—not just to recruit, appeal, urge, exhort, declaim and announce.''[22] Ms. White's critique was aimed at the single-mindedness of most wartime appeals which adopted an adversarial rather than simply informational approach, and as such represents one of the elements of contestation within this transformative moment of the hegemonic order. White argued that such an approach produced propaganda that appealed to audiences via a hard sell technique, and which disparaged the potential for intelligent public education.

It is interesting to note that commercial promotion fits the definition of propaganda devised by the Institute for Propaganda Analysis at this time:"the expression of opinion or action by individuals or groups deliberately assigned to influence actions of other individuals or groups with reference to predetermined ends.''[23] This version of propaganda makes no mention of "controversial subjects," stressing instead the *expression* or *deliberate influence* which applies equally well to government campaigns and commercial promotion, perhaps even to motion pictures. Certainly all three forms shared a belief in the efficiency of dramaturgical persuasion rather than the "explaining" and "reassuring" tactic that Mary Brewster White and others advocated. Director William Wyler once suggested that "every film is propaganda" because of its contribution to the social and political attitudes of its audience. "But, of course," added Wyler, "propaganda must not look like propaganda.''[24] Social scientists Paul Lazarsfeld and Robert Merton identified a wartime malaise they termed "propaganditis" which evolved out of a widespread mistrust for value-laden statements issued from all sides. A typical expression of this phenomenon occurs in the remarks of one test subject:

> I just think it's too sappy to put over on a adult mind. To me it gave the opposite kind of a reaction than it was supposed to give me. I suppose they wanted to make you feel full of patriotism, but I think it gave me the opposite reaction. . . . And then at the end—whistling the Star-Spangled Banner. Everybody believes in the flag, but they don't like it waved in front of their faces.[25]

A close inspection of propaganda campaigns yields an awareness of the inevitable overlap of ideology and propaganda, with the latter term primarily a subregion within the ideological domain. A folder entitled "Womanpower Campaigns," a confidential OWI directive to its community offices ("This is confidential and must not be circulated except to government agencies") provides ample evidence of the need to portray government requests as "natural" and "commonsensical" rather than in violation of traditional values. As ideological discourse, these campaigns undertook the perilous task of masquerading socially aberrant behavior in the guise of everyday life and of "inoculating" the culture in small doses with various new ideas in order to enhance their acceptability. The following statements are all contained within the OWI training folder and were implemented on a community basis, "upon the premise that 'Podunk can best solve Podunk's problems.' "[26] Only partially concealed within the rhetoric are a variety of attitudes towards women which betray a patriarchal, authoritarian voice. After each official statement, a brief analysis of the implied message is offered.

1) "So, of necessity, women are going to war—but more and more and more of them must go soon—fighting the way women *must* fight, with plenty of sacrifice and plenty of WORK. They are taking their places, unhysterically, in the auxiliaries of the Armed Service, in industry, in business, on the farms, in hospitals, in shops. . . ."

Analysis: There are certain unalterables for women in their work roles—notably sacrifice—but they can learn to overcome their hysterical nature.

2) "The 'shorten-the-war' theme is obviously the one which appeals most deeply to women. Mothers, grandmothers, sisters, wives, sweethearts—there isn't one who doesn't want her man back as fast as possible. Working will speed the day—and will help make the waiting easier."

Analysis: Since women are defined by their relationship to men, their patriotic efforts are linked to their personal attachments to soldiers rather than to ideals or abstract values. Going to work will kill time until the men return and normal life resumes.

3) "By an overwhelming recognition of the woman *on the job,* we hope to make all women who are not working wonder why they are not."

Analysis: Women, unaccustomed to social recognition for their work, will respond strongly when their work is positively reinforced. But the most effective incentive for women, the one to which they are most vulnerable, is always a negative one—induce guilt.

4) "The ultimate goal of the September campaign is to associate in the minds of the public the words 'woman' and 'work' just as firmly as the words 'man' and 'fight' are associated."

Analysis: Behavior modification and recasting of sex roles is possible through a vigorous and repetitive public campaign.

5) "any strong, able-bodied woman who is not *completely occupied* with a job and a home is going to be considered a 'slacker' just as much as the man who avoids the draft."

Analysis: Negative reinforcement will also produce results on women who will be expected, as a matter of course, to maintain two jobs instead of a man's singular occupation as soldier or war worker.

6) "Women can stand a lot, and actually they are workers by tradition. It is only in recent years, and mostly in the United States, that women have been allowed to fall into habits of extraordinary leisure."

Analysis: The government is actually doing a great service for women by revitalizing a lost tradition of servitude which they were allowed (by men) to fall into. A great deal of free labor from this durable breed has been wasted.

7) "It is entirely natural for women to work, especially in wartime."

Analysis: Again, the *natural* (rather than conditioned) lot in life for women is hard labor.

8) "One of the principal difficulties encountered in 'selling' women on taking war jobs has been the difficulty in making the appeals personal enough."

Analysis: Women respond to emotional appeals rather than to rational or intellectual persuasion. They must be swindled rather than convinced.

9) "What kind of *hands* have you? Pretty, peacetime palms? Or slightly work-roughened ones— broadened and strengthened and made far more beautiful by physical effort? Are the hands *capable,* can they accept *responsibility,* are they proud of honest dirt?"

Analysis: The old version of feminine beauty is out; in these new circumstances, physical effort is beautiful, dirt is honest—the virtues of womanhood must and can be reshaped.

These excerpts from the OWI training booklet provide a rare chance to observe the inner workings of the machine of state ideology and propaganda. The distinction between the two forms is blurred by the composite character of the project—to mobilize mass action (propaganda) by reworking and enlarging the standard motifs of American cultural life in order to "naturalize" new and necessary standards of behavior (ideology). If we take intentionality to be a key characteristic of the propagandist, there is great import in one of the closing statements of the pamphlet: "The repercussions of this program will be many because they involve complete dislocation of generations of established family routine. The accepted 'American way of life' is undergoing terrific readjustments."[27]

The symbol of the womanpower drive was a torch held aloft by a woman's lightly manicured hand with "WWW" emblazoned on the torch explained by the legend beneath it—*WOMEN WAR WORKERS*. The torch was handed on by the War Manpower Commission to its regional service representatives through suggestions for uniform womanpower recruitment campaigns utilizing community resources. The nationally distributed War Manpower Commission Plan Book, clearly the product of collaboration with the OWI, the Bureau of Intelligence, the Woman's Bureau and other intelligence sources, states its purpose vigorously: "Before the end of 1943, more than one-third of all the workers in the United States *must be women.*"[28] Suggestions are offered on the best techniques for rallying local newspaper support to insure coverage through news releases, pictures, editorials and women's page items. Advertising outlets of every sort are suggested: foreign language and racial newspapers, labor publications, church, club and civic publications as well as daily and weekly newspapers. Cooperation from local radio stations is described as essential. The Washington office promises to supply promotional recordings by "big names" (Kate Smith, Lowell Thomas) for use as one-minute spots, along with five-minute dramatic spots and five- and fifteen-minute interviews with public figures ("dramatically and professionally produced"). Live spot announcements are suggested as are special broadcasts by prominent local leaders (material for such speeches is provided in the Plan Book). Theatrical and non-theatrical films are available for each locale. A four-minute and a one-minute 35mm film, both based on the theme "Wanted— Women War Workers," are intended for screening at local theaters through the cooperation of the film industry's War Activities Committee. Order blanks are provided with the suggested ration of one print for every five theaters. Two 16mm documentaries are described as available for recruitment within the community. Outdoor advertising, via a twenty-four sheet poster ("Victory Is in Your Hands— Apply United States Employment Service") is available through the donated services of the Outdoor Advertising Association of America as are window strips and slogan stencils for display in store windows and womanpower campaign headquarters. One home office suggestion—that the local War Manpower Commission representatives "arrange to have Boy Scouts . . . paint [the campaign] slogans on sidewalks"—evokes an image of a Capraesque America. The Plan Book is literally jammed with ideas aimed at eliciting full-scale support for the war agenda. The wide-ranging strategies mentioned include the designation of a "Womanpower Week," the promotion of work clothes for women ("Women should be convinced that overalls, slacks, and sensible shoes are the order of the day"), the creation of a Roster of Women War Workers as part of the city's archives, even the recruitment of local clergymen as pulpit-promoters of the womanpower campaign. This concert of efforts devised by the War Manpower Commission was one of the many campaigns aimed at influencing and reorienting the major institutions of the private sector: the family (husbands were encouraged to recognize the necessity for working wives, organized child care was introduced); the Church (ministers were eagerly solicited as community spokesmen); the schools (new training programs for women were initiated, medical training for women was instituted at unprecedented levels).

Marxist critics from Louis Althusser to Nicos Poulantzas to Ernesto Laclau have described the conditions and effects of ideological crisis within the state, usually in the context of fascism. "In a crisis all the component elements and conditions fuse, as a whole, into a ruptural unity."[29] The description of a social formation's ideological climate during periods of crisis as a complex and condensed expression of aberrant conditions fits the case of American wartime life.

According to Laclau, the social antagonisms of such historical moments are constituted by "classes in struggle" rather than "class struggle."[30] The ideological climate is dominated by the "popular-democratic interpellation" which has no precise class content and appears to represent no class faction. Consent, that element of the hegemonic order defined earlier as a vital ingredient in binding together antagonistic social forces, is readily available since, at the ideological level, class aims are represented as the consummation of popular objectives. In wartime America, it was the Boy Scouts who stenciled the sidewalk, the normally profit-mad theater operators who volunteered their time and assets, the normally reticent clergymen who preached social action. The desire to achieve full productivity, to fill the factories, fire the furnaces and generate the handsome profit margins was no longer representable as the goal of the owners of the means of production (the Kaisers, Knudsens and the Fords), but the goal of the "people"—that unified body of Americans, for the moment undifferentiated by sex, class or color. While the Henry Kaisers built dynasties of capital, the Rosies riveted (for less money than their male counterparts) and the black GI's cooked and cleaned for the armies of Europe (since blacks were judged unsuitable for leadership positions). Equal status was an ideological construct rather than a condition of life, achieved through a coordination of efforts at every level of government. Mobilization touched every corner of the land—the populist ideology of the war years "healed" every breach in the social fabric. It is important to remember, however, that a "ruptural unity" can never be manufactured, but is instead the product of specific historical conditions. American citizens *were* killed at Pearl Harbor, there *were* raving dictators annihilating entire races of people. This analysis offers proof of a response to these world conditions, the response consisting of a massive and carefully planned ideological program aimed at harnessing and mesmerizing the working people of America in the interest of victory.

The womanpower recruitment campaign was being promulgated with great vigor in the private sector as well. The War Advertising Council, the advertising industry's version of Hollywood's War Activities Committee, was actively educating the business interests of America as to the immediacy of the manpower crisis threatening to destroy the full-throttled productivity revitalizing the land. Realizing the urgency of the situation in mid-1942, the Council published its own "how-to" booklet for advertisers throughout America. The first portion of the pamphlet instructed the advertisers on the range of jobs that needed filling by women, with emphasis on the "unglamorous" job categories—the maids, cashiers, receptionists and department store clerks whose ranks thinned in the wake of the first rush to the high-salaried jobs vacated by men. The idea was that advertising space should begin to include "specially-prepared messages designed to attract women to war-useful employment." By means of a simulated question/answer format, the War Advertising Council booklet provides the ideological strategy for the ensuing campaign, to wit:

Remark: "I have never worked in a factory . . . I know nothing about machines."

Reply: This resistance can best be overcome by likening machinery to household practices with which women are familiar.

Remark: "My husband objects to my taking a job."

Reply: This is one of the greatest resistances. Advertising must combat the feeling on the part of many husbands that a working wife is a reflection on their ability to support her. Advertising must make clear the fact that in war time it is vitally necessary for women to work.[31]

The key slogan of the booklet was "a war message in every ad." For those businesses with neither the time nor the resources for full-scale war advertising, the Council suggested thumbnail messages which could be inserted into regular ads. The suggestion was made that women at work, radiating their new-found sense of purpose, be used as models for advertising copy. One example given is a Camel cigarette ad featuring a Patricia Garner working as a member of a Pan Am flight crew. ("Behind those flags in her hand there's a flag in her heart . . . the Stars and Stripes she's serving by working at a war job. A *man's* job!—but she's the real All-American Girl, 1942 model . . . As Pat says: 'Camels have a flavor like no other cigarette.'")[32] For those companies whose usual consumer goods were converted to war materiel, the booklet suggested publishing, over the corporate name, advertisements designed to educate women on the importance of taking a war job. What's more, said the council, "You will be building up a reservoir of good will that will mean sales after the war." The War Advertising Council pamphlet, by encouraging participation in the nationwide womanpower campaign through corporate funding, combined a patriotic appeal with a pragmatic, businesslike approach. Altruism was successfully coupled with financial gain to further bolster the solid ideological front presented to the nation.

The solidity of the ideological front, the ruptural unity referred to earlier, is testified to by an examination of popular periodicals from 1942 and 1943, particularly the high-circulation products from the Time-Life group. *Life* magazine in particular occupies a unique position within the field of popular culture with its multiple character as a weekly periodical specializing in up-to-the-minute photojournalism (with a pictorial quality far superior to that of newsprint), its eye upon both the warfronts and the Hollywood backlots. During these years *Life* was a vehicle of entertainment—through its human interest stories and detailed coverage of stage and screen—and a mode of instruction for its readership through its suggestions of the new fashion trends growing out of altered lifestyles (e.g., military-style berets for women, stylishly upswept hair for the woman factory worker, and painted-on stockings for the rationed-out female) and helpful tips on wartime etiquette for GIs stationed in England (never take seconds at dinner in a private home and don't steal the "Tommy's" girl). In many issues of the 1942–43 period, it is difficult to distinguish between the advertising copy, with its built-in pitches for the war effort and little outright product promotion, and the feature articles which profiled key Washington administrators like Leon Henderson or Donald Nelson, pictorializing a Women's Army Corps training installation or explaining the physiology of night vision which enabled soldiers to spot enemy aircraft in the dark. The same magazine, in other historical circumstances, may well share an identical ideological function—to promote and maintain a stable and certifiably "American" way of life based on shared patterns of behavior and commodity consumption, but the wartime variant bears a heightened sense of its role, a greater level of "interpellative urgency." But, again, it is important to recall that the perception of propaganda is linked to concrete conditions; in the United States of 1942 and 1943, military iconography and patriotic rhetoric were far less controversial and are therefore not an a priori basis for a claim of propaganda.

The didactic tone of both advertising and entertainment copy in a 1942 *Life* magazine is consistent with the unified, no-nonsense approach to crisis which the Roosevelt administration was attempting to convey in the midst of a war which it was losing. The gearing-up of the industrial base was underway, but, owing to Congressional resistance, the nation was months away from peak production levels, while the Japanese were continuing to defeat the best American efforts in the Pacific. Recruitment of women was slow in developing, there were racial tensions erupting in the overcrowded centers of manufacture, and it was getting harder to find a good cut of meat. Into the breach stepped the carefully-tailored products of mass culture, the result of much plotting and behind-the-scenes collaboration. The films, the magazines, the songs and the advertising displays shared the function of smoothing over the inequities, concealing the imperfections, and minimizing the inadequacies of a struggling nation. The intended effect was organicism, the inevitable and quite natural growth of new habits and new conditions. A 21 September 1942 *Life* article on "War Scooters" illustrates the process, showing how "miniature war machines transform peaceful parks into battlegrounds." The multipage spread offers photographs of seven boys and one girl atop movable war toys made of "non-priority materials": "They have pivoting guns, steer like cars and go like the devil." The origins of such "toys" are never disclosed. Certainly, the sociological angle of documenting a new trend in childhood recreation is absent. The article stands out as a particularly blatant case of desensitizing a populace to the "horrors" of war by reducing war to "child's play," and validating aggressive behavior for young men and women, the future defenders of an embattled America.

Two weeks later, on 5 October 1942, an article appears on "Armies That Win," a brief sojourn into military history that treats the "art of warfare (and) shows the evolution of weapons and the principles that have always brought victory." Armed combat is at once elevated to the status of both art and science. The following week there is a piece on arc welding, an industrial process being used in the assembly of liberty ships and other items of war. Alongside these educational tracts are the pieces aimed at modeling social behavior, like the article in the "War Living" section on 22 February 1943, featuring "Aprons— Stylish housewives now wear them for work and dressed-up parties. . . . Aprons now are so good-looking that women no longer pull them off as soon as they leave the kitchen." This story appears, in retrospect, to be related to the fears of waning femininity among the millions of American women who answered the call of the industrial workplace. In a time of confusion concerning sex roles, *Life* served as a medium of cultural exchange as well as self-conscious arbiter as evidenced by the cover of the 1 March 1942 issue which features two women in white shirts, mannish jackets and bow ties, with the simple caption "Bow Ties." Inside, the explanation is offered that "this year, not only the smart dressers but all busy women seem to have discovered the comfort, style-value and well-groomed look of a suit tailored like a man's. Only the tie remained for them to filch. Now even the tie is gone." But the unisexual image is counteracted by a Coty perfume ad offering the simplest copy imaginable:

> His duty
>   to serve—
> Hers
>   to inspire—
>
>
>   Coty

The visual accompaniment is a cosmetically impeccable female face, well-lit, frontally imaged, but with eyes on a partially figured, heavily silhouetted man in uniform. The woman in the ad speaks to a female audience, but she only has eyes for that man in her life. The sexual roles are clear and traditional. Women do their part by smelling good, by providing a sensuous reward for the toiling man-soldier.

While both ad and feature share a common and equally overt interest in shaping the social attitudes and habits of the readership, there is no unanimity of ideology with a ruptural unity, no uncontested consent. It is crucial in the analysis of cultural products to recognize the multiplicity and contradiction of meanings generated. A unitary purpose produces widely disparate utterances without which culture, through repression, becomes political tract or pamphlet. A similar measure of contradiction is identifiable in the films of this or any period.

A concept of particular significance in Laclau's account of ruptural unity is that of condensation, a term originating in Freud's *Interpretation of Dreams:* the fusion which occurs within the process of representation so that a single image or figure represents in itself many associative chains and is thus invested with a multiplicity of often conflicting energies.[33] Not only is a single issue of *Life* the site of ideological contradiction, but even a single piece of advertising copy contains conflicting meanings which conjure a coherent image, a relatively unified meaning. This is condensation at the level of a single text, a process which will later be noted in the textual analysis of films. A Bell Telephone ad in *Time* magazine in July 1942 provides an example of condensation with regard to several highly charged topics: the "nature" of woman, her role in the war, the division of the sexes, the hope for peace and the role of the Bell Telephone System in the achievement of that peace. The only graphics are the Bell Telephone logo in the lower right corner of the full-page ad and a drawing of a female telephone operator which takes up nearly half the page. Her quiet beauty is augmented by a stoicism apparent around her firmly-set but lipsticked mouth. Her gaze, in contrast to the full frontal pose of the head, is averted—to the future. Beneath the drawing is a poem entitled "We Are the Unseen," written by one Eleanora Dayton Surry, Long Distance Operator, Washington, D.C.

We Are the Unseen

We are the unseen, ever watchful, never sleeping,
Binding the atoms together.
        Not ours the glory nor applause,
We wear no uniform and yet are part of our land's destiny,
        Guarding her secrets well.
We are the unseen, loyal, true to an ideal,
        One God, one country, one flag:
We want no praise, knowing, out there,
        Men have shed their blood that we might live . . .
With others soon to follow them.
        Our reward shall be, one day, with the touch of magic
                at our finger-tips
To send across the quivering wires
One far-flung cry—"Ours is the Victory!"[34]

A place to begin the analysis of the advertisement/poem is with the pronoun "we" (and the possessive adjective "our") used in the title and text a total of eleven times. One of the primary functions of the poem is to enlarge the antecedent for the first person plural from "we/women" and "we/long distance operators" to "we/Americans" and "we/Americans with the help of Bell Telephone System." There is a strong sense of the female in the "we" enhanced by the illustration and the author's womanhood. The adjectives attached to that personal pronoun provide a sense of the regime of meaning within which American womanhood was cast at the time, that is, "unseen," "ever watchful," "never sleeping," "binding," "guarding," "unseen" (again), "loyal," "true," "knowing." This was the woman behind the scenes, ready to fill in for her man but not at all anxious to receive praise for her endeavors. She was archetypally nurturing ("ever watchful, never sleeping") and though hers was the task of "binding the atoms together," she was not one of the atoms herself, since a part of her sacrifice was the willing suppression of her own identity.

Halfway through the poem an ideal constituted by three components now fused into one (God/country/flag) is introduced which offers a bridge from the strict separation of genders enforced elsewhere. Thanks to the Bell Telephone system, the final word of victory will be transmitted to all parts of the nation, instantaneously uniting men and women, soldiers and long distance operators; in short, all Americans who share belief in this triadic ideal, so that the first person plural of the final phrase "Ours is the Victory!" is at last all Americans. The social breach is healed without the loss of traditional sex roles; the sexes maintain their "essential" attributes (men fight; women work) but can be united by shared ideals and the "quivering wires" of the Bell System. For, in the words of the slogan across the bottom of the page, "BELL TELEPHONE SYSTEM . . . LONG DISTANCE HELPS UNITE THE NATION." In an important sleight of hand at the poem's end, the technology that will unite the nation is called "the touch of magic"—a scientific process is transmuted into a feat of prestidigitation incomprehensible to the citizenry, a kind of patriotic offering from Bell Telephone. (The invocation of "magic" is a textbook case of the mythologizing process described by Roland Barthes, robbed of history, hemorrhaged of meaning, eternalized.) Now America is united and victorious, thanks to fighting men, sacrificing and invisible women and trustworthy (albeit unknowable) corporations.

The Film Industry: The Ideological Mission of Entertainment

The segue from wartime advertising to the motion picture industry is a logical one insofar as ideological function is concerned. Every federal agency or trade association charged with coordinating the activities of the private sector with government programs produced a manual, the Bureau of Motion Pictures included. "The Government Information Manual for the Motion Pictures" provides a sense of the ideological guidelines with which the film industry was meant to comply. For unlike *Life* magazine, which could claim the status of world newseye, bringing to Americans images captured from around the globe, the film industry produced unabashed fabrications, a fact which automatically engendered greater scrutiny from official quarters. In examining the ideological potency of the *Life* format, the instructional and informational elements emerge as co-equal with the entertainment values. But the Hollywood film, forever dedicated to the maxim that messages were best left to Western Union, was the medium of ideology par excellence. Because movies were perceived as entertainment, as rewards of laughter and tears, their ability to transmit and legitimize social attitudes, sex roles and behavioral patterns was all the more powerful, given ideology's basis in the "imaginary." (Recall the Althusserian account of ideology as the real experience of imaginary social and productive relations borrowed from the Freudian/

Lacanian concept of the imaginary, the stage of human development preceding the accession to language.) In both instances of the imaginary, psychic and social, a process of misrecognition fosters a kind of complacency through which appearance is taken for reality. On the sociopolitical level, productive relations appear to be the neutral manifestations of market forces. But via historical materialist analysis in the manner of Marx's *Capital,* it becomes possible to derive underlying contradictions which, in turn, produce phenomenal forms. Ideology embraces the phenomenal rather than the generative. In a related way, during the imaginary process of psychic development, the first stage of the construction of the human subject occurs through the misrecognition of a unified persona prior to the attainment of simple motor skills, coordination or elemental language skills. As Lacan writes of the mirror stage, occurring between the ages of six and eighteen months, the infant seizes upon his/her image as the representation of an "Ideal-I," thus situating the ego "in a fictional direction" from the outset.[35] This misrecognition forms the link between the individual and social processes of ego-construction and ideology.

The misrecognition of ideological discourse is experienced in a precognitive, essentially prelinguistic manner through its access to the imaginary of the viewing subject. At least, this is the case when the ideological material assumes the appearance of "entertainment" instead of the related cultural forms of greater self-consciousness: propaganda, educational tracts, historical reenactment. The potency of the cinematic mode (with its visual nexus reenacting the earliest processes of identification) was recognized by government sources who placed far greater constraints on the motion picture industry than on the related fields of journalism or even broadcasting. What's more, the Motion Picture Bureau recognized that the impact of the medium depended on the manufactured spontaneity which induced audience receptivity to the explicit or implicit content (explicit content might be ideas in the form of dramatic dialogue; implicit content might be the attitude that the male protagonist evidences towards his love interest). As a result, the bureau advocated the casual insertion of constructive "war messages" that would not obtrude on the dramatic format:

> At every opportunity, naturally and inconspicuously, show people making small sacrifices for victory—making them voluntarily, cheerfully and because of the people's own sense of responsibility, not because of any laws. For example, show people bringing their own sugar when invited out to dinner, carrying their own parcels when shopping, traveling on planes or trains with light luggage, uncomplainingly giving up seats for servicemen, or others traveling on war priorities; show persons accepting dimout restrictions, tire and gas rationing cheerfully, show well-dressed persons, obviously car owners riding in crowded buses and streetcars. . . . In crowds unostentatiously show a few wounded men. Prepare people but do not alarm them against the casualties to come . . . show colored soldiers in crowd scenes; occasionally colored officers. Stress our national unity by using names of foreign extraction, showing foreign types in the services.[36]

Films were intended to "prepare" Americans for future traumas by the "inoculation" of disquieting imagery placed in relief to the primary action. Showing black officers in a scene meant contradicting mathematical probability, but ideology operates in all cases through selection. In this case, official requests were being made for additions to the pool of selected images that were unlikely but promotional. The bureau suggested that each filmmaker ask himself seven questions at the outset of a production, chief among them the simple query "Will this picture help win the war?" The remainder of the questions were framed in an equally jejune manner, characterized by the casual use of words like "truth" and "propaganda," e.g., "Does the picture tell the truth or will the young people of today scorn it a few years hence, when they are running the world, and say they were misled by propaganda?"[37] The implication was that Hollywood could learn to express itself in the manner of the Office of War Information through "the strategy of truth" which banished the specter of propaganda, an un-American concept. The industry was certainly placed in a double-bind between ideology and propaganda. They were instructed to inject into their films special subject matter and imagery that constituted propaganda by accepted definition (*deliberate* attempts to influence *mass attitudes* on *controversial subjects* by the use of *symbols* rather than force) while being warned to remain ideological (understated, insinuating, covert) in their manner of presentation. The perfect marriage could then be achieved: Hollywood form and Washington content, propaganda cloaked in properly ideological raiment.

In chapter 3, the unique relationship between the state and the film industry was examined by means of Hollywood/Washington correspondence and the examination of the unprecedented level of supervision by the Office of Censorship, the Office of War Information and countless other agencies. It is worth sketching out the theoretical framework in which the cinema/state relationship exists. In the first place, World War II does not represent a break with the customary ties between the film industry and the state, only an extreme case consistent with the changed status of state capitalism—*in extremis*—existing at that time. The degree of syndicalism was unprecedented; the normal distribution of political and economic power throughout a complex network of moderately conflictual, geographically dispersed interest groups was replaced by a far more centralized power base. The standard format simulated a board of directors, with disparate parties (labor, business, women) duly represented, but with the ultimate determinations issued by the chairman—Roosevelt. Given this structure, it is not at all surprising to note that the War Activities Committee of the Motion Picture Industry was a body of powerful men representing the major studios and independent producers, located in Washington, operating under the tacit leadership of the Chief Executive.

Yet at no time has the dominant mode of Hollywood cinema diverged from an ideological complicity with existing social structures through its modeling of behavioral patterns, trends in fashion and sexual roles. The Hollywood system of film production has provided an unceasing flow of images (of people, of institutions), relationships (between men and women, workers and bosses, America and foreign nations) and narrative resolutions (marriage, rags-to-riches, the spiritual apotheosis) which have consolidated and valorized the culture that is its global referent. Of the tragic, the melodrama and the noir films, which appear to challenge this view of the Hollywood film as stabilizing agent, it can be said that the social conflict is characteristically displaced to a discourse of misdirected desire or imbalanced family relations, "personal" rather than "social" inadequacies. One might also argue that the tragic or despairing film, by giving voice and form to social tensions and private anguish, offers a safe, communal release or catharsis in the manner of mimetic forms. According to Louis Althusser's theory of the ideological state apparatus, institutions either public (the police, the military) or private (the church, the family, political parties, trade unions or cultural institutions like the cinema) provide an objective field within which contradictions can safely be expressed while concurrently maintaining and reproducing the prevailing relations of production. The primary distinction between public and private ideological state apparatuses is that the former category (the police, the military) functions predominantly through repression and only secondarily through ideology, while the private institutions function largely through ideology, that is, through the manipulation of shared beliefs, popular imagery and the modulation of social practices (fashion, sex roles, slang) and only secondarily through repression (excommunication, censorship).

In the case of the Hollywood film, the reproduction of existing social relations is quite literal since the cinema is a system of representation which depends upon the effects of recognition and identification for its audience impact. The very "reality effect" which defines this mode of cultural production and separates it from, for example, the avant-garde tradition of anti-narrative and non-representational figuration, guarantees its potential as a medium of social control. By linking the viewing dynamics of its style of cinema to the psychic processes of projection, introjection and identification (enhanced by the creation of the star system, glamour, picture palaces, etc.), the doyens of the Hollywood industry established a popular and highly profitable cultural form exhibiting powers of social control far in excess of the expectations of the Edisons, Armats, Dicksons or Lumieres. Furthermore, to call the Hollywood cinema an ideological state apparatus is not to make a claim for conscious connections between the industry and the ruling class or state power along the lines of a conspiracy theory (based, perhaps, on the fact that L. B. Mayer was an intimate friend of Herbert Hoover). Rather, the claim is that the American cinema constitutes a field of ideological discourse characterized by an uneven and fluctuating relationship to state power and authority. At certain moments of its history, the "relative autonomy" of this cultural institution has seemed an undeniable fact (e.g., during the self-expressive sixties with its tendency toward uncensored speech, nudity, and slow-motion violence at a time when many Americans remained wedded to a sensibility of restraint). During periods of profound ideological crisis such as the World War II period, however, a very different relationship obtains between culture and politics. At such times, a confluence occurs, a "flowing together" born of a common concern for the perpetuation of existing social relations and the hierarchical distribution of wealth, status and power. For while the ideological call to arms may stress the popular-democratic character of the struggle ("One Nation Under God, Indivisible, with Liberty and Justice for All"), the leaders of government and of industry share a vested interest in the continuation of state capitalism far more compelling than the honored traditions of separation of public and private or church and state. As Antonio Gramsci observed, such distinctions are internal to bourgeois law, existing within the domain of liberal humanism, the ideological mantle of capitalist democracies.

Furthermore, it cannot be claimed that the World War II period represented a clean break in the relationship between the film industry and other institutions. External pressures of a similar sort had been leveled by the government during World War I, while significant alterations in the codes of film practice had resulted from the combined efforts of church and community from 1930 to 1934. The various production codes and the creation of the Legion of Decency as an internal mechanism for censorship of movie content represent the significant effects of an external moral coalition upon the industry. Although the pressures of the Catholic Church exemplify the influence of one private institution upon another, rather than a public institution upon a private, this case provides another instance in which a "relatively autonomous" cultural form responds to social forces— from the private sector in the thirties, from the public sector in the forties.

The theoretical model suggested here places the film industry alongside other institutions (the church, the family, the schools) as a functional support of state power operating primarily through the complicity of its ideological practice. It is clear that a rather different relationship was perceived by many observers during the World War II period as evidenced by the fears expressed regarding the propaganda potential of the screen, even upon the state. Such a position was taken by Albert Benham of the National Council for the Prevention of War: "The far-reaching influence of the motion picture makes it a potent factor in any critical period of public opinion. It not only influences public opinion, but, in influencing it, goes far toward determining government policy."[38] The ideological state apparatus argument should by no means obscure the effectivity of the film industry upon the state, so that an accurate theoretical model would allow for mutual effectivity, a reciprocal relationship of determination that recognizes the shared interest of cultural institutions and government in the perpetuation of fixed market relations. But the influence of either term of the relationship may well be experienced as predominant at any given time, depending upon the specific historical context and the perspective of the observer.

Archibald MacLeish, Assistant Director of the Office of War Information, accused Hollywood of bearing a "primary and inescapable responsibility" for America's misunderstanding of events leading to war and of the war itself.[39] In one short statement, MacLeish grants an autonomous status to a cultural institution as distinct from the state, a strong influence upon Americans by that institution, and outright culpability for popular misconceptions based upon that influence. It is interesting that MacLeish was willing to acknowledge that the film industry was producing more effective war information than the Office by that name, which he helped to direct. In any case, there can be little doubt of the central role which the cultural institutions as mass media played in promoting the sudden alterations in lifestyle effected by government policy. William Chafe's appraisal of the effects of cultural forms upon the wartime woman allows for no equivocation: "None of the changes in women's work could have occurred without the active approval and encouragement of the principal instruments of public opinion."[40]

Woman as Ideological Construct

Having undertaken working definitions of ideology and of propaganda, and having suggested the theoretical linkage between the American film industry and state power during the Second World War, it remains to offer a sense of the prevailing ideological currents with regard to women. The women's history section of this study elaborated on the altered fortunes of American women of this period and the underlying economic and political conditions that gave rise to them. It became clear that the public images of the female were in flux, for men and for women, but the depth of this redefinition and its effects upon sex roles, the concrete patterns of gender-specific behavior, were less clear. In order to derive meaning from the various Hollywood representations of women, to place them within a context of historical and ideological specificity, it becomes necessary to attempt a chronicling of dominant currents of thought with regard to women of that period, for films, as popular culture, produce their dramatic effects by means of restructuring and realigning recognizable characters, situations and ideas whose currency provides a key to audience interest. At times, the values presented are residual (as, for example, the 1920s melodramas of D. W. Griffith, which grappled with an essentially Victorian moral/ethical system); at other times, they are emergent (e.g., the topical films of the early forties concerned with the conflicts of the new working woman, conflicts whose novelty was to fade into obsolescence in the postwar years). But before one can offer informed readings of the wartime films, it is helpful to outline the ideological domain out of which Hollywood's wartime representations of women emerged.

Ideology, or mythology as Roland Barthes reframed it in his seminal *Mythologies,* tends to portray its objects as "natural," "inevitable," and devoid of developmental history. The characterization of women within ideology has sought at all times to confine the behavior and identity of half of humanity within strict limits—the "nature" of woman. The sudden emergence of Rosie the Riveter caused the conventional wisdom to reframe its notion of essential womanhood to accommodate new conditions, while maintaining many of the most enduring and corrosive stereotypes. One such stereotype, with particular applicability to the cinema, is that of the good girl/bad girl duality in which unchanging characteristics and strict moral alignments are attached to each term. Of course, many female film personae were allowed to bridge the gap between good and bad by any number of devices ranging from classical peripeteia or dramatic reversal to the use of twin sisters as in *The Dark Mirror* or *A Stolen Life*—one pure, the other evil. In other cases, like *Notorious* or *Possessed*, the question of the female's moral status constitutes the narrative center of the film.[41] In a book entitled *Morals vs. Morale in Wartime*, a New York endocrinologist put the stamp of science upon this false distinction (good/bad girl):

> The young soldier on leave with healthy instincts is quite likely to seduce a "good girl" if there is no "bad girl" around or if one is too difficult to find. The "good girl" is handicapped by her emotional attachments, is motivated by patriotism or is uniform-mad. Usually, she knows little or nothing of prevention. . . . The "bad girl" is usually wise. Her past experiences protect her as well as the boy.[42]

Many allegedly "female" traits were attributed to all women, and perpetuated by women themselves. Margaret Pickel, dean of Barnard College, declared in a wartime issue of *The New York Times Magazine* that women "had less physical strength, a lower fatigue point, and a less stable nervous system (than men) . . . by middle age, when men are at their best, a devoted woman worker is apt to degenerate into fussiness or worse."[43] A War Department pamphlet entitled *You're Going to Employ Women* attempted to communicate its zealous approbation of the new woman by coining a rather curious metaphor: "A WOMAN WORKER is not a man, in many jobs she is a substitute—like plastics instead of metal—She has special characteristics that lend themselves to new and sometimes superior uses."[44] Women, by this definition, are a make-shift labor source whose unique traits (unique from men, *uniform* in women) are exploitable. A Civil Service Commission manual was even more to the point in its characterization of the woman worker: "For the purposes of any placement program they (women) must be considered as presenting a problem in placement or as 'physically handicapped.'"[45] In addition to the construction of an image of woman as plastic and handicapped, another female trait was enumerated in an article in a magazine called *Advertising and Selling* which stated: "Give a woman a job and she'll keep doing it, without suggesting any new changes for performance. The average woman is a caretaker, not a promoter."[46]

One cause of this alleged lack of ambition was that women were thought to belong elsewhere and to wish fervently for the domestic life. In the words of a 1944 edition of *Nation's Business:* "The veritable promised land the majority of our present sixteen million women workers want involves falling in love, getting married, making homes and raising babies."[47] The female editor of a popular woman's magazine had ventured a like opinion in 1942: "A woman in slacks is a woman who is right now dreaming of going back to her life as a woman at home!"[48] Such statements certainly influenced the expectations they attempted to gauge, but despite such pronouncements a number of opinion polls indicated a contrary wish among millions of working women, a circumstance already discussed at some length. But the male-dominated world of opinion-makers and government officials held the view, expressed in an Office of War Information survey, that working women were "a wartime fact rather than a desirable development."[49] After all, says the author of *Human Relations in Industry,* a woman was simply "filling in time while she finds a husband and her *real* career"[50] (emphasis added).

Since women were a vital labor supply, it became necessary to lure them into the workplace by likening the new tasks to the more familiar and "natural" ones in the home. Katherine Glover's clarion call to women in her government-sponsored pamphlet *Women at Work in Wartime* utilizes this strategy in order to bridge the old and new.

> A call has gone out for millions of women to exchange kitchen aprons for overalls; for women whose hands are skilled in sewing, in cooking, to turn to handling lathes, cutting dies, and running drills; for women whose eyes are used to fine sewing to learn to trace blueprints, test precision instruments, and inspect plane parts.[51]

One female journalist referred to the new tasks as "factory housekeeping" and reported that women took to factory machines "as easily as to electric cake-mixers and vacuum cleaners."[52] A Woman's Bureau leaflet advised the American housewife, "If you've used an electric mixer in your kitchen, you can learn to run a drill press."[53] The key to effective social modeling through ideology was stated succinctly in Hitler's *Mein Kampf:* "Effective propaganda has to limit itself to a few points and repeat these eternally." This tactic was utilized in the government's recruitment of women for war work.

The portrayal of factory work as the industrial equivalent of domestic labor was but one ploy used to attract women. Others included the repetition of certain key themes: patriotism, glamour, respect, money, romance and fear. Patriotism was always the first theme for all war inducements; the call to arms or to factories was inevitably couched in terms of national security. Money was a secondary consideration that was downplayed for several reasons. In the first place, an intensified inflationary spiral was feared if earnings were emphasized at a time when consumer goods were severely restricted. Also, the government was unwilling to champion its "equal pay for equal work" credo against the hard-liners of business and labor, whose willing participation in the wartime coalition was the keystone of Roosevelt's domestic policy. Glamour was a more malleable theme as transmitted through countless magazine stories and advertisements such as North American Aviation's *"What! An Artist's Model Building a Bomber?"* campaign[54] or the oft-repeated appellation of the female war worker as Glamour Girl of 1942 or 1943. As for respect, womanpower campaigns frequently proclaimed that good Americans should "treat a woman who takes a factory job as an important person, honor her as we honor a soldier."[55] The romance angle was normally the ideological province of fiction (but no less potent or prevalent on that account). A *Saturday Evening Post* story from August of 1942 described a young woman's experience at a national defense training school. After completing the training program, with the prospect of an assembly line job just ahead, she is called aside by her male instructor who confesses: "I love you, rivet knocker! How about you and me getting welded?"[56]

Hollywood was quick to pitch factory romance, as in the song and dance routine "On the Swingshift" from Paramount's 1942 musical *Star Spangled Rhythm:*

> Life is fine with my baby on the swing shift,
> On the line, with my baby on the swing shift.
> He's for me, he's the whole darn factory,
> He gets the love machinery working in my heart . . .
>   He's the beautiful bomber.

The women workers in this factory are clad in satiny, two-piece pseudo-overalls and all are coupled with smiling and attentive young men with whom they sing and dance. Even the term "swing" of swing shift is transmuted into the swing of popular dance rhythms resulting in a portrayal of that most unpopular eight-hour workshift as a sexualized and appealing jamboree.

But fear was not to be overlooked for its capacity to induce active female participation. One frequent variation on the theme required an elaboration of conditions for women under Nazism for whom life possibilities were reduced to kitchen, church and children. A Works Progress Administration radio script from the "This Is Our Enemy" series effectively dramatized the appalling conditions in Germany where women were methodically dismissed from their teaching positions and professional duties, denied educational opportunities and accorded the primary status of instrument of male reproduction. A major source of fear and guilt was related to the highly publicized correlation between inactive machinery and American casualties. A War Manpower Commission booklet was entitled *This Soldier May Die—Unless You Man This Idle Machine.* The ironic object of the call to "man" the machines was indeed the American woman. This approach through negative reinforcement worked as a personalizing appeal since the slogans such as "the more women at work the sooner we'll win" were often preceded on radio broadcasts by the announcement of dead, wounded and missing in action from that community. One OWI ad came right to the point in its attention-getting headline: "Women of _____, are you making these casualty lists longer?"[57] Yet another 1942 example of the scare tactic is furnished by one J. C. Furnas who wrote:

> In the next twelve months, the American housewife must show that she can keep her head and her temper and roll up her sleeves at one and the same time. If she can't, her menfolk fighting on distant atolls are likely to get slaughtered in the hot sun for lack of ammunition.[58]

Once cajoled into the workplace, the woman worker was slotted into the most monotonous tasks, then told that this was the very kind of activity for which she was best suited. "Women," according to the National Metal Trades Association, "are more patient, industrious, painstaking, and efficient about doing the same thing over and over again."[59] Or in the simpler words of a Connecticut industrialist: "They do the monotonous, repetitive work . . . that drives a man nuts."[60] In fact, these deadening jobs were shunted upon women by their male bosses, foremen and shop stewards; an unwillingness to take these jobs was interpreted as an unwillingness to work. Unfortunately, this self-serving myth of innate female fortitude was subscribed to even by women, including the Women's Bureau of the Department of Labor which publicly stated that "women are particularly good at fine processes requiring painstaking application. They have patience and finger dexterity and soon learn to make careful adjustments at high speed with great accuracy."[61] Such is the stealth and potency of ideology that the victims of its deceptions can themselves be recruited into its propagation.

Although women were meant to work hard, they were expected to maintain a low profile in keeping with the popular catch-phrase "the woman behind the man behind the gun." A major ingredient of the female persona has traditionally been self-sacrifice, a theme whose wartime currency was all the more pronounced. The general sense of "Use it up, wear it out, make it do or do without," was promoted for all Americans. The Office of Civilian Defense distributed a pamphlet which expressed the need for a new relationship between Americans and their favorite commodity, the car: "Pleasure driving is out for the duration. As of today we must pool our cars for necessary use, for driving to work, to school, to the shops. We must share necessary rides with our friends and neighbors so that no car goes on the road with even one empty seat. The empty seat is a gift to Hitler. . . . [62]

The war effort was urged as a rallying cry for labor in order to derail prospective job actions. Labor disputes were portrayed as depriving fighting men of the resources they needed to protect themselves. Again, as in rationing and carpooling, a sacrifice was demanded. But female sacrifice was far more diversified, including even the compromise of romantic idealism. A New York physician, Dr. Galielma F. Alsop, had some words of advice for young women in 1942: "Once assured in your own mind, marry him—the soldier, the sailor, the man in the sky. . . . Rise to the heights of the occasion and make the necessary sacrifices with a woman's traditional high courage."[63] In marriage, as in the workplace, the desire of the male had priority over the patriotic female who could do her part by serving diligently or complying without complaint. The days of lengthy romances and honeymoons at Niagara Falls were temporarily over.

Once again, Hollywood played its role as dramatizer of contemporary values by transforming emotional conflict into entertainment. The nameless dance partners for lonely GIs, the starlets who filled the Hollywood Canteen each night in the Warner Brothers production aptly titled *Hollywood Canteen,* sing their version of sacrifice in this refrain:

> I'm getting corns for my country
> At the Hollywood Canteen
> I'm a patriotic jitterbug.

Betty Hutton's comic persona in *Star Spangled Rhythm* describes the call to sexual sacrifice in a song she sings to a jeepful of sailors. (This scene was criticized by the Bureau of Intelligence because of its too-frivolous utilization of a government issued vehicle!) Hutton's song, "I'm Doin' It for Defense" included these sentiments:

> Months and months, you've been drilled,
> Now it's time you were thrilled.
> Start from here, then we build,
> I'm doin' it for defense.
>
> If you touch my lips and you feel me respond
> It's just cause I can't afford a bond.
> If you think you're Cary Grant, brother, relax . . .
> You're just a rebate on my income tax.
>
> Orders are, for today,
> Just relax, come what may.
> Duty calls, I obey.
> I'm doin' it for defense.
>
> Don't get hurt, don't get sore,
> I'm a pal, nothing more.
> This ain't love, this is war.
> I'm doin' it for defense.

The Hutton character's lyrics constitute a manifesto of wartime sexual politics which enacts the most personalized extension of the sacrifice ethic. At a further level of interpretation, one might suggest that Hutton is a representation of the film industry's sacrifice, of which it was deeply aware. The thousands of miles of USO travel, the scores of films distributed at no charge to military audiences by the industry's War Activities Committee, the impassioned bond rallying undertaken by contract stars are all condensed in the person of this blonde bombshell who is giving her all to keep the boys happy.

The female sacrifice ethic was a time-honored staple even within the women's movement of the day. An influential feminist of the twenties, Harriet Abbott, was outspokenly opposed to the choice of career over family, "personal ambition" over the "homely duties." Abbott's "Credo of the Newest New Woman" is a litany of the ideal female traits which formed the boundaries of behavior in a woman's world:

> I believe in woman's rights; but I believe in woman's
> sacrifices also.
> I believe in woman's freedom; but I believe it should be
> within the restrictions of the Ten Commandments.
> I believe in woman suffrage; but I believe many other
> things are vastly more important.
> I believe in woman's brains; but I believe still more in
> her emotions.
> I believe in woman's assertion of self; but I believe also
> in her obligation of service to her family, her
> neighbors, her nation and her God.
> Following that faith we have the most modern expression of
> feminism. The newest new woman deifies not herself,
> but through her new freedom elects to serve others.[64]

Thus far, the ideological currents concerning the nature of women and their connection to sacrifice have been surveyed. But a sense of a more diffuse melange of attitudes and beliefs about men *and* women which contributed to the shaping of contemporary life ought also to be provided. One conception attached to the war years of interest here was a belief in the "maleness" of the era, due, one supposes, to the militancy of the epoch. In the words of Jonathan Daniels, an administrative assistant to the president, writing just weeks after Pearl Harbor:

> The forties are here in which Americans stand on a continent as men—men again fighting in the crudest man terms—for ourselves and also for that destination in decency for all men of which our settlement, our spreading, was always a symbol. In an America grown magnificently male again we have a chance to fight for a homeland with the full meaning of homeland as a world that is fit to be the home of man.[65]

That the geist of a decade should be so vigorously stamped as "male" provides a clue to the ubiquity of female self-effacement, the sacrifice credo and the "otherness" of woman.

But that "otherness" also manifested itself in adoration of the female. For the American fighting man, the prototypical American male of the forties, women were rendered "ideological" by their physical absence; they were dreams, letters, pin-ups and memories rather than flesh and blood. Novelist James Jones describes this special status which the thought of womanhood acquired for the GI:

> But men thought about women. In fact, women were probably always in their thoughts when they weren't actually in combat or immersed in work, getting ready for combat. When the presence of death and extinction are always just around the corner or the next cloud, the comfort of women takes on a great importance. Woman is the antithesis of war. Soft, pliable, decent, clean, sensitive, understanding, and great to fuck. One might live with a woman day after day and this opinion might wither, but living without them at all in the midst of the hairy angularities of other men enhanced it. Just how warlike, aggressive and bellicose women might be faded as their proximity faded.[66]

The fact that images of women so often adorned the "nose art" of American military aircraft points to the other pole of female "otherness." If women were goddesses, they were also hellions—explosive and destructive. The instinct to "put the blame on Mame" (originally a song performed by Rita Hayworth in *Gilda*) is usually attributed to a postwar sensibility, but the backlash against women was rooted in the blind adulation of the female unknown.

The separation of male and female created by military service had its opposite in the increased proximity of the sexes in the workplace. The codes of formal behavior began to disappear in the factory setting. A Women's Bureau official noted after an extensive tour of a California shipyard that men barked orders at women, refused to pick up their tools when dropped and withheld the deference associated with traditional male/female relationships.[67] Other signs of the resentment which many felt toward working women were the recurring reports of immoral conduct by female factory workers and the rising incidence of juvenile delinquency which was so often blamed upon absent mothers. Of course, the "latchkey child" syndrome was exacerbated by another ideological subcurrent (mentioned previously): women were unwilling to use the childcare facilities that were reluctantly made available to them. In the words of a government official in 1943, "There is a positive aversion to group care of children in the minds of working women. To some it connotes an inability to care for one's own; to some it has a vague incompatibility with the traditional idea of the American home; to others it has a taint of socialism."[68] Here again is a case of a popular notion which works against the best interests of the people who share it. Public campaigns to facilitate the acceptance of changing patterns of behavior were frequently inadequate with the result that entire social programs died for lack of response. The fact that an element of ideology appears to be dysfunctional for those who believe it is never adequate grounds for its denial. The refusal to utilize childcare resources by women who needed such facilities is one of many such cases of self-destructive beliefs.

Because women were accustomed to serving the family, it is not at all surprising that the most common reason given by new recruits for their decision to enter the work force was to provide for family support (84 percent), while only 8 percent offered "self-expression" or dissatisfaction with their traditional roles in the home. It was the next logical step to perceive the woman worker as a helpmate of a new sort, the woman who could contribute to her family's welfare in a novel way. With such a self-definition, there would be little drive to achieve equal status in the workplace to replace that of "helper" or "assistant." Women's failure to oppose unfair job classifications, lack of promotion and withheld seniority was due in part to this image of the female as the perennial helpmate. Men were wont to justify their inequitable policies by suggesting that women preferred to stay in the background. A thousand aphorisms could be mobilized for this purpose, including this one from a 1942 book entitled *The Psychology of Supervising the Working Woman*. In it, prejudice is stated as fact: "Women as a rule make poor bosses in a factory or office."[69] In the face of deeply entrenched beliefs regarding sex roles, the naive enthusiasm of government propaganda constituted a pale corrective. An Office of War Information radio broadcast on the subject of female participation illustrates the slighly purple tone of many such propaganda efforts:

ANNOUNCER (*Forceful*): Woman power!

WOMAN (*Poetically*): Woman power! . . . The power to create and sustain life. The power to inspire men to bravery, to give security to little children. A limitless, ever-flowing source of moral and physical energy—working for victory! *That* is woman power!

These examples are the concrete manifestations of the hegemonic domain in which coercion is achieved through compliance. Essentially the cross-currents of attitudes and images attached to women, while representing the perceived relations among men and women, served to obscure many of the conflicts and social tensions which might otherwise, in surfacing, have threatened the stability of the prevailing social structure. Many ideological components were nostalgic, the residue of an earlier phase of American life (and capitalist development). There were fixed beliefs attached to womanhood as an eternal form, many of which were challenged by the course of events, but few of which were radically altered by four years of war. The swing back to traditional roles for women and the misogynist tenor of the postwar era were precisely a shared return to familiar imagery, to the comfort of an unchallenged hierarchy in which sex roles are clear and unquestioned. The violence of this resurrection of values was aided by the unswerving emphasis on the temporary nature of female ascendancy which was based, in turn, on the notion of female service and sacrifice. Aroused and emotionalized at every turn, American women were mobilized out of fear for themselves and for their men, out of the need to support their families, or in an idealized quest for glamour, respect or romance (encouraged and/or dissuaded in each instance by representational forms). Motion pictures were very much a part of the ideological air breathed by these women. The expressed aims of government and the half-conscious elaborations of a complex ideological conjuncture are alike discernible within a large body of films which were concerned with representing women who were, for the moment, the focus of great social concern. It is to these films that we now turn.

Part Two

Texts and Textuality

Introduction to Part Two

Analyzing the Filmic Text

Christian Metz, in his groundbreaking essay "The Imaginary Signifier," disavowed the notion of a "textual system" (developed in *Language and Cinema*) as a fixed ensemble of codes specific to cinema or even to an individual text. Regarding this re-thinking of his theoretical stance as a contribution of psychoanalysis to linguistics, Metz acknowledged the greater importance of the dynamic aspect for his analysis of texts, an emphasis on production rather than product. The very terms Metz calls forth to describe his critical process indicate his recognition of a necessarily arbitrary set of procedures initiated by the critic ("the broadly projective character of the relation the cinema writer often maintains to his 'object' "):[1] "working conveniences," "blocs of interpretation already foreseen or established by the analysis," "sectors of signification," "significatory pressure." Analysis is viewed as "interminable," the textual system possessed of an "indefinite thickness" so that the "perpetual possibility of a finer or else less apparent structuration of a grouping of the elements into a new configuration" persists.[2] Although Metz speaks here of the exigencies of performing close analyses of single texts, the same strictures can be assumed for other, more comprehensive, critical projects—those that seek to determine the larger patterns at work within and across a range of filmic texts.

Thus far, it has been the aim of this work to articulate a contextual framework, composed of the historical and ideological conditions of wartime America, for the analysis of specific film texts. To the methodological paradigm for the previous chapters, the tripartite structure "history/ideology/text," the concept of intertextuality must now be added. For if consideration has been given to the material regimes of history and ideology, viewed as shaping forces in the production of representational forms, the determinancy of filmic representation itself requires critical attention. Mainstream or Hollywood cinema is a field of signification, seemingly open and unconstrained, which is nonetheless organized by conventions of realism, of narrative duration, of genre, and of iconography.

Particularly since the American film industry had achieved such a marked degree of standardization by the forties, evidenced by its consistent level of production (four to five hundred features yearly with an average gestation period of six to twelve months), its long-term contract system for all studio employees, and its level of generic self-awareness, it becomes necessary to evaluate the meaning of a single film text in terms of its articulation or "cutting out" from an intertextual field of related product. Umberto Eco has offered a conveniently specific definition of intertextuality that focuses on the "relay to other images or other texts" but that does not encompass nontextualized discourses or other heterogeneous social practices no matter how formative they may be for the viewing subject.[3] The levels of intertextual connection are vast, ranging from iconic ties (repetition of actors, sets, gestures, even plays of symmetry and asymmetry) to authorial ties (repetition of writers, producers, directors, cinematographers and art directors) to strictly thematic ones including remakes, spinoffs, serialized films from Andy Hardy to Maisie or repeated treatments of related social issues or themes. Because the focus here is upon female representation, it is the thematic/structural principle which will guide the examination of intertextual determinancy.

Yet the chapters which follow and the categories of film texts contained within them remain the "working conveniences" of this critic. While it is altogether true that issues of female representation guide the choice and examination of texts and that these texts respond to the pressures and limits of the historical/ideological field, the organizing principles of these chapters lie elsewhere. Indeed the most imminent of "significatory pressures" at work in the following is film criticism itself; the configuration of texts speaks to the prior categorizations of particularly feminist film criticism. In the end, these groupings are creatures of meta-criticism, responsive to the shape and flux of a very particular historical and cultural practice. The critical discourse becomes in this context a crucial level of mediation for the readings. Rather than offer an apology for this strategy, I would suggest that the meta-critical character of the categories makes of them a more useful set of rubrics—groupings that aid the critical (and pedagogical) enterprise by assembling texts which mobilize a shared problematic or methodological approach.

The filmic categories are contained within three large groupings corresponding to the final three chapters of the book. In the first of these ("Unfree Agency: Women in Ideology"), four distinguishable but overlapping categories share representations of fictional females (often, though not always, thematically central) who function as narrativized links within a chain of social relations. In this chapter, the represented woman is placed within ideology in its most global formulation. Specific issues of enunciation or female subjectivity addressed elsewhere are displaced, in part because these figures are largely absent, in part because of the primacy accorded the broader framework of social life within the narrative.

Herein can be found such categories as "Woman: The Martyr or Source of Inspiration," "Woman: The Helper," "Woman in the Family Melodrama," and "Moral Tales for Women."

"Subjectivity at a Distance" considers the construction of the female subject in greater detail—the fabrication of fictional personae as well as the implications for the construction of "real," historical subjectivity for women. This particular problematic has occupied the special attention of feminist criticism at least since Laura Mulvey's important 1975 essay, "Visual Pleasure and Narrative Cinema." The women of these three groupings, foregrounded if negatively cast, are constituted through their radical alterity from the male subject-center: "Woman: The Inscrutable Female," "The Evil Woman," "Woman: Object of the Look."

The final chapter, "Figures in/of Enunciation," offers a critical intervention rather than an extension of preexistent models. For in the latter of two sub-groupings are contained instances of determinate discursive authority delegated to women. The power of enunciation within the filmic text has generally been considered beyond the pale of female possibility within mainstream cinema. Based upon the rather special historical conditions of the wartime moment, however, it became increasingly possible for the woman-in-discourse to engage in limited instances of direct address or to control the flux of narrative or of image-production through the agency of her subjectivity. These forays against the borders of the representable (the cinematic "vraisemblable"—the ideological currency of ideas, values and expectations that can be popularly accepted as the "real"), limited and conditional though they may have been, offer a sense of the potential for resistance within the hegemonic domain while suggesting the need for a greater elasticity of critical parameters. The first of the two sub-species ("Thematic Presence/Enunciative Absence") testifies to the degree to which the represented woman could dominate the text at the level of the diegesis without altering the terms (and limits) of patriarchal discourse. The latter grouping, entitled "Enunciation against the Grain," takes up the examination of the limited instances of discursive authority described above.

The categories contained in each of the three chapters are thus examined for their characteristic fixing of the female, with attention given the variations of treatment within the general pattern. This textual positioning can then be correlated with the social and ideological positioning of real women within the culture of the time. Finally, individual texts of each grouping are analyzed in some detail for their specific play of elements. (The films examined in each category are listed beneath the heading with the remaining texts of the grouping to be found in the appendixes.) These elements include the properly intratextual (among them, the circulation of meaning within the film through the repetition and variation of gesture, dialogue and incident; the elaboration and resolution of narrative tension; the significant instances of figuration; and the transgressions of formal and narrative codes), the intertextual evinced within a particular category (elements that resonate within and across the groupings), and the contextual, those of history and ideology.

The categories offer yet another aid to the historiographical project undertaken here through their isolation of particular ideological currents whose historical dimensions and variations can thus be examined through the filmic representations. Assuming that there is some base determinancy between concrete historical conditions and cultural products, it becomes possible to chart the relative frequency of the distribution of texts within a given domain. It can be demonstrated, for example, that within the limits of this sampling the representation of woman as inspirational source was far more likely to occur in 1943 than in 1941. The incipient empiricism of this approach should not, however, be viewed as an end in itself, rather as another parameter of determination distinguishable in a temporal mode.

In this work I focus my attention on the first two years of American war involvement, 1942 and 1943, and upon the film production of that historical moment. The decision to focus on a two-year period was necessitated by practical considerations of length, yet it was clear that the films themselves could not be grouped so strictly by year of release. In the first place, the lags among germination of idea, production and exhibition meant that 1943's idea could, quite routinely, become 1945's film. Furthermore, the studios were prepared for war contingencies with a healthy stockpile of films, so that a 1942 release might well have been conceived and produced one or two years previous. Finally, the charting of historical determinancy for cultural products is feasible only if the study examines, to some extent, the output of adjacent years. Discontinuity, after all, can only be distinguished and evaluated in terms of continuity. Consequently, half of the films screened and examined were actually released in 1942 or 1943 with the remaining number released in the years prior to or following that two-year period (see appendixes for the historical distribution of films sampled).

At this stage, it is necessary to inspect the term "spectator" as used here. It is not my intention to posit a unified and undifferentiated male spectator in the manner of the more doctrinaire feminist literature.[4] In fact, the historical evidence gathered herein outlines the conditions of female spectatorship during the war years, a concept which has hitherto been insufficiently understood and written about. Nevertheless, historical and sociological research alone cannot hope to define the concrete character of spectatorship which, like subjectivity, is both historical and psychological, but, unlike subjectivity, is defined both in the aggregate as a social phenomenon and in the individual as a psychic and perceptual process (cf. Metz's "The Imaginary Signifier" and "Fiction Film and Its Spectator," inter alia). Despite the temporary encroachment of the female within popular consciousness encouraged by economic gains, the burgeoning of women's fiction and heightened familial authority, the presumption of white, adult, middle-class male spectatorship (patriarchy as manifested in the production/consumption cycle of cinema) constituted a set of pressures and limits upon representation in Hollywood films. While such a statement is no more than a mere beginning, a suggestion for further investigation, the linkage between historiographical work and spectator studies is a crucial one. This study examines the borders of male spectatorship as hegemonic, seeking the circumstances in which the female spectator becomes a condition of the text as well as a box office statistic. Yet it is through the construction of a precise historical framework that these moments of rupture can be comprehended not as mere formal anomolies, but as the products of a particular social formation and its ideological domain.

5

Unfree Agency: Women in Ideology

This chapter examines four overlapping categories of film texts which offer representations of women occupying intermediate positions within large systems: of work, of family life, of a moral or theological system. Here the woman is important for the linkage she provides within a chain of social relations. While the construction of the female persona may in fact constitute a major movement of the film, it is the maintenance of social institutions and the circulation of individuals within these systems that occupy the primary attention of the film as ideological construct. An analysis of the female characters of these categories must explore their positioning at two levels: that of the narrative (how the woman is structured *for* the text) and of ideology (how the woman is structured *by* the text, itself a reworking of the social field).

Woman: The Martyr or Source of Inspiration

Joe Smith, American (1942)
The Great Man's Lady (1942)
So Proudly We Hail (1943)

The first category of the four is constituted by those films in which women, often martyred for the cause, are seized upon as inspirational sources for action. At this juncture, it is worth recalling the Coty perfume ad discussed in chapter four which crystallizes the wartime responsibilities of each sex: "His duty . . . to serve—Hers . . . to inspire—Coty." The Office of War Information's "Woman Power" broadcast, in attempting to praise the intrinsic strengths of the American woman, served to reinforce the strictured notion of the female as inspirational source: "Woman power! . . . The power to create and sustain life. The power to inspire men to bravery, to give security to little children . . . " In terms of participation in the war effort, the fictional females of this category range from actively engaged (*Flight for Freedom*, 1943; *So Proudly We Hail; Joan of Paris,* 1942) to purely inspirational for their men (*Joe Smith, American; Caught in the Draft,* 1941). In the midregion of this grouping are the films whose work it is to valorize the sacrifices and personal struggles of women whose efforts seem, on the face of it, to be far less crucial and life-threatening than those of their male counterparts (*Mrs. Miniver,* 1942; *The Great Man's Lady; Roughly Speaking,* 1945). On the contrary, *Mrs. Miniver,* William Wyler's award-winning tribute to female indomitability, offered proof of the greater dangers of the domestic front. In this film, hand-to-hand combat, even death, is experienced by women at home despite the public attention given the male warrior. Woman is both fighter and nurturer, the one who sacrifices her life and the one who insures the continuity of the social fabric. It must be added, however, that the films of this category need not dramatize wartime issues (although most do). Both *The Great Man's Lady* and *Keeper of the Flame* (1942) are concerned with the conflicts and contributions of the woman-behind-the-great-man, in non-war settings.

The historical connections between sacrifice and womanhood as intensified by war have been outlined in chapters two and four. It is worth noting in this context that, of the twenty-three films in the "Martyr" category, nineteen are from 1942 or 1943, making this the most intensively clustered grouping of all. Whether or not the thematic material of these films is directly war-related, the questions raised and the values represented were compelling and immediate for contemporary audiences.

The representation of woman as passive inspirational figure occurs in MGM's *Joe Smith, American,* a film bearing this dedication:

> This story is about a man
> Who defended his country.
>
> His name is Joe Smith.
>
> He is an American.
>
> This picture is a tribute
> To all Joe Smiths.

Judging from communiques between MGM's Ray Bell and officials of the Bureau of Motion Pictures, Office of War Information, it is clear that MGM intended to tell a story about Everyman (see discussion of this exchange in chapter 3). Robert Young plays this "average Joe," a crew chief on an aircraft assembly line, who is unpretentiously all-American and heroic. The film plays the populist culture game of portraying a man who is both average—"one of us"—and extraordinary—"the best of us." The Capraesque assumption that such Americans are the backbone of the country is a variant of the essentialist "melting pot" mythos that seeks to obliterate the distinctions of class, race and gender.

Self-effacing though he may be, with his "average" family—a pretty, unassuming wife (Marsha Hunt) and cowlicked son—and familiar cast of working buddies and neighbors, Smith is chosen for a highly classified work detail installing bomb sights. He is kidnapped and methodically tortured in an effort to pry secrets from him; a series of flashbacks are consciously induced by Smith to ward off the pain of his beatings. It is primarily through these retrieved images of comfort that wife Mary comes to be defined and her wifely/motherly virtues appreciated. These memory pieces and the mini-revelations they awaken in Joe serve to construct a female representation mediated through one "typical" male subjectivity. The production is, in its entirety, mediated at yet another level, as a particularly conscious process of writing: MGM producing promotional material for an edgy bureaucracy.

Mary Smith, modest as her name, is first presented as the conservator of the home (the space within which she is confined throughout the movie, except in memory and in a brief hospital sequence). Early in the film, Joe complains that the family never eats on the dining room table, to which Mary replies that the table is for company. When Joe retorts that they never have company, Mary admits that she is afraid to use such a nice table for fear of scratching it. In a moment of emotional release at film's end, a boisterous crowd of friends and family celebrate Joe's heroism at this table. Wifely conservatism—the unheralded skills of scrimping and making do ("Use it up, wear it out, make it do or do without")—initially represented as bordering on the obsessive, gives way to spontaneity and emotional connectedness. Yet in both cases, Mary's concerns are focused outside herself, on an unflawed tabletop or on her husband. As elsewhere, there is little sense of Mary's concern for herself, her identity outside that of wife and mother.

In the area of parental discipline, Mary defers to Joe, who complains: "You always make me the heavy." When Johnny is punished for withholding information from his parents, Mary sneaks into his bedroom to give him a clandestine sandwich and glass of milk. Unbeknownst to Mary, Joe makes a similar trip, only with a slice of watermelon and a glass of milk. Joe, not a hard man, hasn't the heart for real harshness with his eager-to-please son (Darryl Hickman), but it is Mary's nurturing capacities, silently performed, that keep the family functioning. At times, Mary's acquiescence borders on outright oblivion. When Joe is given his top secret assignment, he is warned that he can divulge the details of his work to no one, not even his wife. Joe bridles at this suggestion. How can his longer hours and the effects of his more stressful work be withheld from Mary? The spectator might well expect this area of potential conflict to develop into a major strand of the narrative hermeneutic, but it does not. Nevertheless, because Mary is depicted as a compliant soul who tenders unconditional support to her husband, her silence in this instance is not at all inconsistent with her characterization.

The flashbacks, which reconstitute Joe's blind date with Mary and the internal monologue that chronicles her virtues, contribute to the construction of the wife as passive, undemanding helpmate. When they first meet, Mary is demure, picture-pretty, and a good listener as Joe speaks enthusiastically of his secret plans (he talks of going to China). But Mary is firmly rooted in the home. The semic ensemble attached to her is produced through Joe's self-induced recollections of half-forgotten virtues ("You forget how early she gets up to make your lunch")— she irons his clothes, she darns his socks while he's bowling, she's beautiful even when she's scared. Hers is a fragile strength, though, evidenced by her fainting when Joe yanks out Johnny's loose tooth. Another flashback concerns Joe's impatient hospital vigil at Johnny's birth. The announcement of a successful delivery is greeted by a fellow sufferer's congratulations ("Good work, Joe"); even in childbirth, it is Joe who receives credit while Mary is the unimaged instrument of Joe's fatherhood. Smith draws strength from these memories even while his fingers are being crushed by pliers.

There are present-time scenes of Mary intercut with the torture sequences during which she grows more and more concerned at her husband's absence. At last she learns that Joe has been taken to the hospital. When, despite his injuries, Joe insists on tracking down his captors using his sensory memories of the abduction (although blindfolded, he has made careful note of major auditory "landmarks"), Mary understands and accepts his need to act out his revenge. Her line of dialogue is the summation of her role in the family and, more particularly, in Joe's life: "I'll go home and wait for you." The long-suffering wife, the silent support of the family, the embodiment of fragile strength, expecting little gratitude for her labors, receiving less (except under these crisis circumstances) . . . this is an apt pre-war profile of the American wife as developed in popular culture. *Joe Smith, American* was among the first films to address war-related themes on the homefront, having been produced in the weeks prior to Pearl Harbor. The altered dimensions of female power and visibility coupled with the growing willingness by the studios to portray women's newly-tested capacity for work and achievement produced determinate alterations in the range of Hollywood's female representations. This development can be recognized in the analysis of two other films of this category.

There is no wartime film which heralds the direct participation of women more enthusiastically than Paramount's *So Proudly We Hail,* the tale of eight Army nurses who survive the drubbing of American forces on Bataan and Corregidor. This 1943 release announces itself as a facsimile of real events by the unadorned credit ("Based on records of the United States Army Nursing Corps") and the specificity of its temporal frame (the narrative begins on 5 May 1942, as the group of nurses arrives in Melbourne). The film is structured as a framed flashback with a therapeutic motivation; the central female character, Lt. Janet Davidson, otherwise known as Davie (Claudette Colbert), has been rendered catatonic by her ordeal and the loss of her husband, Lt. John Summers (George Reeves). The attending physician attempts to probe into the past through the shared narration of Davie's comrades in order to uncover the causes of the psychic disturbance.

Despite the hermeneutic centrality of Davie's psychosis, however, the nurses as a unit constitute the narrative focus in a manner similar to *Tender Comrade* (a 1943 release discussed in chapter 7), the female group and its conjoined efforts overshadow any single dramatic conflict. *So Proudly We Hail* is, in effect, a female combat film which offers a stratified range of characters and types cohering into a fighting unit, with the senior officer (Lt. Davidson) occupying a dominant narrative function.

The effects of sexual difference mark the film as a distinctive variant of the combat picture while offering insights into the perceived parameters of female behavior and temperament under the most intolerable conditions. From the outset of the framing sequence, the women are valorized as heroines whose cravings are to be satisfied. Although these women sound very much like the cynical dog faces of any other war picture ("What is a heroine, anyway?" . . . "Someone who's alive, I guess"), there are significant gendered elements which recall the standard contours of Hollywood's female representations. As the women prepare themselves for reentry into normal life, taking their first tentative steps in high heels after months of combat boots, one nurse wryly comments, "High heels . . . the things we do to trap men." The extended flashback, which explains the need for such re-education, chronicles a process, namely the ongoing struggle to maintain a sense of female identity along with a level of professionalism despite the dehumanizing conditions produced by the elements and a cruel enemy.

The film's construction of the Army nurse is notably oxymoronic. The question can be posed: How can a trio of Paramount's most lustrous stars—Claudette Colbert, Paulette Goddard and Veronica Lake—be made to retain the sheen of glamour that attracts audiences while convincingly replicating the lives of the most battle-hardened, unglamorous females—women who live for weeks on end in tunnels dug 400 feet beneath the bombed-out surface of Corregidor? The Colbert character is the focus of the gender problematic; her nickname "Davie" connotes a soft boyishness, a gentle androgyny. Colbert's commanding officer, known simply as "Ma," is a stern but grandmotherly presence who enforces regulations but is willing to bend the rules to allow Davie to marry her Lt. Summers just before the evacuation of Corregidor. Davie's attitudes toward her own womanhood are complex in their inscription. She is the daughter of an officer now deceased, and her language is sprinkled with militarisms ("Mind if I bunk with you?," "Let's trench over here"). When a disagreement between Goddard and Lake escalates into a fight, Davie intervenes in the tradition of all stalwart top sergeants: "Forget it and shake hands." Davie is capable of chastising her charges with a withering (and sexist) remark ("You talk like a bunch of old women") while concurrently conveying a sense of the maternal, as when she promises to take special care of young Rosemary, whose immigrant mother's fears are thereby allayed. Davie also insists on borrowing a skirt for the brief wedding ceremony amid the bomb blasts; she clings to the vestiges of her femininity even as the American fighting forces crumble about her.

In a world defined by an abridgment of family ties and the sense of an entire generation's destruction, the rebuilding of society becomes another kind of duty to be performed. In the words of the grief-stricken Ma, "We've gotta get it right this time." The benediction of Chee, the Chinese man who performs the wedding ceremony, is a part of the suturing action which the marriage becomes; his three wishes: long life, good luck and an abundance of children. The ceremony is the linkage of generations at the hour of despair; Chee's gift of a piece of 2000-year old jade connects the act of union with a comforting human lineage that places personal suffering in relief. The change in Davie is dramatic. In an attempt to convince Davie to evacuate Corregidor despite Summers' disappearance, Ma chastises the once admonitory lieutenant, "Stop talking like an hysterical school girl." Davie has come full circle.

Her female vulnerability and her role as wife and mother firmly established, Davie sinks into a speechless state on board the rescue ship. It is only a letter from John which the doctor reads aloud that begins to rouse her. A slow pan over the women's faces reveals that all are tearful as the doctor's narration of the letter is progressively doubled, then replaced by Summers' own voice. Concurrently, John's face appears in the left-hand corner of the frame, first clear, then in soft focus, finally with full resolution. At this point, the narration is fully John's. His voice and his imaginary presence fill Davie with renewed hope and courage as a bright plume of fire replaces his face, frame left, leading to the final dissolve. Although the nurses themselves are depicted as inspirational figures from whom their male comrades and the audience can draw strength, their own source of moral and emotional sustenance is ultimately male. The words and image of a man rekindle the commitment to life and to the shared struggle. The power of this inspirational force is achieved through the romantic connection, the bonding of male and female, which is the nexus most characteristic of Hollywood's formal/ideological mode.

So Proudly We Hail addresses other moral/ethical issues which are gender-related. The Japanese are depicted as ruthless enemies who bomb hospitals and abuse their female captives. The American fighting force, on the other hand, is here represented largely by women whose steady hands and gentle sensibilities humanize the combat zone. This feminization is metonymic; the womanly qualities valorized through the film are made to extend over the entire fighting force. In a shipboard sermon delivered en route to Bataan, in which he compares the Japanese and American mentalities and strategies of war, the chaplain glories in the notion that "we are sentimental . . . that makes us the stronger." Faith and sentiment, traditionally female qualities, are attached to the soldiers by a montage of close-up reaction shots. As the chaplain speaks, face after face is imaged in quiet contemplation, men intercut with women, stars and principal actors intercut with nameless GI faces. At this moment, the film performs a blurring of gender difference and of fictional/nonfictional representation.

For the most part, however, the nurses' womanhood constitutes a focal point of the filmic narrative. The women are requisitioned oversized men's overalls on Bataan; a brief but giddy "fashion show" of the government issue attire reminds the viewer of the male/female disparity and of the distance between these female personae and their studio contemporaries as objects of visual pleasure for male and particularly female audiences. Largely absent are the trappings of costume and hairstyle which offered the semblance of glamour for the filmgoing woman worker. The lighting codes that do remain intact (back-lighting, eye-lighting, "softening" effects) serve to mitigate the severity of the Veronica Lake character, for example, whose unsmiling manner and tightly upswept hairdo offer sharp contrast to the peek-a-boo eroticism or little girl sexiness of former roles. Paulette Goddard is cast as the staunchest supporter of femininity; she wears a black negligee to maintain her own morale. Despite these cosmetic constraints, the nurses are ineluctably perceived as women; in fact, their womanhood is a major ingredient of their military usefulness. When, near the collapse of Corregidor, Davie suggests that her unit has outlived its usefulness and should be moved to safety, the male commanding officer elucidates the role of a nursing corps at a battle front: "You're doing more for morale than anything else in this sector. Just seeing you girls around is almost enough." This assessment of the female as male morale-booster rather than female worker is accompanied by yet another indication of a sharply drawn notion of sexual difference, here in the guise of chivalry. In the colonel's words: "Don't worry, when the time comes I'll get you out. Or else I'd never be able to look my wife or any other woman in the face." The remarks are the twin vestiges of the patriarchal domain which denies the functional potential of the woman in order to use her as a spur to male interest then compensates by pledging benevolent protection. In neither case is the woman's intrinsic value as worker and sovereign guardian of her own life recognized.

If the combat nurses are meant to embody an inspirational/sacrificial function, there is one sequence—the most frequently cited moment of the film—which manifests that function most clearly. The Veronica Lake character (Olivia) is initially portrayed as a "frozen-faced ghoul" possessed by hatred of the Japanese ("I'm going to kill Japs, every blood-stained one I can get my hands on"). Her fiance had been riddled with bullets at Pearl Harbor ("I couldn't see him any more, just blood") and she remains aloof and angrily self-destructive throughout the first third of the film. The restoration of compassion and a renewed willingness to live ("At least I don't want to die any more; there's too much to do") is a subsidiary project of the narrative which reaches its climax during the hasty withdrawal from their installation on Bataan. Suddenly, the women are trapped in their quarters by the Japanese, cut off from their escape vehicle with only one grenade to fend off the advancing enemy. With the safety of all at stake ("I was in Nanking, I saw what happened there," says one nurse), Olivia steps forward and grabs the hand grenade with the words: "So long, Davie, thanks for

everything . . . it's our only chance . . . it's one of us or all of us . . . good-bye.''
A lengthy, high key close-up of Olivia's face images her state of grace—the out-
ward signs of transcendance (the perfect calm of the features, the resolution behind
the eyes)—recall Michele Morgan as *Joan of Paris* and all the other Joans from
Geraldine Ferrar (De Mille's *Joan the Woman*) to Marie Falconetti and Florence
Carrez (of the Dreyer and Bresson versions). Olivia lets down her blonde hair
and, in close-up, pulls the pin on the grenade before walking slowly toward the
enemy. Her back to the camera, she is encircled by the aroused Japanese in the
moments before the detonation destroys them all.

   This sacrificial act is noteworthy in two respects—one that reinforces the
ideologically dominant representation of women, the other which contravenes
it. Olivia's action is figured in sexual terms; the body whose pleasures had been
annulled by the destruction of its erotic object becomes the vehicle of retribution. For Olivia's sacrifice, swiftly conceived and fearlessly executed, is
nonetheless predicated on her sexuality. She is the apotheosized femme fatale
using her powers of attraction for the public good. Significantly, however, Olivia's
heroism benefits other women; she is an inspirational figure for her female comrades rather than for a male constituency. In the vast majority of instances in
this category, women are martyred or perform inspirational feats to spur the
militarism of their men (*China*, 1943; *Five Graves to Cairo*, 1943; *Joan of Paris*,
1942; *The Mortal Storm*, 1940; *Mrs. Miniver*). In *So Proudly We Hail*, the
crucial moment of self-sacrifice is by a woman, for women.

   The female personae of the film maintain an unparalleled level of durability
and authority, often physical, often connected to men. During the escape from
Bataan, the two female leads (Goddard and Colbert) take full responsibility for
their respective mates (Sonny Tufts and George Reeves); Goddard knocks out
Tufts and rows him away after he decides to go down fighting while Colbert takes
the oars of another boat containing her unconscious lover. While embracing the
familiar tenets of love and marriage and finally placing recuperative power in
the words and spirit of the absent husband, *So Proudly We Hail* suggests seldom-
seen female possibilities founded in a strength and autonomy connected to a labor
process. At the level of social reception, the film was no doubt a source of inspiration for the millions of hard-working, underpaid and underappreciated
American women. Whether or not this circumstance makes of the film a reac-
tionary appeasement to potential female dissatisfaction is a judgment to be rendered
elsewhere.

   The last group of this category is constituted by those films in which the
behind-the-scenes heroics of the female protagonists (usually in support of their
husbands) have escaped the notice of the world. The work of these films is to
bear witness to the achievements of these neglected warriors for whom social
recognition remains unavailable. The dutiful sacrifices of the wife/mother are
fully absorbed within the family system while the husband/father issues forth into battle and glory. *The Great Man's Lady* conforms to this narrative/thematic

pattern in its retrospective examination of the life of a 100-year-old woman, Hannah Sempler Hoyt, who may or may not be the legal spouse of Ethan Hoyt, the founder of a major American city. The 1942 film, although framed in a contemporary setting, sprawls rather self-consciously across a huge chunk of American history, beginning in 1848 in Philadelphia, moving through the years of westward expansion and the coming of the railroad to the development of the skyscrapered metropolis. While the film addresses itself to the timely issue of the unsung woman (viz. "the-woman-behind-the-man-behind-the-gun" slogan so vigorously endorsed through government promotion of the war years), *The Great Man's Lady* seeks to universalize and historicize its theme in broadest strokes, exemplified by its brief prologue: "Not only behind great men, but behind the ordinary guy—you will meet a Hannah Hoyt. In her own small way, she will be helping, pointing the road ahead, encouraging her man to reach his own pinnacle of success."

This inscription provides an ironic preface for what follows since Hannah, working in more than a "small way," is revealed to be the true promulgator of events while Ethan Hoyt's pinnacle of success is anything but his own. The film is a framed flashback of character revelation in the *Citizen Kane* mode in which the ancient Ms. Sempler (Barbara Stanwyck) narrates "one hundred years of memories" to a young female reporter writing a biography of Ethan Hoyt (Joel McCrea). In fact, the film is linked more directly to *The Man Who Shot Liberty Valance* than to *Citizen Kane* for its re-evaluation of the exemplary founding father of the West and its discovery of misplaced immortality. Ultimately, the young reporter in *The Great Man's Lady* agrees with Ford's newspaperman in *Liberty Valance* ("When fact becomes legend, print the legend") and drops the biographical project after three years' research.

The Stanwyck character is an outspoken and energetic activist whose advice and support are the bedrock of the Ethan Hoyt legacy. While the female personae in *Joe Smith, American* and *So Proudly We Hail* received the praise and admiration of their peers, the perception of Hannah Sempler Hoyt's power to inspire is reserved primarily for the spectator. For Hannah, in contrast to Greer Garson's Mrs. Miniver or the Rosalind Russell character in *Roughly Speaking*, is denied any recognition for her deeds even within a family context. The circumstances of her anonymous martyrdom are revealed only through the narrative.

As disclosed in flashback, Hannah was a romantic young girl from a proud Philadelphia family. She ran off with an equally adventurous Ethan Hoyt to build a bold new settlement out west—Hoyt City. Hannah's precipitous exodus severs the bond with her own family while her marriage to Ethan takes place alongside their covered wagon during a thunderstorm, a ceremony on the run much like that of the Colbert/Reeves union in *So Proudly We Hail*. From the start, McCrea's broad-shouldered bulk and hesitant manner play off of Stanwyck's ebullience. If Hoyt is the man of iron who can wrest civilization from nature, it is only by virtue of Hannah's brains and will, for it is she who plants the seeds of thought in Ethan's mind, she who shoots the wild rabbits for their dinners on the prairie, she who salvages their land claim when Hoyt allows himself to be swindled. "We'll build a city here, you and I," says Hannah as she gazes on the unblemished western horizon. In a brief superimposition that is essentially a flash forward, the skyline of the Hoyt City to be appears before their eyes; it is Hannah's force of will that conjures this vision. Years later, when Hoyt despairs of finding silver on his Virginia City claim, it is Hannah who recognizes signs of the precious metal stuck to his boots. At her urging, Ethan returns to his claim, thus inaugurating the great Colorado silver rush. As always, it is Hannah who is responsible for the breakthrough, Ethan who acts it out and receives the credit.

When in the early days, the Hoyt fortunes at low ebb, a railroad man offers to buy a three-quarters interest in Hoyt City, it is Hannah who runs him off with a knife. Years later, after their paths have separated, Hannah intervenes once again to dissuade a now prosperous and politically active Hoyt from selling out to the railroad. This man, whose unwavering honesty is to become a key ingredient of his legend, tells Hannah, "I took the easiest way, like I've always done, except when you were around to keep me straight." The interim events that connect these twin temptations form a web of melodramatic upheavals. Ethan has misunderstood the relations between Hannah and the gambler Steely Edwards (Brian Donlevy) and, not realizing that she is pregnant with his child, abandons Hannah in a fit of jealousy. Because of her devotion to Hoyt, the man of destiny, she refrains from revealing the truth, knowing her pregnancy would divert him from the furious swirl of activity arising from the silver strike. Hoyt City must be financed even at the cost of her personal happiness.

Soon afterward, Hannah's newly born twins are lost in a flood and Ethan, thinking her dead as well, remarries. Her reappearance at the moment of his near sell-out comes on the heels of a divorce decree which she has arranged to save the reputation of Ethan Hoyt, public servant. She has never stopped loving him, never stopped reinforcing his imperfect moral judgment, but has had neither husband nor child to appreciate her invisible sacrifices. Like the Stanwyck character in *Stella Dallas,* Hannah is content to observe the fruition of her labors from afar, confiding in Hoyt, "I was proud of you, prouder than a cat with a dozen kittens." Hoyt is her child, the product of her ministerings, for Hannah is denied the companionship and sexual gratification of wifehood. "You gave me the strength and the courage," says Ethan; "But you did it alone, Ethan, all alone," is Hannah's reply. She is the quintessential martyr, fastidiously self-abnegating, unable to accept even the slightest reward for her efforts.

When at last the flashback narration is completed, the young woman writer is aghast at this revisionist view of local history. Together the two women gaze upon the newly dedicated statue of Ethan Hoyt, city father, proudly astride a charging horse. The reporter's parting observation: "I think the wrong person's on that horse in the square . . . it ought to be you." In a final flourish of self-effacement, Hannah takes from her purse the yellowed marriage certificate drawn up in a prairie thunderstorm so many years before and tears it up. A tiny smirk of self-knowledge (and masochism) animates Stanwyck's face as she looks up at the bronzed figure—fade to black.

The Great Man's Lady offers a transcendental version of martyrdom. Hannah Sempler Hoyt is portrayed as a purely sacrificial figure whose rewards are not of this world. It is further testimony to her strength that self-knowledge is adequate recompense for her toil; she shuns the approbation of the world in true Christian fashion. The film itself is the only valorization the protagonist receives, yet in its telling it reinforces the tradition of the suffer-in-silence female of real flesh and blood for whom no films will be made. As such it is a bitter and ironic testimonial to womanly virtue.

Woman: The Helper

Pacific Blackout (1941)
Watch on the Rhine (1943)
Pride of the Marines (1945)
Lost Weekend (1945)

Throughout the analyses of the texts of all categories, it has been necessary to allude to the historical groundwork in order to situate the textual readings in a material/ideological context. In the case of this category ("Helper") it is worth reviewing the ideological environment within which the woman-as-helpmate theme was produced. Prior to the war, the Economy Act of 1933, in its denial of government employment to two family members, helped institutionalize the notion that women workers were purely supplemental. During the war years, female laborers were frequently hired by the absent husband's employer, the better to justify the wife's immediate termination upon her mate's return. The relegation of the Women's Advisory Committee of the War Manpower Commission to observer status on the policy-making board, even in the determination of women's issues, testifies to the strictly ancillary role of the committee. The litany of traditionally female job classifications offers further proof of the indelibility of the female assistant stereotype: nurse (not doctor), secretary (not executive), waitress (not maitre d'). As mentioned in chapter 2, government investigations discovered countless instances of women doing skilled work while classified as "helpers"; the dictum that "women, as a rule, make poor bosses in a factory or office" crystallized an attitude that effectively stifled upward mobility for the woman worker.

In terms of narrative function, the female has long been utilized as the hermeneutic provocateur, the protagonist's assistant/companion who provides the crucial, usually overlooked linkage of fact or interpretation (often through "woman's intuition"). The closest approximation to equal status for women in the detective genre might be Nick and Nora Charles of *Thin Man* fame; more often as in *The Glass Key* (1942), *Ministry of Fear* (1943), or *I Wake Up Screaming* (1941), the female offers aid and comfort to the crusading male figure through her sexual presence while providing an alternative trajectory for the narrative (that of the romantic discourse). This paradigm has changed little over the years and appears to have been but moderately deflected or transformed within the World War II context. Of course, there have been any number of fictional female sleuths, ranging from Nancy Drew to Miss Marple, but the vast majority of hard core "truth seekers" in cinema have been men (this would include active/aggressive hermeneuts beyond the detective species—those avenging murders, engaging in espionage or tracking down assailants).

But the assistant detective is only one of three sub-groupings considered here. Women are represented as adjutant figures in a more historically specific way during this period: as moral/spiritual supporters of men during the struggle and as rehabilitators of men in its aftermath. These are exemplified by *Pacific Blackout, Watch on the Rhine* and *Lost Weekend.*

Pacific Blackout was released in the last weeks before Pearl Harbor and was criticized for its alleged discrediting of defense preparedness on the home front; set in Seattle, the film includes a lengthy and unexpected power failure and a near-successful bombing raid on the city. Consequently, the film begins with a polite disclaimer and high praise for the Civil Defense program. In terms of its narrative construction, *Blackout's* hermeneutic knot is triply constituted: Robert Draper (Robert Preston) is framed for a murder which he must set straight or die (threat to the individual); he suspects his plight is connected to his work on anti-aircraft range-finders (threat to the nation); and he is aided by a female benefactress placed in opposition to the woman responsible for his false conviction (romantic enigma). The much-maligned blackout is a vital element in the narrative scheme as it provides the occasion for Draper's escape en route to Death Row early in the film. He stumbles upon a whimsical young woman with a plain-Jane name, Mary Jones (played by Martha O'Driscoll), who is searching for her dog and who instinctively comes to his aid, despite his handcuffs and obvious fugitive status. Mary is a telephone operator who works the night shift (the mere notion of a working identity for a woman is a mark of the historical moment) and exhibits a curious assortment of gendered characteristics: she is blonde and rather sweet-looking, but wears a fedora-like hat and a tailored dress that connote mannishness. She seems at times to be in the mold of the "dizzy dame" but she is capable of much sensible behavior, as when she succeeds in freeing Draper from his shackles. He has found a metal file and tries this tedious method while Mary grabs an ax and cleaves his bonds with a single blow! She faints dead away but one suspects even this sign of fragility as she prolongs the swoon in order to remain in Draper's arms. Mary Jones is a canny young assistant, indeed, who seems motivated by a personal agenda of desire.

Draper bids Mary farewell (he must go it alone) and steps into a boarding house to get some rest. Just when the desk clerk's suspicions are dangerously aroused, Mary enters, offers convincing explanation and escorts Draper upstairs. A quick phone call and Mary discovers her evening-long absence has cost her her job. In answer to Draper's puzzlement at her motives, Jones replies, "I'm a very impulsive person . . . you looked as if you needed help." This reply does little to assuage Draper's bewilderment: "One woman perjured herself on the stand trying to send me to the electric chair . . . and now you pop up out of nowhere and risk yourself trying to help me . . . can you tell me how two women could be so utterly different?"

Mary Jones and the perjuring female, Marie Duval (Eva Gabor), are placed in positions of antagonism and parallelism through their relations to the male protagonist. They are opposed through their names (guileless, all-American *Mary* Jones versus inscrutable, accented *Marie* Duval—domestic/foreign variations of the same name) and motives (Jones' apparently selfless aid is linked to erotic attachment; Duval, it turns out, was blackmailed into betrayal out of concern for her family in Occupied France—there is no romantic connection with Draper). Yet Draper's naive question ("How can two women be so different?") underscores the functional parallelism of the paired females vis-à-vis the central male figure (the film's subjective vortex) for whom their womanhood remains an issue. The final distinction between the two women regards their respective fates: Mary flourishes, Marie is killed. Indeed, the film resonates with the undercurrent of xenophobia which animated America prior to its entry into the war.

Mary continues to perform feats of well-timed heroism. The desk clerk enters their room, gets the drop on Draper and calls the cops before Jones smashes a vase over his head, launching another leg of their odyssey. As she nimbly scampers down the fire escape, Mary remarks, "I like to run . . . you should see me steal bases." A running gag in the film relates to Mary's appetite; she is always hungry. "Are you always eating?" asks Draper at one point. "Yes, but I never get fat, don't worry," she replies. An air raid signal sounds and the pair get shuffled into a bomb shelter. Mary is off to settle things with Marie Duval, and as she scurries off she calls to the non-plussed Draper: "Good-bye dear, take care of the baby!" When at last the plot is fully uncovered and the antagonists are identified, the threat-to-the-nation thread remains to be resolved, for a bombing raid has been called in on the Midas Munition Plant. Draper's quick thinking averts the disaster, but it is Mary's cleverness that saves Draper's neck. She arranges for a telephone operator pal to overhear the evildoer's confession/explication over the wires just before the cops arrive, thus insuring Draper's release. With the threat to person and nation overcome, the film ends with Draper taking Mary for a few hamburgers at a local drive-in.

Pacific Blackout constitutes a near-parody of the male protagonist/female helper paradigm. Playing against the Robert Preston character's stolid brand of male problem-solving, young Mary Jones offers a creative spontaneity of action that both resolves conflict and animates the elaboration of these resolutions. While Mary is not the source of the enigma (it is Draper, the man of science, whose work has been turned against him and his country), she is the pixy spirit who teases it along, unblocking conflict and promoting a general sense of levity otherwise missing from the proceedings. A working girl with a healthy appetite, spunk and athleticism to burn, Mary is a light-hearted representation of the American girl consistent with the free-wheeling, slightly isolationist mood of the immediate pre-war months when American heroes were blithely battling Fascism as Yanks for the RAF or as Canadian volunteers. The succeeding two variants of the woman helper are far more serious in their relationship to conflict and resolution.

Watch on the Rhine is the earnest account of the character and heroics of one man who, in the spring of 1940, had been fighting Nazism from the beginning and who foresaw the worldwide conflagration that lay ahead. Kurt Mueller (Paul Lukas), his wife Sarah (Bette Davis) and their children arrive in the United States and proceed to Sarah's family home, a plantation estate outside Washington, D.C. This is the home of Sarah's mother, Fanny Farrelly (Lucille Watson), widow of a one-time associate justice of the Supreme Court whose stern portrait surveys much of the dramatic action. Based on Lillian Hellman's successful play of the same name, the film exhibits a theatricality of spatio-temporal rhythms (the drama respects the Aristotelian unities) which are in keeping with the succession of speeches by the dramatis personae, many of which are concerned with directly ideological matters.

Most of the philosophical questions raised pertain to the willingness of individuals to expose themselves to personal danger and sacrifice for the sake of ideals—in this case, anti-Fascism. Released in 1943, the film avoids the controversy aroused by the play (whose pitch for commitment predated the American entry into the war). Of interest here is the manner in which duties are apportioned within the family context, specifically the function of the woman in the shared struggle for a better world. There is a virulently patriarchal structure in evidence throughout the film which links the generations of Farrelly women, Fanny and Sarah. Both women are outspoken and demonstrably strong-minded, yet each yield their place to the men in their lives. Old Joshua Farrelly, despite his strictly iconic presence, continues to bear the ponderous weight of Law upon his furrowed brow. Sarah's Kurt is a man of deferential reserve who inadequately conceals the self-righteousness of his beliefs. When asked his trade, Mueller replies, "Fighting fascism, that is my trade." The solemnity with which his philosophy is intoned makes Mueller a rather overbearing figure not unlike his portraitured father-in-law: "I must make my stand. I can do nothing else. Amen."

The officious tone of Kurt Mueller's pronouncements are counter-weighted by his narrated exploits; a member of the resistance for seven years, he has been wounded in Spain and carries the bullets of fascism within his body. His life has been saved by a comrade-in-arms, Max Freidank, chief of German resistance forces, and he must return to Europe to attempt Freidank's rescue. Before doing so, he dispatches Fanny's houseguest, Count Dubrankowicz, who works for the other side. This matter is accomplished with the world-weary air of a professional nearing his end. Gallantly, with little speech-making, Mueller sets off on his suicidal mission while Sarah stays behind to tend to her humorless sons, Joshua and Boudu. It is her lot to pack off the former to his sacrificial purpose, in the footsteps of his soon-to-be martyred father. Then she busies herself in the instruction of young Boudu, explaining the procedures for becoming a man, outlining the inner resources of courage and determination which she displays but is barred from utilizing because she is a woman. Sarah's role appears to be a rather limited one: to assist in the struggle against fascism by making, nurturing and resolutely supporting men who do battle with the forces of evil.

While there is a certain logic to some division of labor within the family, the character of that division is conditioned by ideological contingencies. Moreover, the circumscription of the female function is not uniformly mandated by historical precedent. Hellman's own short story "Julia" celebrates the great courage of a woman with a husband and child, like Sarah an expatriate American, whose direct involvement in the anti-Fascist movement costs her her life. Indeed, the strict demarcation of sexual roles in *Watch on the Rhine* is an atavistic feature most notable for its power to bridge the generational gap between mother and daughter. Initially appalled by the unremitting pressures of the Mueller family's nomadic existence and the absence of the simplest childhood pleasures for her grandchildren, Fanny comes to respect Sarah's life, her dedication to the messianic teachings of her husband ("It's a fine thing to have you for a daughter; I would like to have been like you"). Yet this unshakable loyalty to Mueller becomes inseparable from a kind of subservience which denies Sarah her full right of speech. On several occasions, as she is in the midst of explaining herself to her family, Kurt interrupts to speak for her, *ex cathedra*. The words of the great man are valued above the personal expression of his wife. The sense of gravity that surrounds both Mueller and the late judge and the authority accorded them within the family are linked to a notion of sexual difference. As rock-steady as the women may be, theirs is a support role connected to their womanhood as part of a gender-conscious family structure which is meant to be replicated by following generations.

The third and final version of the female helper in the wartime Hollywood film relates to the rehabilitation of the ten million returning vets. During the war years, women had been characterized as the moral and spiritual wellsprings of their fighting men, or else as their clever but respectful assistants. Now the responsibility for the restoration of the depleted male fell to the woman as well. Of course, the readjustment issue was of great concern to both sexes, exemplified by a War Advertising Council pamphlet entitled "How Your Advertising Can Help the

Veteran Readjust to Civilian Life.'' Prepared during the last days of the war in conjunction with the office of War Information, the Council's suggestions were intended to unify the approach of postwar advertising messages; to wit: ''Ads should be written to give the impression that the returning veterans will be all right and act all right unless the actions of civilians make them act and feel otherwise.''[1] The pamphlet urged that this sense of responsibility, shifted onto the civilian population, be inculcated in all advertising copy, while encouraging an upbeat no-nonsense approach: ''Avoid sloppy sentimentalism. Remember that veterans may read these ads too, and most veterans resent being cried over.''

Yet the particular importance of the woman in the rehabilitative process becomes apparent in the pamphlet. In a sample advertisement which had been published by the drug and cosmetic industries (with, one may presume, its predominantly female clientele in mind), the various civilian attitudes towards the returning vet are dramatized in cartoon fashion. Five of the six stereotypes are criticized for incorrect behavior; all but one are characterized as male. ''The Greeter'' is the man who offers a smile and a handshake, but no job. ''The Bloodhound'' can't wait to hear all the gory details of combat (''It's o.k. sailor, you won't shock *me!* Ever knife a Jap?''). ''The Patriot'' brags about his financial sacrifices to the veteran while ''The Rock'' begrudges him his ninety day cooling-off period before resuming civilian life and work. Only ''The Clutch'' is a caricatured woman, overly emotional around the returnees (''practically blubbers (while) leaping to help some disabled veteran over a pebble''). The ''Blue Ribbon Citizen,'' on the other hand, is a beaming, fresh-faced woman with all the right emotional responses. ''Like all good people, she asks no questions, weeps no tears, doesn't stare at disabilities. To her, a returned veteran is an abler, more aggressive and resourceful citizen than the boy who went away. She's proud of him, proud to know him. Anxious to be of real help. She's the kind of person we should all be.'' The femaleness of this prototype is implicit; she is helpful but silent, proud of the man, anxious to reward him. The unspoken reward is, of course, her sexuality and service through the marriage tie. The ideal post-war woman is the one who can be a sexy mother figure, for the twin attributes of the rehabilitating female are seduction and nurture—the former to revitalize the sexual identity, the latter to soothe the traumas to mind and body.

During 1945 and 1946, a veritable cycle of films was produced which spoke to the resettlement problem and the issues which it raised between men and women. Among these are *Pride of the Marines, The Courage of Lassie* (1946), *From This Day Forward* (1946) and *The Best Years of Our Lives* (1946). In each instance (with a slight reshaping in the case of the Lassie film), men who bear the scars of war experience or who have great difficulty in settling back into jobs and civilian life receive the aid and support of wives or prospective wives. The flashback structure of *Pride of the Marines* allows for the depiction of the boy/girl relationship prior to separation, the roots of female loyalty which will blossom into maternal devotion as a result of protagonist Al Schmidt's blindness. The aptly named

The Reception Committee–

(KNOW ANYBODY HERE?)

The Greeter. A one-man brass band. "Nothing's too good for Our Boys!" he always says. And that's what he gives them. Nothing ... except a big hello. Help? "That's the Government's job," he says.

The Clutch. One like her in every town. Always leaping to help some disabled veteran over a pebble. Practically blubbers while she's doing it. Succeeds in making the veteran feel he's ruined for any normal life. Or career.

The Bloodhound. "It's OK. Sailor, you won't shock *me!* Ever knife a Jap? How does it feel to be bombed?" The War's just one big adventure story to him. But it hasn't been for the sailor. He wants to *forget* it—not *talk* about it.

The Patriot. Always talking about all the things he goes without. Mentions the War Bonds he buys as though he were doing the *Government* a favor. This makes veterans (who've been buying plenty of Bonds themselves) wonder whether we had the right people in foxholes.

•

Prepared by the War Advertising Council, Inc., in Cooperation with the Office of War Information and the Retraining and Reemployment Administration.

The Rock. He's nerveless. The Iron Man. War hasn't affected *him.* Can't understand why discharged veterans are allowed 90 days to relax before going back to their old jobs. Can't understand why they should need time to get over the War. He doesn't. Combat Officers would love to have this type in their care for a while.

Blue Ribbon Citizen. Like all good people, she asks no questions, weeps no tears. doesn't stare at disabilities. To her, a returned veteran is an abler, more aggressive and resourceful citizen than the boy who went away. She's proud of him. proud to know him. Anxious to be of real help. She's the kind of person we should all be.

"How Your Advertising Can Help the Veteran Adjust to Civilian Life" Pamphlet prepared in cooperation with the Office of War Information and Retraining and Reemployment Administrations by the War Advertising Council. Postwar advertising campaigns such as this one sought to couple product promotion with values clarification. The "Blue Ribbon Citizen" was the woman who could rehabilitate the returning vet through a combination of seduction and nurture.

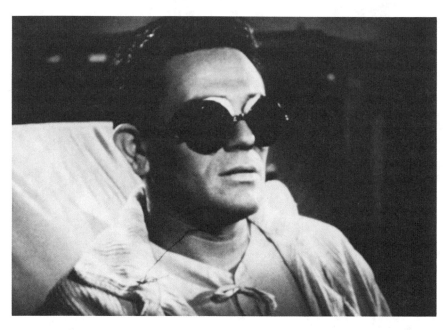

Pride of the Marines (Warner Brothers, 1945)
Al Schmidt (John Garfield)—sightless, bitter, unwilling to accept dependency on a loving woman—faces postwar life in emotional isolation. For men like Al, rehabilitation means learning to acknowlege weakness, learning to allow women to offer support and comfort.

Ruth (her "whither thou goest, I shall go" ethic alludes to the Biblical antecedent, the name itself denoting kindness) has the right answer to the familiar question, "Will you wait for me?": "You'll have to pry me loose, I'm the sticking kind." When Ruth comes to visit him in the hospital after a grenade has exploded in his face, Al is remote, wordless, unable to express the tangled emotions inside. After Ruth leaves a nurse tells him, "A guy could lean on a girl like that." "A Marine don't lean on anyone, if there's leanin' to be done," says Al. "It's the female sex that's the weaker, isn't it?" Al's question addresses the core problematic of all these films: can the female learn to be the stronger without appearing to be so? Become the silent rock, tucking the manchild into bed, watching over him as he sleeps?

The Best Years of Our Lives features three men from varying class backgrounds, each of whom require the gentle ministerings of a woman. Myrna Loy, Theresa Wright and Cathy O'Donnell each put their man to bed at various points in the film to lighten the suffering of drunkenness, nightmares and severe handicap, respectively. But, as in *Marines,* the woman must foster the illusion that it is she who is the truly needy one. The last word in *Marines* is the direction given the cabdriver—"Home!" For the home is the space dedicated to nurture, the woman's domain, the site of her construction (place of the "homemaker") in which the rebuilding task can be effected in earnest. Home is the horizon point toward which this group of films makes pilgrimage, the word around which a nation's hopes for regeneration coheres.

Lost Weekend, while diverging from the direct treatment of the soldier's readjustment, reconstitutes the male/female therapeutic relationship in civilian terms. Here the crisis of male strength is alcoholism; a talented young writer (Ray Milland), tormented by his dependency and self-destructiveness, fights to regain his spiritual equilibrium with the aid of a good woman (Jane Wyman). The Billy Wilder production situates itself as a social problem film through its opening shot, a pan of a cityscape which comes to rest on one building, zooming in on a bottle of whiskey suspended on a string from Milland's window. This is the account of one personal struggle among many, but the dynamic of the conflict, in terms of its exposition of male/female relations, is identical to the GI readjustment films. Once again, as in *Pacific Blackout* and *Pride of the Marines,* the naming of the woman is significant: the appellation Helen St. James indicates the saintliness required for the female function. Helen's loving and forgiving nature is as intrinsic to her as Don's infirmity is to him. "You're trying not to drink," says Helen, "and I'm trying not to love you."

Not that all women are equally endowed with the curative urge, evidenced by the person of Gloria, a barmaid who is largely victimized by the feckless Milland (he takes money from her in exchange for a kiss and false promises). Helen is altogether different; a paragon of discipline and middle class virtue from Toledo, she has met Milland at the opera (narrated in flashback, some three years after the meeting). He is so affected by her exemplary ways that he stays dry for weeks. It is only when her family comes to New York for a visit that the pressures become insurmountable and Don reaches for the bottle. When Helen realizes the extent of Milland's alcoholism, she dedicates herself to defeating what she takes to be her rival for Don's affections, for she is a fighter. In words nearly identical to Eleanor Parker's in *Pride of the Marines,* Helen tells Don, "You don't know me very well if you think I'll give up now." Don's brother, Wick, counsels otherwise, "Let go of him, Helen, give yourself a chance." Yet, throughout the three years that have transpired, she has remained loyal while Don attempts to exorcise his personal demon by transmuting his suffering into art. He is constantly engaged in the struggle to write his autobiographical novel, *The Bottle.*

The culmination of Don's battle with himself is his descent into the Dante-esque environs of an alcoholic ward of the city jail. As terrified as he is by this vision of hell, he soon steals a quart of rye to soothe his agony and renew the self-destructive cycle. Meanwhile, Helen has waited up all night for him outside his apartment. She literally bludgeons her way into his consciousness by her un-willingness to let go. "Don, let me in, Don . . . I won't go away." When at last she has gained entrance and gazes upon this empty husk of a man, she re-mains undaunted. "Don, put your arm on my shoulder." Her man has not been maimed by the enemy or blinded by an exploding grenade, but he is a walking casualty nonetheless who is lost without this beatific female presence with will enough for two people.

Helen's particular brand of nurturing is part nurse, part cheerleader. Her erotic self is rarely asserted; indeed, sexuality only surfaces in the film as Don's ticket to another bottle of booze via the enamored barmaid. There is an evangelical tone mixed with a progenitive strain of self-actualization therapy evidenced by Helen's speeches at the film's conclusion. "The only way to start is to stop," preaches St. James the healer. "There is no cure besides just stopping . . . you've got talent and ambition." Still shaken and uncertain, Don bleats a reply, "What do you expect, a miracle?" "Yes, yes!" is the pious rejoinder. "Put it all down on paper, get rid of it that way . . . tell it all . . . to whom it may concern . . . and it concerns so many people." At this point, Helen reaches out and reverses Don's cigarette, placing the filtered end to his lips. The wrong-ended cigarette has been a recurring signifier of Don's misguidedness, of his inverted values and self-esteem. Helen's gesture is the penultimate movement of the film—corrective yet essentially noninvasive. The last move is Milland's: he drops the cigarette into his glass of rye.

Lost Weekend represents the third form of female assistanceship located in the wartime cinema: helper as healer. This popular culture variant of American womanhood is tied to a precise historical moment, the initial months and years of postwar readjustment during which every effort was being made to smooth

Let There Be Light (1946)
Army nurses wave their cheerful farewells to busloads of psychically bruised GIs, newly healed and released, in John Huston's long-suppressed documentary. Although most of the filmed therapy sessions are "man-to-man" (one stern, male psychiatrist is even addressed as "sir" by a soldier in the throes of sodium pentathol), the largely absent female figures (mothers, sweethearts, nurses) emerge as the primary source of care, emotional sustenance, and gentle healing.

the return of the disoriented, often mentally or physically disabled GI into the mainstream as husband, father, worker and consumer. The fictionalized versions of this process accentuate the role of the woman as the personalized agent of regeneration, acting out of sincere affection and enlightened self-interest.

John Huston's long-suppressed documentary *Let There Be Light* (1946) investigates the plight of the emotionally disturbed vet without recourse to the dramatization of cure-by-romance. As a piece of nonfiction, the film testifies the more forcefully to the prevalence of the woman-as-healer dynamic within postwar culture. In Huston's film, a group of men at one rehabilitation center are followed through a series of therapeutic processes administered by army psychiatrists. It is interesting, however, that one of the most emotionally loaded scenes occurs during the initial interview of one overwrought soldier who begins to sob uncontrollably when he speaks of his girlfriend. She is the one person who ever understood him, whose emotional support furnished him with the strength to overcome the trials of war. Toward the end of the film, the same GI is briefly shown in animated discussion with a young woman on the grounds of the sanitarium; resumption of contact with his "sweetheart" as he calls her is a crucial part of his therapy. Yet the Huston film was not released for more than thirty years, the starkness of its theme and the severity of the disturbances shown were

deemed to be insufficiently counterbalanced by the optimism of the film's conclusion in which the men are cheerfully bused out of the complex, leaving behind
a phalanx of smiling, waving nurses. The therapeutic solution to the readjustment question posited on the screens of America was implicated at a deep structural level with the conventional narrative format and with one construction of
character in particular: that of the woman/nurturer dedicated to reassembling the
keystone of Hollywood's fictional world, the romantic couple.

Woman in the Family Melodrama

The Great Lie (1941)
Penny Serenade (1941)
The Clock (1945)
A Stolen Life (1946)

A great deal of critical energy has been expended in recent years in the analysis
of the melodrama and its cultural/psychological context and antecedents. The term
has exhibited an excessive variability of meaning, however, with many critics
applying the "melodramatic" label to any Hollywood film that interiorizes and
personalizes social/ideological conflicts while actively soliciting the emotional,
often sentimental, response of the audience. There is, of course, a fundamental
validity to this criterion, broad as it may be. One need only think of the frequency of representations of sexual violence which have, since *The Birth of a Nation*,
traditionally constituted the permissible arena of social conflict, that titillating
displacement of class and racial tensions that incorporates the play of desire, power
and revenge between men and women.

Melodrama is often loosely attached to what are called "women's films"
(those that develop an explicitly female subjectivity) or "weepies" (films that
touch a common core of suffering and loss, usually in a female audience). A working definition of melodrama might well suggest a characteristic narrative structure. For the melodrama as narrative entity achieves a congruity with the perceived
rhythms of human experience—the amplitudes of emotional expression extending
the structure of strict narrative causality.[2] Moreover, the site of conflict for
melodrama is the home, the battleground within which actions (and emotional
levels) rise and fall. The motivation of this film type is the constitution or restoration of the conditions of reproduction of society, focused upon a single
microcosmic unit. The specifics of this trajectory are determined in large part
by the historical/ideological context within which a given film is produced.

The high melodramatic period of the Hollywood film is most often considered
to be the 1950s, encompassing as it does the most accomplished works of Sirk,
Minnelli, Ray and Vidor. It is undeniable that the war years produced nothing
comparable to the complex orchestrations of the best "domestic" melodramas

of the 1950s: *Written on the Wind* (1956), *Bigger than Life* (1956) or *Home from the Hill* (1960), films whose splashy color and intricately choreographed planes of action, centered around the home, responded to the dizzying prosperity and concomitant heightening of family tensions of that period. The melodramas of the early war years primarily focused upon the possibilities of romantic union rather than the disillusionments of a utopia achieved. If the modality of the "high melodrama" is ironic (the American family after the fall), that irony can only be understood in connection with the effects of inquisition and paranoia: the Iron Curtain, the blacklist, the fall-out shelter. The relative naivete of the wartime melodramatic mode—comic and low-mimetic—is an extension of a general concern for refiguring in reassuring terms the romantic yearnings of a generation at war.[3] Another pole of the wartime melodrama is tragic-transcendental, a mode in which loss is actively theologized, relocating the terrain of martyrdom from the battlefield to the American family (here, the entire family grouping shares the mantle of martyrdom, e.g., *The Human Comedy*).

Contributing to the nebula that surrounds this category has been the widespread misapplication of the term "family romance." In its original Freudian context ("Family Romances," 1908) the notion of family romance was limited to the imaginative elaborations of children with regard to their parentage.[4] Describing the several stages of this phenomenon, Freud suggested that the commonly noted tendency of the child to replace his/her parents with an idealized mother and father (of higher class or status) was motivated by ambitious and erotic impulses. Intense sexual rivalries generated in the Oedipal phase contribute to the desire to remove or transfigure the objects of hostility. A later phase of this complex occurs after the accession to sexual knowledge; the child (in fact, the paradigm as described works only for a male child) fantasizes sexual indiscretions by his mother and even constructs scenarios whereby siblings are rendered illegitimate. There are a range of variations of fantasies alluded to in Freud's brief essay, but for present purposes the salient point is the absolute focus on the child as the source and subject of "family romance."

Conversely, the term has been endowed with a far more generalized context and utility in the hands of film theorists. Stephen Heath, in an essay entitled "Contexts" (*Edinburgh Magazine,* #2), extends the notion of family romance to include "continuing fantasy activity round the topic of family relations generally,"[5] corroborating the usage by an elliptical appropriation of the original text: "its many-sidedness and its great range of applicability enable it to meet every sort of requirement." In fact, Freud's reference ("its" antecedent) was to the malleability of childhood fantasy formation—e.g., the bastardizing (hence legitimizing as erotic object) of a sibling of particular sexual attraction to the fantasizing subject. Heath's usage is based upon the linkage between this childhood tendency and the conditions of fabular production in toto (via "imaginative activity"). Pushing his reading ever further, Heath suggests that the etymological connection between romance and roman (novel) authorizes the appropriation of family romance to indicate the psychic source for the endless play of narrative/ideological positionings within a fictionalized family domain, site of so much of classical cinema. The argument is itself something of a romance, one that constructs a wished-for-parent in order to prove its own legitimacy.

The distinction to be made in terms of cinematic melodrama is precisely between those fictions which move across generations and are, properly speaking, family romances (for, in Freud's words, "the whole progress of society rests upon the opposition between successive generations")[6] and those which are intragenerational (usually between husband and wife). As previously stated, forties melodramas are typically far more concerned with the creation or restoration of the conditions for family than the fifties variants in which questions of patrimony and generational conflict take precedence.

A significant number of films of the early forties did, in fact, center on the pursuit of an idealized family structure in which a child plays a crucial role. Interestingly enough, the children present in the family configurations of these melodramas are most often babies. Even if these children are older, they are rarely endowed with subjectivity but are instead the *occasion* of narrative conflict rather than its promulgator. Often the question of legitimizing the child is the prime hermeneutic vector; consequently, adoption, with its entanglements of law and emotional uncertainty, becomes the subject of a number of films: *The Great Lie* (1941), *Penny Serenade* (1941), *The Lady Is Willing* (1942), *Journey for Margaret* (1942), *To Each His Own* (1946), *Anchors Aweigh* (1945). At a time when the resurrection of the family nexus was the highest priority, it is historically apt that the family romance should fixate at this incipient stage. Moreover, the demands of instant regeneration appear to have encouraged representations in which a kind of grafting or recycling of offspring provides the solution to dislocated reproductive sexuality. For their part, the films of the mid-to-late fifties most often examine families with children of an advanced age bearing significant subjective status: *Bigger than Life* (1957), Tarnished Angels (1957), *Splendor in the Grass* (1961). It should be noted in passing that the fictional time frame of such films is of little importance (many are set in other historical periods); rather, it is the congruence of represented family relations with contemporary social patterns (in this instance, in synch with the baby boom) that is noteworthy.

Penny Serenade (1941) is a provocative case study of family romance in that its narrative and ideological conflict center is constituted through the mismatch of the idealizations of husband and wife. Each of them has a specific notion of family life in mind; the disjunct between the two versions drives the couple apart. At the outset of the film, Julie (Irene Dunne) is on her way to the airport—she is leaving her husband—when a series of flashbacks are triggered by a "special" tune ("You Were Meant for Me"). Through a dissolve from the label of the spinning disc, her first meeting with Roger Adams (Cary Grant) is narrated. After intermittent returns to present time, his marriage proposal on New Year's Eve and their hurried post-nuptial consummation on board a train are presented in flashback. Adams is a journalist en route to a long-term assignment in Japan.

These narrative elements are curious in their prefiguring of so many filmed partings during the next four years. Adams's departure deadline is a matter of professional commitment. Yet the impulse marriage, the rushed intimacy and the unlikely impregnation that results, coupled with the particular destination, make *Penny Serenade* the forerunner of many wartime romantic narratives. The festivities surrounding their fateful first encounter to the strains of "You Were Meant for Me" are engendered by a New Year's Eve celebration but are otherwise identical to the kind of frenzied activity (part elation, part fear) that intensifies the last moments of the departing GI. In the next flashback segment, Julie has joined Roger in Japan but difficulties arise when Adams exhibits a flair for profligacy. Having received an inheritance, he is anxious to quit the newspaper and travel before the baby's arrival. Clearly, Roger seeks the pleasures of romantic coupledom while Julie is ready for motherhood and family responsibilities. Julie's apprehensions concerning Roger's wanderlust are interrupted by an earthquake in which the baby is lost. Here, as so often in melodrama, a prematurely elaborated emotional crisis is settled by an act of God or nature only to reemerge later at an escalated level. A far greater sedimentation of experience (of the characters and of the identifying spectator) is required to intensify the clash of emotions.

When Roger and Julie return to the United States, the couple's disparate plans for the future drive them farther apart. Roger wants to buy a small newspaper despite the poor financial odds and to shower Julie with extravagances while she wishes only for a child. Her family fantasies were aroused on their first date by a Chinese fortune cookie and have only been redoubled by her tragic loss. The answer is adoption if only they can appease the adoption agency's Mrs. Oliver, archly played by Beulah Bondi. Although Roger cannot fully share Julie's enthusiasm, he does indicate his preference: he wants a two-year old boy. Adams' choice is consistent with other masculine characteristics: his restlessness, his unwillingness to be restricted by a nine-to-five job or to be examined by the adoption agency. It is Julie's determination to satisfy her maternal instincts that convinces Bondi to entrust an infant girl to them. But, after a year's probation, they are on the verge of losing little Trina due to Roger's failure with his newspaper.

The demise of the business is figured in characteristic melodramatic terms. Little is made of the depression context during which so few small business enterprises survived (particularly home-grown newspapers). Rather, Adams' plight is represented as a just sentence for his male hubris. In a scene rare in the annals of Cary Grant performances, Roger pleads his case before the judge with tearful eloquence; he will work for anybody and do anything if only they can keep Trina. His vision of family has now begun to conform more closely with Julie's and he is prepared to sacrifice for that vision.

Through a series of flashback dissolves, Trina is shown first to be a healthy pre-adolescent member of a conventional family unit, then suddenly stricken by an unnamed illness. Her death leaves Roger and Julie detached and sullen. With the loss of the child, the shared family romance is dissolved. Their struggle to achieve the family ideal—through a failed pregnancy and the battle to receive and maintain custody of Trina—has constituted the binding force of the couple's relationship. Julie's preparations for her imminent departure are interrupted by a telephone call from Mrs. Oliver. By some happy coincidence, she is able to offer them a curly-haired, blue-eyed two-year-old boy. The couple is thus reunited through the realization of Roger's original family fantasy.

Penny Serenade presents a version of family melodrama in which an accommodation of familial idealizations of husband and wife occurs, a process conditioned by the volatility of their shared experience. Given the traditional framework of gender typing, it is the man who receives the bulk of the credit for the compromise, from pleasure-seeking to family planning and responsible custodianship. The reply to Roger's adoptive preference for a two-year-old boy (a prepackaged Butch to play ball with in the back yard) is a doomed little girl for whom he must fight and humble himself. As a reward for the sacrifices of the male, for whom such sacrifices are judged more remarkable, his original idealization is eventually bestowed upon him and the marriage is regenerated. What is left unsaid, and certainly accounts for the unsettling impact of the drama, is the lack of recuperative capacity intrinsic to the romantic couple itself. In classical Hollywood versions of love and marriage, there is inevitably some source of tenderness or memory which can be tapped in order to facilitate the final embrace. Here, as in so many homes across the land, the cement of the man/woman relationship is extrinsic, resting upon the *idea* of a child (any child) as a shared and externalized focus for their love. The spectator may well ask, "If Cary Grant and Irene Dunne cannot sustain a marital romance without the benefit of a child, what hope is there for us?" The unspoken reply, of course, is "Have children!"

If *Penny Serenade* examined the conflict and gradual unification of projections of husband and wife, another version of narrativized fantasy relations involves a clear-cut separation between the sexes in which the male and female imaginaries remain mutually undisclosed. Such is the case in two Bette Davis vehicles, *The Great Lie* (1941) and *A Stolen Life* (1946). In both films, Davis is out to snare a man whose emotional priorities regarding marriage and fatherhood are unfathomable because inadequately expressed (in line with the encoded male preference for action over declaration). An important facet of these two films is the primacy which the male figure retains (George Brent in *The Great Lie,* Glenn Ford in *A Stolen Life*) despite his lack of subjective presence. Many feminist critics have pointed to the procession of female personae in Hollywood films who have remained objects of narrative (and of the male gaze) rather than fully endowed subjects, incitations to action rather than the true agents of events. In these two films, the female protagonists are the energetic shapers of narrative. But (and this is crucial) the fictive female is endowed less with the power of emplotment than with a will toward machination, usually against other women: Davis versus the Mary Astor character in *Lie,* Davis versus her twin self in *Life.* The point made by Christine Gledhill (that "women as women" rather than as blank slates, pawns or scheming tricksters are unrepresented in mainstream cinema) remains largely unchallenged by the forties melodrama.[7]

For all their inscrutability and passivity, the men of these two films provide the impetus for all the assertiveness and aggressivity; the elaborate patterns of deception which are the substance of the narrative hinge on these ciphers of consciousness. Much could be said of the man's position in this self-destructive circuitry—his power to incite the turning of the woman's aggressive energy back upon its sister-self. Thus, even in his absence, the male controls discourse, imbricated as it is within the patriarchal order. Julia Kristeva offers grounds for this evacuation of the feminine in her very definition of woman as "that which is not represented, that which is unspoken, that which is left out of meanings and ideologies."[8] Clearly, neither access to subject status nor centrality of narrative function is sufficient to reverse the submission of the woman within a discursive regime unwilling to challenge an "easy" verisimilitude, to refigure the prevailing relations of power among men and women.

Like *Penny Serenade, The Great Lie* raises the issue of the binding power of the child for the married couple. The trajectory of the Davis character's desire is circuitous due to the unlikely turn of events and her response to them. She has wed Brent but not before he and Astor have consummated their own technically unlawful union (Astor's divorce decree was not final). When Brent is lost over Brazil, Astor, now pregnant, agrees to exchange her future child (once again, instant fertility is the handmaiden of the hermeneutic code) for Davis's lifelong financial support (Astor is a concert pianist, selfish, ill-tempered and highly unsentimental). When Brent returns from the dead months later, the question arises as to how strong a factor true (versus bartered) motherhood will be for the husband-object who is also the determiner of female fates. For Astor now re-enters the picture, hoping to snare Brent with the revelation of her biological connection. This despite the fact that it was Davis's ministerings through the pregnancy that prevented Astor's hard-living ways from endangering the child (Davis has arranged for an isolated western retreat in which the reluctant mother goes cold turkey on scotch, cigarettes and late-night revelry).

Davis's family romance has been a solitary one prior to Brent's return. She is content to buy a piece of her husband to sustain the family fiction, a process which has already entailed a degree of secrecy (the western retreat). Brent's unforeseen resurrection rekindles Astor's own scenario of desire; for her, the child represents the one chance to realize her own "romance," which is coupledom. Unlike her rival's, the child has no position in her idealization. The moral valences

A Stolen Life (Warner Brothers, 1946)
In this film Bette Davis plays twins locked in mortal combat over taciturn Glenn
Ford, whose character occupies a controlling position within a circuit of female
self-destruction. The formidable posers of the woman's aggressive energy are
turned back upon her sister-self.

of the two family romances are clear to the spectator. Nevertheless, Davis realizes
that both husband and son are in jeopardy should Astor's claim prove convincing, nor is she willing to risk all by revealing the unvarnished truth. Despite Davis's
monumental avoidance ploys, Astor at last forces the issue, producing a moment
of constructed ambiguity—the audience is meant to be uncertain of the husband's
choice. Whom will he punish, whom will he reward with the mantle of male
sovereignty and the perquisites of name, motherhood and manor? One begins
to anticipate a Solomon-like proposal of child-cleaving to determine the true
mother, but Brent opts for the heart-felt mother (Davis) with only a stern chiding
for her deceit. In this filmic instance, a unique reformulation of Freud's account
of fantasy-construction and imputed illegitimacy occurs. As in *Penny Serenade,*
the child has no part in the structuring of projections; for Brent, who has had
no direct contact with the child, the baby functions as ''son-ideal.'' The key circuit of social power is father-son with the two women vying for a position within
that circuit. Davis assumes that her validity within the family rests upon her role
in the paternal linkage; she is sanctioned in this belief by centuries of patrilineal
precedent. Instead, purity of maternal instinct triumphs over biological necessity. As with the adoption scenario, the conditions of familyhood and the effects
of and motives for parentage (often of an aberrant variety) are being explored
within the melodramatic format. What can children mean for the couple, indepen-

A Stolen Life
Kate—the good twin—is pinioned between her seductive alter ego, Pat, and their shared erotic object, Bill, in a triangulation of composition and desire.

dent of the attachment to the child-as-person (in neither film discussed is the infant known to the parent(s) in question)? As a force in the union of men and women and the formation of units we call families, what level of determinancy can be attributed to the regenerative instinct?

The Bette Davis character in *A Stolen Life* is, in fact, two characters—Kate, the sweet and selfless twin with whom we are meant to identify, and her seductive and cold-hearted alter ego, Pat. Here the female protagonist's idealization is not intergenerational, but is instead the product of her desire for Bill (Glenn Ford), a pipe-smoking lighthouse keeper's assistant, a virile man of nature whose material wants are few. The family connection in this melodrama is between Kate and her identical twin, of whom we know nothing until some twenty or more minutes into the film. Our surprise is matched by Bill's soon afterward when he spends an afternoon with Pat in the mistaken belief that she is her sister. He is fond of Kate, but he is bewitched by Pat, whose mission it becomes to steal Bill for herself. This she accomplishes while Kate can do nothing more than languish in tortured silence, unable to match her sister's seductiveness, unwilling to confront Bill's shifting interests head-on. Kate is the idealizer, Pat is the doer. Moreover, Pat's motives are presented as utterly impure; she acts out of greed and vindictiveness.

The twin dynamic in *A Stolen Life*, although apparently analogous to that of *The Dark Mirror* (identical twins constituted by a clear bifurcation of good and evil) is quite disparate (see discussion of *The Dark Mirror* in chapter 6). Here, the good twin is the voyeur, her virtue unappealing to the stolid male of her choice. Pat's ruthless self-interest is also a self-assurance which is undeniably appealing to its erotic object (and, in an unsettling way, to us as spectators for whom the "sweet" Bette Davis character is far less riveting). The post-war female indict-ment is even more damaging here than in *The Dark Mirror* which suggests the biological inherency of female sexual rivalry. Olivia de Havilland's murderous half was driven to dark deeds by a history of frustrated eroticism (her "better half" was always preferred), but Pat is the favored twin from the beginning, whose desire to monopolize the men (as the mythic Cronos monopolized the women) is spiteful and unquenchable.[9] It is precisely a case of *need* versus *desire*. To represent such a devastating brand of sisterhood is corrosive enough, but add to that the real attractiveness of this perfect female narcissism; the result is an indictment of the basis of male-female sexual chemistry. Good is boring; energetic female narcissism—amoral, all-devouring—once directed upon its object choice, is irresistible. Characteristically, a glimpse of Bill and Pat kissing seals Kate's resolve to flee the summer home of the family friend (Charlie Ruggles) and return to the city; word of the engagement follows in short order.

The fantasy activity of the film is indeed related to Freud's exposition of family romance insofar as the child's idealizations are said often to be correc-tives for intense jealousy and rivalry toward siblings. Such is the case in *The Stolen Life,* when the two sisters take to sea and, in the midst of a pounding storm, Pat is washed overboard and drowns. At the first level of fantasy, Pat's death is Kate's wish fulfillment. But in attempting to pull her twin back into the boat she has been left grasping only Pat's wedding ring. When Kate regains con-sciousness hours later, she finds that all assume that she is Pat; she is offered the choice of two identities. The second level of fantasy—the assumption of the wifely role—is achieved by a mere continuation of Kate's passivity. She allows herself to become Pat but in so doing achieves a further level of wish fulfillment, for she becomes the assertive and sexually active person she could never be. Ironically, her final act of "Kate-ness"—wide-eyed acquiescence—insures her metamorphosis into "Pat-ness."

The dream turns nightmare when Kate discovers that Bill has been planning to leave Pat because of her feckless infidelities. When all seems hopeless, Kate goes to family intimate Ruggles, who has suspected the truth all along. As with the Davis character's deceit in *The Great Lie,* Kate is but lightly reprimanded for her efforts to realize a wished-for union via a macabre masquerade. Bill, who was forced to give up the lighthouse to support Pat's extravagances, meets Kate at the windblown scene of their first encounter to say that she is forgiven, it was always her from the start. He is back to his natural environs, she has achieved her vision despite the fact that Bill's emotional makeup remains as opaque as ever. Ford is a ruggedly handsome cipher throughout, a condition which only accen-tuates the subjective centeredness of the film, an elaboration of one woman's unspeakable desires: sororicide and incest. That the sister in question deserves her death or that "virtue prevails" provides no consolation for one concerned with the character of female representation and the vilification of the feminine in the postwar years.

Indeed, female fantasy formation undergoes significant alteration in the five-year span encompassed by these few examples (1941-46). By the end of the period, the woman's family romance is as likely to embrace destructive as regenerative impulses, bespeaking contemporaneous attitudes toward female culpability. This trend is counterweighted by the "Woman as Helper" category in which the woman repairs and consoles her man; the conflicting thematic currents of these post-war years make this period far more complex than many critics have acknowledged, wholly focused as they are on the film noir problematic.

While the questions of adoption and legitimacy gained a kind of preeminence among intergenerational family idealizations of the period, the impulse toward the regeneration of the family—the romantic couple beleaguered by war's exigencies—remained the core of the family melodrama. Romance thus becomes the pre-condition for a restored social order through the nexus of family. Hollywood has never strayed far from the romantic idyll and its culmination in matrimony, thus replicating the prevailing social relations while imaging the perpetuation of its market audience. However, a level of urgency vis-á-vis coupledom becomes recognizable during the war years, recasting the idyll into passion play; women in particular are made to struggle for their union.

Hence, a film such as *I Love a Soldier* (1944) narrates one new GI wife's struggle to establish a family all on her own. The defining space of the melodrama is the bourgeois home. In *I Love a Soldier,* as in so many other wartime melos, the female protagonist's (Paulette Goddard's) efforts to create some semblance of a home—temporary, makeshift and tentative though it may be—becomes the immediate, externalized focus of the reconstitutive struggle. Goddard takes a small apartment in the town adjacent to husband Sonny Tufts's army base, settling for occasional opportunities to transform a cheerless attic apartment into a family space. Yet another instance of the GI wife rising to the challenge of the day occurs in *Over 21* (1945), in which Irene Dunne, a mature woman and accomplished writer, is forced to leave New York and set up housekeeping in a ramshackle bungalow community on the edge of the army base at which her fortyish husband (Alexander Knox) is stationed (a well-known newspaper editor, he has enlisted in spite of his publisher's pleadings). Dunne, the model of wifely support and ingenuity, makes a cozy home from nothing and smooths her husband's ruffled self-image (he's twenty years older than the other officer candidates) while penning Knox's daily newspaper column (unbeknownst to him). An indomitable and resourceful woman, Dunne's greatest challenge arises when Knox learns of the ghostwriting; the difficulty is not so much in the doing of the deed (her columns expand the newspaper's readership) but in the protecting of her husband's ego. This, too, is the burden of the woman attempting to maintain the family connection.

Of course, such films as these take up the problematic of the contemporary family in a direct way. Other films, such as Vincente Minnelli's *Meet Me in St. Louis* (1944), refigure the family-under-siege discourse, removing it to a comfortably distant past in which a solid patriarchy ruled benignly with the interests of stability and continuity uppermost. *St. Louis's* turn-of-the-century time frame enables the affirmation of the family to be bolstered by a general optimism for a dawning age of technology, where sparkling electric lights displace the grim realities of technology-at-war.[10]

Minnelli's film of the following year, *The Clock,* examines its milieu head-on. From a dreamy adolescent ensconced in Victorian comfort in *Meet Me in St. Louis,* Judy Garland now plays a New York working girl who trips over the foot of a rather average-looking soldier who is on a two-day leave and ends up marrying him before he returns. The film overlays verisimilitude with fairy tale, producing a fantasy (two average people touched by the magic power of romance) rooted in the urban rhythms of Manhattan—overcrowded, anonymous, overly bureaucratized. On the side of verisimilitude, the film is notable for its monumental tracking shots through Penn Station at beginning and end which effectively frame the microcosm in a "full" world capable of swallowing up private dramas, in the manner of King Vidor's silent classic *The Crowd.* On the other hand, *The Clock* dallies with a Capraesque vision of magical Americana, complete with a sprightly milkman (Capra regular, James Gleason) who assists and encourages the couple in their headlong dash to the altar. The pressure which time exerts throughout the film is at once the well-crafted compression of drama and the recognition of "real" time constraints in the experience of forced separations between women and their soldiers.

The Clock is a melodrama whose fabular structure is conditioned by the emphasis on its contemporary setting. Indeed, the couple's odyssey through the streets, parks and subway stations of Manhattan to the justice of the peace earns its audience's benediction by virtue of the post-war vision which this pair evokes. She—a secretary in the sales division of some vast corporation sharing a modest flat, three years in New York from the American heartlands, a working girl whose romanticism has not yet been stamped out of her. He—a self-conscious but boyishly appealing kid from "Mapleton," "green as grass" by his own admission, pleased with the escalators in Penn Station, modestly insistent in his pursuit of this girl. He wants to "put up houses" after the war ("I like building things with my own hands"); in fact, he wants to start "a little business of my own back in Mapleton." Like the Dana Andrews character in *Best Years of Our Lives,* Joe's metier is to be construction—building for others and for himself (he tells Alice about the home he plans to build for himself on the piece of ground he's already picked out). These plans are shared for his companion's benefit, but they firmly establish Joe's worthiness as a stable, productive even visionary site of identification for the 1945 audience. Certainly, there could be no more appropriately charged occupation than this for one bearing the representational onus as the rebuilder of society. For the social framework rests, at least in terms of the melodrama, on the family whose locus is the home. Joe will build homes.

It is also significant that Joe plans to begin "a little business of his own." As recounted in chapter 1 of this work, the years of wartime consolidation witnessed the final death throes of the small business as the economic backbone of America. The years to follow brought the full blossoming of the diversified corporate conglomerate; Joe's dream would be even less obtainable in 1955 than it was in 1945. That staple of the American self-image—the freeholder, the self-sufficient man of local commerce—could, by this time, be counted among the fairy tale elements of the film.

The couple's first encounter occurs on a Sunday morning—Alice's day off— and, as Alice boards the bus for home Joe runs after it, pleading with her to break her date for that evening. Wartime melodramas abound in such ill-matched contests between lovers and the mechanized conveyances which spirit away their paramours (Robert Walker [Joe] watched Jennifer Jones run after *him* and his train in *Since You Went Away* the year before). Just prior to their parting, Joe has rather awkwardly bestowed his cigarette lighter upon Alice, an act whose spontaneous generosity and naivete touch her. She yells to him over the roar: "Under the clock at the Astor at 7:00."

The reasons which Paulette Goddard initially poses to herself in *I Love a Soldier* as she falls in love with Sonny Tufts—the reasons why soldiers are to be kept at arm's length—are recited to Alice by her concerned roommate, Helen: "It doesn't make sense to make friends with a stray soldier . . . a girl's gotta look out for herself. . . . They leave ya in a few days and then what've ya got?" Despite the warning, Alice ditches her erstwhile suitor, Freddie, and appears under the Astor clock at 7:25. In a conversation soon afterwards, Joe asks, "Don't you want to get married someday, maybe?" "Oh, that . . . not for a long time anyway," is the reply. Not, at least, for another twenty-four hours.

This New York fairy tale picks up steam when, in the wee hours of the morning, the couple encounters Al Henry (James Gleason), the milkman. Garrulous, friendly, optimistic, Al is really from Indiana. Like the couple, Al bears the stamp of populism; his small-town humor is sorely tested by the big city. When he is accosted by a drunk, the romantic duo finishes his route for him and helps him home. Al is the Proppian donor who repays the protagonist's generosity with magical assistance. For when Joe confesses to the milkman and his wife (whose basement flat is the urban equivalent of the gremlin's humble cottage): "I don't think it's fair to the girl, a soldier getting married," Al offers a morsel of wisdom—a person can learn as much about another person in a minute as in a lifetime. This is the missing piece in the romantic puzzle whose constraining parameter is time.

Armed with this knowledge, the timelessness of Eros, the pair continue their

The Clock (Metro-Goldwyn-Mayer, 1946)
The civil ceremony that joins Joe (Robert Walker) and Alice (Judy Garland) in hasty matrimony is but one of Hollywood's many unromanticized wartime unions. A "true marriage" can only be achieved through a play of imagination; minutes later—and in silent communion—they reenact the ceremony in an empty church chapel.

odyssey, soon encountering the most severe test which the city has to offer. Having called in sick, Alice guides Joe through the labyrinths of the subway system at rush hour only to be caught up in the crush of Grand Central Station and separated. She goes to the USO while he searches aimlessly. In the immediacy of their connection, they have failed to exchange last names (what need have prince and princess for last names?). Joe is en route back to the clock at the Astor Hotel when they spot each other amidst the trammel of Penn Central. In a panic, Joe blurts out: "Look, please, please, will you marry me?" They rush off to arrange the nuptials only to find that their nemesis (the city) offers further contestation: a three-day wait for the blood test. It is the sprightly Al Henry to the rescue once again; his cousin is able to secure a waiver for the delay. The magistrate is only just collared as he's stepping into the elevator at the close of the day.

What follows is one of the most ironic wedding scenes in the American cinema since Keaton's *His Wife's Relations,* in which Buster finds himself married to a woman twice his size as a result of a wedding ceremony (in Polish) which he has mistaken for a civil proceeding. Here, as the magistrate intones the ritual, a subway train passes by, drowning out every word. The city has achieved its symbolic triumph; the couple stands dazed in the aftermath. "I guess I don't feel very married," says Alice. "It was so ugly . . . it didn't . . . " Her words are cut short by uncontrollable sobs. Spotting another wedding party, they enter the now-empty church where they reenact the ceremony, consecrating themselves in a dramatically lit two-shot. The organ music that fills the chapel is also the product of their shared imaginary. Alice pronounces her vows: "Oh, Joe, I love you . . . I'll love you till the day I die." At this moment an altar boy approaches, snuffing out the candles and ending the scene. Again, the useful reference film is *Best Years of Our Lives* in which the Dana Andrews and Teresa Wright characters unofficially share the wedding vows of the Harold Russell and Cathy O'Donnell characters by means of a carefully orchestrated composition in depth. Their gazes locked, they come together from across the room to seal the private union with a kiss. The post-war world was envisioned as demanding the "true" bonding of well-matched souls able to overcome whatever stumbling blocks were placed before them. Conventional ritual could not equal the intensity of the self-ordained marriage.

The Clock's finale is preceded by a quiet interlude of coupled intimacy. In the few hours before Joe's departure, the newlyweds have taken a hotel room. Dressed in their robes, they speak with looks and signs of love; the musical theme is faintly domestic. Joe asks Alice not to dwell on the separation; Alice replies that she is certain that they were meant to be. The tone of the scene expresses the thematic "sacred love," the momentary idyll snatched from time, and is reminiscent of the early morning scene of quiescence from *Romeo and Juliet* just before the newly sanctified couple are parted forever. The tragic possibilities of this moment in *The Clock* are downplayed in favor of a suggestion of domestic joys to come.

The parting is connected to the idyll not by a luxurious lap dissolve but by a straight cut which emphasizes the harshness of the juxtaposition. The train station is jammed with departing GIs whose wives and families cling to them until the end. Alice and Joe part with the simple words, "See you soon." As Alice walks from the platform back into the cavernous space of Penn Central, the camera cranes back and up, mingling the protagonist with the multitudes. This is the companion shot of the opening track through the same location; the "one of many" theme is thus economically and symmetrically expressed. Minnelli, anxious to convey the typicality of his tale, returns the focus from the personal struggle to the broader social canvas from whence it came. On Alice's face is a look of confidence consistent with the upbeat parting words, "See you soon." A kind of beatific glow emanates from that face as she walks out into the world, into postwar life and toward the new challenges and rewards that lay ahead. The milling crowds of soldiers and sailors engulf her solitary figure and she is in fact lost in the crowd. This final signification of grace is oddly resonant with the fade-out of *Stella Dallas,* a pre-war melodrama which finds the Barbara Stanwyck character merging with the throngs of Manhattan, beaming with a transcendence born of her perfect act of self-sacrifice (she has insured her cherished daughter's happiness and upward mobility by casting her off, content to watch the daughter's wedding through the window from a rainy nighttime street). The philosophical gulf that separates Stella and Alice is the gap between the social mobility imperative of the Depression years and the familial cohesion imperative called into service for the postwar era.

The Clock offers a curious mixture of fictional modes in the Fryeian sense— mythic/romantic and low-mimetic. There is a strong component of myth or romance distinguishable, a sense in which Joe and Alice follow the path of the mythic hero or knight errant, seeking safe passage through the eddies and whirlpools of the urban landscape with the help of a latter-day Merlin. Conversely, *The Clock* locates the odyssey in a very concrete contemporary environment, taking great interest in the surface and rhythms of Manhattan foundering in the wartime crunch of concurrent oversupply (of people and desire for consumption) and undersupply (of housing and commodities for consumption). The low-mimetic impulse toward verisimilitude, the lust for that impression of reality the better to anchor the fable in common experience, is somewhat at odds with the fairy tale qualities of the piece. Certainly the tension between the two modalities helps make *The Clock* one of the more idiosyncratic melodramas of the war years.

Moral Tales for Women

Kitty Foyle (1940)
The Gay Sisters (1942)
The War against Mrs. Hadley (1942)
Without Reservations (1946)
Young Widow (1946)

This last of four categories of wartime female representation is constituted by those films in which a markedly proscriptive function with regard to female behavior can be determined. This said, it must be noted that the premise of this entire study has been that the women's films of this period were infused with an ideological cogency consistent with the volatile profile of the American wartime woman. As a result, a degree of advocacy can be located in most of the films discussed; moreover, the formative power and social influence (through the play of projection, introjection and identification) of films that simply imply standards of female behavior through characterization, without a trace of polemics must also be recognized.

In these films are assembled the texts whose interpellative urgency (to borrow a term from the earlier discussion of propaganda) is most notable, an urgency related less to social action, as is the case with propaganda, as to socially constructed but privately held attitudes and values, the true terrain of ideology. Many of the family melodramas invited the spectator to judge the causes of human (usually female) suffering or to view the results of "ill-conceived" actions (*King's Row*, 1941; *Duel in the Sun*, 1946; *The Great Lie; A Stolen Life*). The more upbeat tales of romance offer resolutions, primarily via the marital bond, which heartily endorse certain forms of coquetry, humility or traditionally feminine virtue (*State Fair*, 1945; *Seven Sweethearts*, 1942; *Shop around the Corner*, 1940; *The Major and the Minor*, 1942). These melodramas, whose visions traverse the tragic/comic axis, give dramatic shape to tumultuous events of a sort recognizable from personal experience. They sustain a sense of spectacle, events-in-themselves whose social implications and emotional resonances we are invited to contemplate. In a limited sense, these melodramas can be regarded as "intransitive" insofar as they are posed against the films of this last grouping, whose female protagonists are most frequently embroiled in a discourse of charged didacticism—some lesson is learned, some taboo is enforced. The identifying spectator is thus urged to imbibe the usually moral corrective as an antidote to sorrow, isolation or turpitude. Quite frequently, the case can be even more graphically stated: "If you want that man, here's how to get him." But whether the film enacts approach (to the rewards of love and family) or avoidance (of bitterness, loneliness or even death—*Shadow of a Doubt*, 1942; *The Stranger*, 1946; *Sorry, Wrong Number*, 1948;

the pitch of advocacy is relatively intense. Rather than encouraging the passive contemplation of emotionally charged events, these films invite a more active response.

As has been the case throughout this analysis, the historical dimension plays a determining role in the frequency of occurrence and the character of the content of these "moral tales." Judging by the graph of distribution for the "melodramas" and "moral tales" (see appendix C), there is a radical peaking in 1942 and a miniaturized duplication of that pattern in 1946. Based upon the far greater concentration of films screened for this study from 1942 and 1943, the 1946 peak can be judged to constitute a significant second wave of post-war moral tales. For while there were certainly important lessons to be taught and models of behavior to be proposed for the war years, there was no less urgency in the reshaping of social patterns for the postwar world, perhaps more so. The fundamental shift was from a positive brand of advocacy ("join in, get active") to an increasingly negative pole of endorsed behavior ("don't forget femininity or the needs of men, don't be overzealous").

By way of covering the range of issues confronted by these films, I propose three sub-groupings for analysis: the prewar tale (e.g., *Kitty Foyle*), the directly thematized war variant (e.g., *The War against Mrs. Hadley, Without Reservations, Young Widow*), and the moral tales whose admonitions are figured in terms of familial imbalance (*The Gay Sisters; Shadow of a Doubt; Woman of the Year; The Hard Way*, 1943; *The Princess O'Rourke*, 1943; *Mildred Pierce*, 1945). Many of the remaining texts of this grouping could be amorphously assembled beneath some general rubric such as "What Every Woman Should Know." Nevertheless, the temptation to reduce the idiosyncrasies and complexities of these films to ideological one-liners is to be avoided. After watching June Allyson, Gloria De Haven and Van Johnson romp through MGM's *Two Girls and a Sailor* (1944), one might conclude that a man may be attracted to the extroverted sister (De Haven), but is likely to marry the demure one (Allyson). In many cases, a film's moral imperative is simply far less important than its general mode of elaboration or the performances contained within it. *Two Girls and a Sailor* provided a showcase for MGM's talent (Jose Iturbi, Jimmy Durante, Gracie Allen, Lena Horne) just as much as *Stage Door Canteen* (1943) for which Sol Lesser had assembled the likes of Katharine Hepburn, Harpo Marx, Paul Muni and Merle Oberon. The minimal narrative of the latter film involves an ambitious young starlet's realization that her dreams for stardom are ultimately less compelling than the affections of a well-scrubbed soldier named Dakota. Unquestionably, few spectators would recall in great detail this narrative thread that connects the cameo appearances of major stars washing dishes and waiting tables.

Likewise, it is misleading to isolate the ideological implications (which are substantial) of *Two-Faced Woman* (1941) from the effects of the persona of Greta

Garbo in an atypical and career-ending role. She plays an independent, outdoor-sy woman who must masquerade as her own beguiling twin to seduce her husband into fidelity—the comic version of Bette Davis' exploits in *A Stolen Life.* In such cases of star performances (particularly for glamour figures like Garbo, who were reduced to the exploitation of their own iconography), the typical play of *identification* which underlies a film's ideological potency is potentially subordinated to a play of *fascination* for the star; a kind of fetishization may begin to replace introjection on the part of the female spectator. At the very least, films which feature major glamour figures often exhibit this tension between spectacle and narrative—with the latter's connectedness of actress and spectator—so that the behavioral implications for the female audience are considerably diminished. (Dietrich's role in *The Lady Is Willing,* 1942, as a domestic female, may be placed alongside the Garbo performance.)

Despite all disclaimers, a significant number of the "Moral Tales" films can justifiably be analyzed as public preachments for specific modes of female behavior. The pre-war example, *Kitty Foyle,* announces itself as social treatise by its full title: *Kitty Foyle: The Natural History of a Woman.* The film sets out to examine what it terms as the "comparative newcomer to the American scene," the white-collar female worker, and the pitfalls she encounters. The crucial issue appears to be the age-old philosophical conundrum free will, now recast in a specifically female mold, both as liberator and as unfamiliar burden. In a conversation early in the film in which a group of young women debate the relative virtues of their rather unglamorous lives as wage earners, one woman poses this question to Kitty (Ginger Rogers): "Isn't independence worth anything to you? After all, what's the difference between men bachelors and girl bachelors?" Kitty replies, "Men bachelors are that way on purpose." The assumption is that many women workers would gladly exchange their white collars for aprons. Certainly the statement signals an awareness of the fact that, no matter how forceful a presence the woman may be in the marketplace, the power to opt out of it still remains with the man, the proposer of marital partnerships.

Before long, Kitty is forced to make a choice of her own. Significantly, her choice is transformed from working or not working to one man or another man and, of equal importance, one moral station versus another. The question of employment rapidly recedes in favor of this moral dichotomy; once again, the Hollywood film places the originally foregrounded social issue in soft focus as private emotional issues take precedence. Kitty's faithful but unexciting boyfriend, Mark the idealistic doctor, has just this night proposed to her. Life with him will be filled with moments of altruism exemplified by their evening's date in which he delivers a baby (with minor assistance from Kitty) instead of taking her out to dinner. The alternative, appearing unexpectedly that same night, is the dashing sophisticate, her old flame Wynne Strafford from a Philadelphia Main Line family, who asks her to set sail for Buenos Aires with him at midnight. The hitch: Wynne is married and can't promise that he'll divorce his wife. Although her first response is a willing suspension of choice ("Oh Wynne, don't ask me anything, don't let me think, just take me with you!"), Kitty begins to engage herself in a moral dialogue as she packs for the imminent departure.

This internal dialogue is waged between the rough equivalents of id and superego. "Marriage isn't everything" says one faction of Kitty's divided self while the other tells her, "You'd be happier with Mark and that little piece of paper." But the decision is ultimately arrived at through a recourse to personal history; much of the remainder of the film is the flashback narration of Kitty's troubled relationship with Wynne and the discourse of class conflict which has accompanied their relationship. Kitty's memory takes her back to age fifteen and her life with her drunken, down-and-out Irish father. The unavoidable reference here is to Freud's notion of the family romance discussed earlier, for young Kitty has recurrent delusions about princes and the Lady of Chalot and Cinderella—magical exit routes from her depressed surroundings. When she takes a typing job with a magazine, she immediately becomes enamored of the aristocratic publisher (Strafford) who is everything she is not. When the magazine succumbs to the ravages of the Depression, Wynne is forced to retreat to the family fold, that is, the very old and very wealthy banking empire that passes for a family.

Although Wynne expresses concern for her well-being, Kitty is vocal about her ability to manage for herself: "You needn't worry about me. I'm free, white and twenty-one . . . no one owes a thing to Kitty Foyle, except Kitty Foyle." In a return to the present, Kitty wistfully recalls, "So you joined the New York white collar brigade." Once more in flashback, Kitty reconstructs her first encounter with Mark and her discovery of his noble professional aims: he longs to heal sick children who can't help themselves. Her growing respect and affection for him is cut short by Wynne's re-emergence. He proposes, she resists due to their conflicting class backgrounds, but finally acquiesces. Although the terms of Wynne's trust stipulate that he must remain in Philadelphia, Kitty soon realizes that she cannot co-exist with the stuffy, circumscribed Strafford world. Longing for her new husband's support, Kitty receives far less than she had hoped for ("You can't just square off at them"). She returns to New York with faint hopes that Wynne will follow, and when he does not, she files for divorce.

In true melodramatic fashion, Kitty has become pregnant, but just as she prepares to tell Strafford, she learns that he has become engaged to a Philadelphia society matron. Again in present time, Kitty's internalized discourse continues in voice-over as she recalls her plans to name the child Tom Foyle, musing, "This is what women want. It isn't men . . . not really . . . it's something down inside them that's the future." But the child dies and only her career remains; she becomes a successful couturier, opening a shop in Philadelphia. It is now 11:35 and she must decide between two lives in the persons of two men. In a burst of rationality and moral clarity, Kitty slams her suitcase and rushes out of the apartment to find Mark and accept his marriage proposal.

Kitty Foyle proposes a curious moral dilemma for its audience. On the face of it, the choice between married life with a solid, unglamorous but idealistic young doctor and an extended fling in South America with a rakish sophisticate is no contest, given the traditional middle-class audience which the film addresses. The complication resides in the previous marriage and pregnancy with the fancy man which strongly reinforces the ties, particularly in light of Hollywood's propensity toward reuniting once-married couples if the passion remains. But Wynne is remarried and wishes to remain so with the result that concupiscence replaces reunion as his motive. The fact that Kitty is simply not in love with Mark provides another jolt to the conventional pattern of romance in which correct partners are those who share a sincere love. Kitty chooses the boring but legitimate man whose devotion is strong, realizing, pragmatist that she is, that it is a far more secure position for a woman to be more loved than loving. In the film, man/woman relationships are strongly contextualized as *occupational* for the woman who must look to "job" security and stability for the children who are her first priority. Ultimately, the question of choice or free will is revealed to be illusory given the material constraints of conflictual class backgrounds, preexistent ties to family and fortune and the cruel tides of fate which can take away one's first-born. The one autonomous female choice, that of the single working girl, is depicted as drudgery from the outset, with the suggestion that it really is a non-choice, a self-abnegating necessity for those who can't find alternatives. The intrinsic value of productive labor and public participation by women is not yet an issue in this 1940 melodrama. The lesson of the film—play it safe, choose security over passion—becomes less a moral tale than a program of female self-interest.

The directly thematized moral tales represent Hollywood's attempt to take an active role in popularizing war themes specific to female participation. Films as diverse as *Joe Smith, American, Ladies Courageous* and *Since You Went Away* (to be considered in chapter 7) can be examined for their treatments of contemporary life on the home front and the manner in which the fictionalized women of these films learn the importance of their own roles in the war effort (ranging from inspirational wife to ferry pilot to patient spouse and mother). In all cases, the lesson remains that a nation at war requires each citizen to recognize her unique role and stick with it for the duration. In most instances, as with the three aforementioned films, the theme is developed through action (even if Mary Smith's "action" in *Joe Smith, American* is simply to inspire her husband to withstand the torture of enemy agents). The moral tales are more firmly issue-oriented; their didactic tone establishes the primacy of an ethical discourse which displaces the proairetic vitality of a *Joe Smith* or *Ladies Courageous*. The key process is an internalized one, a coming-to-consciousness of the female protagonist.

Stella Hadley (Fay Bainter) is a singularly unsympathetic character in MGM's *The War against Mrs. Hadley,* a woman overendowed with money, pride and petty prejudice. The film's ideological motives are twofold: to prove the necessity of democratic values and dedicated group action for all and to humanize the very rich at a time when widespread privations threatened to intensify class tensions. No studio could have been better suited to this latter task; MGM was, with Paramount, the most consistent purveyor of images of the very rich. *The War against Mrs. Hadley* produces what Roland Barthes has termed an "inoculation effect," a process by which an unpopular concept is introduced into social discourse in a small dosage in order to neutralize its negative charge. The spectator is given ample reason to detest this smugly patrician Mrs. Hadley—indeed, the film encourages this reaction—in order that more deep-seated antipathies to the privileged classes may be swept aside in the tide of sympathy which is eventually generated for her. Rather than deny the grounds for class tensions, the film sustains them in a limited way in order to level them on emotional grounds by film's end.

Ensconced in her Washington, D.C. mansion, the staunchly Republican widow of a newspaper magnate, Stella Hadley is utterly self-absorbed. Like so many other World War II narratives, the film begins on December 7, only its significance here is that it is Stella's birthday. She is surrounded by her hard-drinking son Teddy, daughter Patricia, a handful of family friends and a full complement of servants. When the radio announces the Pearl Harbor attack, Mrs. Hadley's consternation is aimed not at the Japanese, but at the maid who drops the dishes (her brother is stationed at Pearl). The chauffeur is drafted, the butler becomes an air raid warden, Teddy is transferred to active service and Pat meets an all-American but workingclass GI (Van Johnson) while doing canteen duty. Stella's world is slowly unravelling to her dismay and incomprehension. For her part, Patricia is intent on shedding the stumbling block to romance, her aristocratic upbringing. When she brings home her boyfriend Mike, he is intimidated by the disparity between their backgrounds. "So you live in a small house and I live in a big house," says Pat. "Is that any reason to treat me as though I suddenly had the measles?" The film itself takes up the metaphor of quarantine, inoculation and cure.

Indeed, Stella remains in self-imposed quarantine for much of the film. She is angry with her would-be suiter (Edward Arnold), a well-attached military man, who has arranged Teddy's overseas assignment; she refuses to do Red Cross work with Laura Winters, an old family enemy; and she resists the blackouts at every turn, feeling that the war is being waged against her personally. A rabid anti-New Dealer, she is convinced that the wartime measures are intended to humiliate her class ("Oh dear, it's just like the French Revolution"). Mrs. Hadley is further outraged during a visit to Pat's canteen by the slang and low-class manners of the soldiers. When Pat marries Mike against her mother's wishes, Stella stays home. Her growing isolation is imaged in a slow reverse track which reveals Mrs. Hadley, alone in a huge empty room, reading a letter from her son.

The breaking point occurs when Teddy receives the Distinguished Service Cross and Mrs. Hadley is called upon to be interviewed as a morale boost for other GI wives and mothers. Laura Winters' son has been killed in the same action that resulted in Teddy's DSC. In an act of contrition, Stella goes to her arch-enemy's home and, in consoling her, breaks into tears. This is the moment of annihilation of the protagonist's hubris, but only at the expense of someone else's tragedy. Mrs. Winters delivers the speech that expresses the theme the film has struggled towards: "None of that matters now . . . fights, political differences, anything . . . All that matters is that you and I, all of us, work together to make what Tom died for something fine and lasting." The denouement follows in a rush of reintegration—Stella forgives then marries Arnold, receives a letter of congratulations from former nemesis FDR, goes to visit Pat, Mike and baby in Phoenix and even decides to put her car in storage for the duration. Arnold's parting line as the revitalized Stella rushes out the door: "Those Japs and Nazis better look out, now that Stella's in the war."

Our patience for Stella Hadley's moral re-education, our willingness to observe the gradual leveling of resistances to democratic principles enforced by the rigors of war, is certainly reinforced by actress Bainter's iconographic presence. On the screen since 1934, Bainter specialized in playing decidedly sympathetic women. She was Mickey Rooney's beloved mother in *Young Tom Edison* (1940), an understanding, matronly figure in *Our Town* (1940) and Tess Harding's sagacious aunt in *Woman of the Year* (1942). In the two years after the release of *Mrs. Hadley,* Bainter was a dispenser of war orphans in *Journey for Margaret,* Mickey Rooney's mother once again in *The Human Comedy,* a tough but endearing commanding officer of nurses in *Cry Havoc* and the midwestern mother and mincemeat champion of *State Fair.* Bainter's Hadley is a blue-blooded snob whose potential for kindliness can never entirely be obliterated due to the residue of the actress' historical persona. This condition contributes to the ease by which the film's ideological ploy is rendered. While it appears that Mrs. Hadley is learning to embrace democracy and war participation, the audience is concurrently being taught forbearance for the privileged few who are more to be pitied from behind their cheerless iron gates.

Without Reservations (1946) and *Young Widow* (1946) are products of the post-war reassessment of the American female. With the returning tide of long-absent soldiers, women were asked to step aside from their jobs, relinquish their dominance within the family and take their places alongside (or, more likely, behind) their men. Marriage, spiritual renewal, and the salving of old wounds were themes much in evidence in these years, along with the darker side of that vision personified by the "noir" women who betray rather than heal, are ruthless rather than compassionate: *Double Indemnity* (1944), *Scarlet Street* (1945), *The*

Killers (1946), *The Razor's Edge* (1946), *Leave Her to Heaven* (1946). *Without Reservations* and *Young Widow* represent two diverse instances of advice for women interested in joining that great army of middle-classed marrieds. *Reservations* suggests the forms of female behavior most likely to snag a "real" man (in this case, John Wayne) while *Widow* traces the necessary path toward revivification for a woman obsessed with her heroic but dead husband.

Claudette Colbert, the wittiest and most self-sufficient of heroines throughout the thirties and forties, is a successful novelist enroute to Hollywood at the beginning of *Without Reservations*. Her book, a wartime bestseller, centers around a single character, one woman's version of the ideal man: a Marine pilot, strong and silent with a trace of poetry in his soul. Seated across from her on the train are two Marine Corps officers, Wayne and his buddy Don De Fore, who carry with them a copy of the novel. Up to this point, Colbert and her Hollywood producer have been in a quandary over the correct choice for the lead of the film version of her book; Colbert is convinced that the success of the project depends upon casting just the right man for the role. When this rough-hewn, straight-talking captain begins to tell her how wrong the novel's protagonist is (unaware as he is of her true identity), she begins to become enamored. His forceful manner and the respect he commands from De Fore and the other men, coupled with his no-nonsense grappling with her on all issues, begins to convince Colbert on two related fronts: Rusty is the man for her film and Rusty is the man for her life.

What follows is an elaborate series of ruses that allow Colbert to continue the concealment of her identity while staying on the train long past her Chicago connection in order to hold on to Rusty (hence the title *Without Reservations*). The hallmark of the Colbert persona is intelligence—she is always smart enough to know when to surrender herself to the man she desires even if she is brighter or wealthier than he (*It Happened One Night, The Palm Beach Story, No Time for Love, So Proudly We Hail*). Rusty finds the intellectualism of the novel in question repugnant; the tone of Wendell Wilkie "One Worldism" apparent from the excerpt he reads aloud strikes him as phony and decidedly unfeminine. When Colbert's fame catches up with her at last (she is surrounded by an autograph-hunting mob of literary ladies in a midwest town), Rusty's manhood cannot endure the assault to his presumed dominance; he stalks out to try to forget her. It is not until weeks later, with both of them now in Los Angeles (she in her Hollywood Hills bungalow) that Rusty swallows enough of his pride to pay Colbert a visit.

This is, in fact, the film's conclusion since Wayne's decision to see Colbert constitutes the great male compromise. She, however, is determined to make the necessary adjustments which are, of course, major: soft-pedal her intelligence, downplay her success, yield to his opinions, etc. Wayne, the man of action, is seen not engaged in the wartime exploits which have resulted in the medals pinned on his chest, but in a civilian world requiring different kinds of skills. Colbert, a success in the civilian world, is in love with the man of action and is willing to sacrifice parts of herself to have him, the romantic hero of her own creation. Mercifully, we are spared the experience of their encounter (the film ends as he arrives at the door), for the sight of Colbert's self-censorship in the interests of retaining this traditional man would be painful. The solution here is troubling since the person most adept in the peacetime context, most prepared for the changing times, is also the major compromiser simply because she is a woman. Implicit to this romantic itinerary is the too-familiar motif of the tamed female, the woman who must learn to temper her power with pragmatism or worse is simply humiliated by a man and made to love it (*The Taming of the Shrew*). *Without Reservations* suggests that the candor and iconoclasm which were fine while the men were away may prove costly for romance with the return of the status quo.

Young Widow is a readjustment film in the tradition of *Pride of the Marines, From This Day Forward* (1946), and *The Best Years of Our Lives* with the twist that the candidate for rehabilitation is an emotionally wounded woman, the young widow of the title. Joan Kenwood (Jane Russell) is the widow of an aerial photographer shot down on what was to have been his final reconnaissance mission. Joan is first shown disembarking from an ocean liner filled with jubilant soldiers. The camera dollies in on the woman's face which offers a solemn contrast to the welcome home celebration and the strains of Auld Lang Syne. The placement of the female protagonist in the midst of the returning soldiers, intensified by the intercutting of stock footage of real GI homecomings, establishes her as the female equivalent of a male returnee, one whose wounds have not sufficiently healed. A journalist returning from her London assignment, she had begun her career in tandem with her husband, Barry, writing captions for his photographs. Everything in her world now reminds her of him; rather than return to her old job with a New York newspaper, she goes home to the family farm in Virginia.

Through conversations between Joan and her Aunt Sissy, it is made clear that Joan is the most recent in a long familial line of widows whose husbands died heroes, the most notable being her great-grandfather, a Civil War hero. A genealogy is thus proposed within which this young widow's identity is constructed. Like the pioneer women whose memories were resurrected as inspirational models for the female factory workers in *Priorities on Parade* (see chapter 7), the war widow lineage is here alluded to for the comfort and continuity which history can supply. Both the joys and sorrows of women have always been connected to their men is the implicit postulate of this sequence. If a woman's emotional self is experienced through her connection with a man, Joan Kenwood's professional life has also been a function of her husband's career. We are told that Joan's journalistic start was as the captioner of Kenwood's news photographs. She is the dutiful wife dusting and polishing her husband's work. Ever the helpmate, she has followed in her man's wake, tidying up the stray shards of meaning dispersed by his lens.

Life on the farm is difficult; the memories are inescapable. The camera simulates Joan's point-of-view as it haltingly scans the bedroom closet filled with "his" clothes, "his" camera, "all those little things." That special record she plays is torture; instead she submerges herself in activities—cooking, riding a tractor, rowing a boat . . . but never forgetting. Aunt Sissy reminds her that she must love again, but the reply persists, "There'll never be room for anyone in my heart but Barry."

On the train ride to New York, a young pilot begins to flirt with Joan with predictably cold results. The apartment she shares with her friend Peg, whose husband is in a submarine somewhere in the Atlantic, is also home to several displaced servicemen, including the amorous Lieutenant Jim Cameron. Joan is also pursued by her ex-boss, Peter Waring, who tells her, "I was thinking how much better you'd look in my lonely penthouse than behind a typewriter." Waring contents himself with her friendship while Cameron emerges as the romantic hopeful.[11] While returning from a concert, Joan and Jim watch in horror as a frail old lady falls onto the subway tracks; Cameron saves the woman in the nick of time from the wheels of the hurtling train. Here is the quintessential rescue of the melodramatic tradition which in this case strengthens Cameron's claim upon Joan's resistant heart. But instead of plucking his lady fair from nature's precipice (the ice floes and waterfall of Griffith's *Way Down East*), Cameron, the modern hero figure, saves the aged surrogate from a rampaging urban machine.

In variance to the hermetically privatized emotionalism of the standard melodrama, *Young Widow* hastens to historicize its problematic. One of Joan's co-workers, Gerry, and her fiance Bob, arrive for dinner and a discussion ensues in which Gerry discloses her refusal of Bob's marriage proposal based upon his intended enlistment. Joan's advice is to honor Bob's wish, with the words, "I'd do the same thing all over again." Joan's loss is rendered as emblematic of the sorrows of a generation, a stance which the film never abandons. Despite certain pleasurable, even romantic moments with Cameron, her sensory self is linked to the memory of her past at a very deep level. Although Jim conveys his understanding of Joan's emotional plight, he confesses his love and argues for an end to resistance most convincingly: "There's only now and we're alone in it." But when he kisses her, she hears Barry singing.

It is through recourse to the broader social nexus that Joan's access to desire is restored. Roommate Peg's husband has returned without one of his legs and Joan witnesses the bravery and indomitability of the couple. Peg counsels Joan to rush to the airfield to tell Jim that she will wait for him. With the possibility of desire's return thus enforced, Joan arrives at Mitchell Field as Cameron's aircraft passes overhead; she mouths the words, "I love you, I'll wait for you." Through a miraculous contraction of cinematic space, Jim "sees" Joan's words from within the speeding plane, as evidenced in a close-up reaction shot. Her friend Peter, who has driven her to the airfield, offers the last gesture of the film—

he raises two fingers in a victory sign to Joan, now flushed with the renewal of life's passion.

What is most arresting about *Young Widow*'s historical determinacy is its reliance upon the larger patterns of social life as a "way out" of a personal-emotional cul de sac. Trapped within a circuitry of desire which can only be triggered by a single idealized (and lost) male, Joan seems doomed to take her place among the widowed martyrs of her family heritage. So deeply embedded in past experience, the structuring of the protagonist's desire denies the possibility of access to sensory pleasure. The touch of a man, particularly a "desirable" one, automatically re-cathects Barry and thus reproduces the pain of his loss. This cycle is broken from the outside by the therapeutic example of the roommate Peg. She has lost a part of her lover, but is able to substitute a vision of the whole desired object, precisely the one formed as an idealization in the husband's absence. Joan is thus encouraged to replace her lost object with another (who has previously evoked Barry) enabling an unbroken circuit of pleasure and desire to recommence. But despite the therapeutic imaging of the second couple contained within the narrative, there is a larger social discourse addressed by this cure; the vicissitudes of thousands of Americans are alluded to, forging a kind of national solidarity-in-loss. It is thus the function of the film to perform the ritual gesture of rekindled passion as a simulacrum for the masses. In this sense, Joan's cure can be attributed to historical necessity as forcefully as to diegetic motivation.

6

Subjectivity at a Distance

Laura Mulvey's statement that "woman . . . stands in patriarchal culture as signifier for the male other," bound within a symbolic order that renders her the bearer rather than the maker of meaning, helped to inaugurate a decade of impassioned feminist film criticism.[1] Feminists had long argued that women were culturally located outside history, that the "eternal feminine" was a construct that defined the male through difference, thus posing itself as a kind of empty set, the "non-male." Mulvey and others (notably Claire Johnston in her "Women's Cinema as Counter-Cinema" published two years prior to Mulvey's 1975 essay) reframed the debate in psychoanalytic terms, arguing that the woman, in signifying castration or lack, inaugurated the production of language within the symbolic order but could hold no place within it. In Christine Gledhill's apt summation: "Female sexuality cannot be expressed; the symbolic activity of language and culture is set into motion in an attempt to liquidate the very lack that women are said to represent. For women themselves to attain mastery within this system, they would have to want to liquidate themselves. Hence the enigmatic silence of women."[2]

Yet, far from concluding that woman remains ever "the unnameable, the unsaid," the work undertaken here offers testimony to the instability of the represented woman at one moment in her history, the difficulties posed by altered economic and social conditions for the replication of patriarchal culture. It remains for the final chapter to examine the most noteworthy instances of such instability within the regime of filmic representation. Here, the represented woman—inscrutable, evil, fetishized—remains largely consistent with the global categories identified by feminist criticism. Having said this, it still seems important to retain the specificity of close analysis across a range of texts within a determinate material context as a necessary corrective to theorized totalities. The categories that follow invoke the critical models in question, attest to their veracity, but attempt to insert the particular within the general. A brief return to the realm of historical/ideological determinants helps furnish that framework of the particular.

The sudden rise to prominence of the public image of the active female—Rosie the Riveter, Tillie the Toiler—obscured the fact that two-thirds of the Rosies were employed prior to Pearl Harbor. Yet, in matters of mass cultural production, it is popular image rather than historical fact that dictates. Here, Hollywood's expression of American womanhood achieved a degree of congruity with popular journalism, the pages of *Time, Life* and *The Saturday Evening Post,* according to whose coverage the shift from pot roasts to soldering irons was instantaneous and pervasive. The key to this obfuscation lies in the class character of the glorified American woman featured in *Life,* et al., and, even more cogently, in the advertising copy of these periodicals. For it was through the promotion of a youthful, smiling housewife ringed about in her kitchen by an assortment of modern conveniences and labor-saving devices that the American corporate structure hoped to maintain a grasp on its ever-expanding horizons. There was little doubt that the family unit was the economic nucleus for mass consumption, evidenced by an ambitious businesswoman's pronouncements in a book entitled *Selling Mrs. Consumer:* "Every business day approximately 5,000 new homes are begun; new 'nests' are constructed and new family purchasing units begin operation. . . . The founding and furnishing of new homes is a major industrial circumstance in the United States." It was a crucial marketing strategy that the mainstream American woman identify with this representation of an idealized self—idealized as the owner and operator of mass-produced commodity durables. This ego ideal was white, glowing with good health and high spirits, often aproned, almost certainly a mother of children whose happiness could be insured by the purchase of skates, sparkling white crinolines and a mix-master for whipping up layer cakes.

The disruption of business-as-usual was effected only in response to crisis times, with the American woman converted from consumer to producer. Yet another result of female migration into the industrial workplace was the dissolution of an historical fiction, shared by males of all classes, that the human labor that fueled the shops and factories was skilled and artisan-like, imbricated in the age-old traditions of craftsmanship. This notion was in keeping with the aspirations for upward mobility shared by all industrial workers, for the more skilled the job, the higher the pay scale, the more elevated the status. Management concurred in this scaling, for its hold over the worker was reinforced by the division of labor and the fragmenting of a unified workers' front. Into the breach stepped the middle- as well as working-class female who soon came to realize what had long been the case. The skill and training required of the apprentice-master-craftsman system had increasingly been supplanted by swiftness and endurance as the key ingredients of industrial-line work. In case after case, women found that the cries of "no experience" and the requirements for extensive training programs which had been used as weapons against female recruitment misrepresented the circumstances. In most cases, even specialized tasks such as welding and riveting necessitated little more than a few weeks of on-the-job training. Several of the women interviewed in Connie Field's powerful documentary *The Life and Times of Rosie the Riveter* (1980) mention the initial shock they felt with the recognition that their jobs, exclusively male, jealously guarded through rites of seniority, were more monotonous than skilled.

To the combination of disjuncts within the family configuration causing redistribution of authority and responsibility, anxieties regarding child-rearing, juvenile delinquency and the effects of female mobility on the modeling of future generations, and the ever-greater concentration of economic power in the woman (increasingly both consumer and producer), can be added the previously-mentioned dislocations of the corporate (and patriarchal) domain, all of which contributed to a growing male uneasiness. In terms of psychoanalytic theory, the woman poses an inherent threat to the man as a pure instance of sexual difference through the visually ascertainable absence of the penis. For Laura Mulvey, "the woman as icon, displayed for the gaze and enjoyment of men, the active controllers of the look, always threatens to evoke the anxiety it originally signified."[3] This theorized dramatization of the castration threat can be viewed, by the very presence of the woman, as a kind of psychical grounding for these many levels of male dissatisfaction and half-formed hostility manifested during the period. Here, too, is the psycho-social foundation for the connections between the apparent passivity of "other" status (that is, female inscrutability) and the outright allegation of wrong-doing (the evil woman). A kind of double bind occurred within patriarchy resulting from the clash of escalating anxieties produced by the ever-swelling female presence and self-sufficiency and the necessity for utilizing womanpower to win the war. With victory and the maintenance of order assured, there was no stopping the pendulum of aggression against the "new woman." The accusatory character of the "Evil Woman" category blossoming after 1945 is historically linked to the manifest confusion of its antecedent, "The Inscrutable Female."

Woman: The Inscrutable Female

Across the Pacific (1942)
Cat People (1942)
The Fleet's In (1942)
Andy Hardy's Blonde Trouble (1944)
Laura (1944)

The films of this category ("Inscrutable Female") are characterized by the construction of female personae whose origins, intentions and activities are imperfectly understood by the male protagonists, who dominate narrative action and organize the hermeneutic elaboration of the film. In its most elementary form, this film variant poses a general problem of knowledge for the desiring male, who has difficulty in evaluating and predicting female behavior, as evidenced in *Andy*

Hardy's Blonde Trouble. In this episode of the durable MGM series, Andy's problem (always, as here, represented as a stepping-stone to manhood) is initiated by the appearance of twin sisters who, like Hardy, are en route to college and who pretend to be one person. This confusion of identity is displaced by the real crisis of desire: Andy falls for the Bonita Granville character, who has become enamored of the college dean, an attachment which, in Hardy's experience of teenage romance, is indecipherable. The film's hermeneutic is thus founded in an illegibility not at all shared by the spectator for whom Granville's attraction to the refined father figure played by Herbert Marshall is perfectly familiar. The film's resolution peremptorily returns Granville to the generational fold. This return is signified by a kiss bestowed upon the cowlicked Hardy, whose response (a hoot and whistle directed at the camera) indicates the resurrection of the desexualized erotic discourse, the hallmark of the Hardy series. In this instance of female inscrutability, Andy's adolescent sensibility is at stake. The gap between the male center of narrative and the female object is thus trivialized while the spectator is placed at a safe distance from the sexual problematic—Andy will understand women when he grows up, just as we have.

The Mary Astor character in *Across the Pacific* is also an enigma throughout the film, but in this case the audience shares protagonist Humphrey Bogart's position of knowledge, which only gradually identifies Astor's Alberta Marlow as friend or foe. A strong intertextual reference to *The Maltese Falcon* (same collaboration of John Huston, Sidney Greenstreet, Astor and Bogart) helps render Alberta "a wily female" who may or may not be a hayseed from Medicine Hat, who may or may not be in league with Greenstreet, who may or may not be in love with Bogart. Bogart is himself a mystery man for the first portion of the film, when it appears that he has been courtmartialed from the service less than a month before Pearl Harbor. But it is not long before Rick Leland (Bogart) emerges as an undercover agent and Greenstreet's Dr. Lorenz emerges as a Japanese collaborator. It is the woman and her position within the dualistic male system which prolongs the elaboration of the two-pronged hermeneutic (erotic and political). During the war years, the twin components of political allegiance and romantic attachment were frequently conjoined to problematize (in narrative terms) and eroticize the female persona. A kind of condensation (commitment to man/country) was thus effected which reinforced the sexualized character of female war participation of the sort illustrated by Betty Hutton's song, "Doin' It for Defense" from *Star Spangled Rhythm* (1942) (see pp. 207–8). The double inscrutability of the Astor character thus has a kind of aphrodisiac effect upon Leland just as it does for the male protagonists of *Berlin Correspondent* and *My Favorite Blonde* for whom the deferment of knowledge is also a deferment of sexual gratification.

Richard Dyer, in his essay entitled "Resistance through Charisma: Rita Hayworth and *Gilda*," asserts that, above all else, women in film noir are unknowable and it is this unfathomable quality that exerts a fatal attraction upon the hero.[4] In this formulation, the evil character of the female as femme fatale, black widow or seductress is less crucial to the construction of noir's generic domain than this "otherness" from the subject-position of the male. Yet, Dyer goes on to argue that, due to the combination of residual identification produced by Rita Hayworth's previous roles and the suggestion of sado-masochism and homosexuality in the Glenn Ford character, the standard polarities of knowledge and normalcy are reversed—Gilda/Hayworth rather than Johnny/Ford is substantially valorized. A corollary of Dyer's position might suggest necessary distinctions among variants of female inscrutability in cinema, based in part on the relative coincidence of knowledge positions for audience and character. Dyer alludes to the importance of a privileged moment in *Gilda* during which the audience is momentarily privy to the character's private thoughts as she sings "Put the Blame On Mame" to the men's room attendant, her trusted confidant. Johhny hears only the end of the song (which is a critique of female culpability), and he remains consistently less informed than the spectator as to the quality of Gilda's inner life.

In *Across the Pacific,* the Astor character is equally opaque to protagonist and audience, her moral status hanging in the balance. In the "Evil Woman" category, in which the female is fundamentally untrustworthy, the spectator often witnesses female malefaction well before the hero does, as in *Leave Her to Heaven* (1946), in which the Cornell Wilde character discovers his wife's crimes long after they have been imaged. The range of positions available to the female in the moral scheme of film narratives is thus related in part to the mode of revelation of her narrativized actions and intentions and the relationship between the availability of this knowledge to the spectator and the male protagonist. The knowledge coefficient for the spectator is characteristically limited by the object-status of the female within narrative; it is rarely her voice-over, her flashback, her point-of-view that are given.[5]

The inscrutable female is often the absent female, as in much of *Laura* in which the painted image of the Gene Tierney character mesmerizes the detective sent to investigate her murder; the narrative impulsion is all but immobilized by the detective's obsessive gaze. Laura's return from the dead destroys the male idealizations whose signifier is the portrait. Detective Mark MacPherson, who begins to fall in love with this portrait, is unhindered by any real knowledge of the woman, while Laura's absence allows Waldo Lydecker to "narrate" her to MacPherson in the early portion of the film ("She had charm . . . vitality. Men admired her; women envied her"). Lydecker's projections are all the more satisfying for the purity of their imaginary construction ("I read my articles to her; her listening was more eloquent than speech.") Even after Laura's resurrection, it is only with the greatest difficulty that she extricates herself from Waldo's version of her ("The best part of myself, that's what you are," says Lydecker to Laura). Her erotic attachment to MacPherson, while not the aggressive sensuality of the prototypical noir female, provides evidence of an autonomy threatening enough to goad Lydecker into action. He attempts to destroy the woman whom he can no longer control. Thus the narrative play of *Laura* is composed of a systematic construction and dissolution of the female persona's inscrutability which is actively willed by the men competing for her. The film's conclusion displays little interest in the results of female desire except insofar as one recalls Lydecker's earlier remark: "With you a lean strong body is the measure of a man and you always get hurt." The suggestion is that Laura's erotic impulses are simply not to be trusted, based as they are on her own imaginary rather than Lydecker's. Unlike several of the films of this category whose heroines, as represented, have little if any latitude as desiring subjects simply because their narrative function requires that they remain ciphers, Laura's Imaginary is effectively displaced by a series of male subjective positions (Lydecker, MacPherson, Shelby Carpenter) until the end. Her involvement with MacPherson is but an accession to one of several male scenarios while the results of her decision are of little interest as compared to the contortion of events incited by Tierney's image and the silences so energetically interpolated by the men around her.[6]

Female inscrutability in this group of film texts, then, is based upon an inability or unwillingness to ascertain the dimensions of female desire by the male subject who bears a variable relation to the knowledge-position of the spectator. Andy Hardy's puzzlement is comically treated precisely because of the gap between the audience's sophistication and Andy's ineptitude in deciphering female romantic behavior. *Across the Pacific* (and, to a lesser extent *Berlin Correspondent*) depends upon the opacity of female desire for one level of its hermeneutic elaboration and thus suspends substantive knowledge of the female until its resolution. In both *Gilda* and *Laura,* the discourse of female desire is effectively displaced, and in the former text, forcefully repressed by the agency of male desire. In *Gilda,* the presence of the female body, a vision of taunting plenitude, requires an active suppression while Laura's absence, and simultaneous presence as pure representation, furnishes a kind of screen for male projection.

Yet another variant of this paradigm occurs in *The Fleet's In* (1942) in which the female protagonist, played by Dorothy Lamour, undergoes a process of domestication, fusing exoticism with wholesomeness, in order to become not a desiring subject, but the idealized object of male desire. Lamour is the Countess of Swingland, the toast of San Francisco, a nightclub performer whose exhibitionist appeal is intensified by the mystery that enshrouds her, her tantalizing physical presence reinforced by the absence of a name. A very young William Holden is a wide-eyed sailor, Casey Kirby, who must garner a kiss from the Countess to win a bet and, in doing so, inaugurates an unlikely romance. This comic masquerade is developed through an alternation of opposing facades organized around the paired notions of naivete and sophistication. Kirby is a sailor, one of a particularly jaded breed, who is, in fact, a high-minded country boy whose ingenuous character is belied by the terms of the wager (naturally, he is only helping out a friend). The Countess, who should be a world-weary show girl, is capable of becoming "all . . . kind of fluttery and dizzy" when she kisses Casey. Because the sailor avers to his mates that the Countess is "good and kind and wholesome," that is, precisely who he wants her to be for his idealized object, the Countess must become what, in accordance with the Hollywood idiom, she really already is. In this instance, the exotic and inscrutable femme fatale conforms to the male erotic scenario, and with great willingness, because by becoming the wholesome lass of her sailor's fantasy, she can recover an unsullied version of herself endorsed by the standards of patriarchy. Thus, the tainted city girl is morally resuscitated by becoming an idealized version of herself; unfettered female eroticism is defused by a willing accession to its containment.

Richard Dyer's claim for the requisite "otherness" of the female noir figure leaves unmentioned the variable processes of signification which produce quite disparate versions of this figure. In the first place, the representation of alterity may occur at two textual levels: diegetically, with or without a marked differential of knowledge between spectator and male protagonist and, discursively, as through the use of "mysterious" music or the isolation of the female through lighting or composition. Then, too, woman may be constructed as "other" through the imputation of another character, as through the projections of one or more male characters thus freed to organize their libidinal itineraries independently of their erotic object. Yet another variant of alterity occurs in Jacques Tourneur's *Cat People,* in which female otherness is represented as an uncontrollable force of nature inflicted upon man and woman alike. Here the otherness is graphically realized as metamorphosis; the female protagonist is descended from a line of Serbian witches who can take the form of cats and who destroy any man who dares kiss them. From the outset, the inscription of this female power is enforced as elemental; Irena's tortured sketch of a caged leopard which she tears in half in the first scene is reunited by the wind. Her appearance in a pet store sets off a frenzied response among the animals. "You can't fool a cat," says the shop owner, "they seem to know who's not right."

Irena's otherness is not a sign of malevolence in the classic noir mold described by Dyer. In ideological terms, this mode of female inscrutability is the more corrosive for its location not in the mind, but in the "spirit" of the female character ("It is not my mind that is troubled"), in the blood that runs through her veins. She, more than any other character in the film, is victimized; she is unknowable to herself and envies the average woman on the street who can make her husband happy without fear of devouring him. Furthermore, Irena's condition of otherness is heavily overdetermined so that it is not possible to read her hereditary power/curse unitarily as the signifier of unbridled and liberating female libido, despite the encouragement of sensory associations (her scent is "strong, sweet") and the opposition of domesticated female sexuality represented by a second female, Alice ("I know what love is . . . it's understanding . . . just the two of us living our lives together . . . happily, proudly . . . it's enduring and

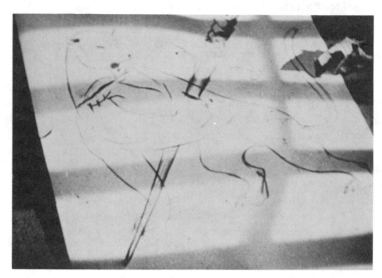

Cat People (RKO, 1942)
Female self-destructiveness is starkly imaged in this film. The impaled leopard,
sketched by the identifying female protagonist, is the wicked beast slain in
legend by the Marmaluke king. By film's end, this pose will be uncannily
duplicated in the fallen woman herself.

everlasting''). For Irena is also characterized by a powerful current of self-
destructiveness; masochism is thus implanted as another, equally elemental, feature
of a protagonist gendered in excess. Hers are the traits of a hypertrophied
"feminine."

Irena's sketch of an impaled leopard displayed at the opening of the film is
a metaphorical version of her own death. She owns a sculpture of King John (who
drove the Marmalukes out of her country) imaged in the act of spearing a cat.
She worships this icon of male dominance and self-mutilation. Irena knows that
the panther is, according to biblical exegesis, a wicked animal. She does not fully
understand, however, the compulsions which lead her to feed her pet bird to the
caged leopard in the zoo. While these two conditions may well be regarded as
within the domain of the superego and id, respectively, it is the entanglement
of the counter-discourses of psychoanalysis and theology which produces the den-
sity of the film's textual and hermeneutic elaboration.

On the simplest narrative level, a psychoanalytic reading is discouraged by
the presence of a smug and desirous male psychiatrist to whom Irena goes for
help ("These things are very easy for a psychiatrist," he says). Her denial of
a psychic basis for her tortured state can be read either as disavowal or as authorial
advocacy. In terms of its connotative impact, the compositional strategy of this
scene is marked by a stylization whose meaning is overdetermined. Under hypnosis, Irena's face is bathed in a perfect oval of light with all else in darkness.

This literal disembodiment may be read as underlining the radical disjunction of mind and body (Irena's inability or unwillingness to trace her actions to their origins in the unconscious), may favor the suggestion of the primacy of psychic processes as the key to Irena's troubles or may be read theologically as a moment of grace for a tortured soul. In a figure such as this one, a multiplicity of readings can be said to coalesce.

The notion that Irena's unknowable powers are beyond her control, the emanations of pure evil lodged in her body, is undercut in the later stages of the film when the cat-metamorphosis is triggered by sexual jealousy towards Alice, the other woman. From the deft matching and overlapping of the aural and visual traces of bestiality (a cat's snarl dissolves into the squeal of air brakes, paw prints merge with human footprints), it is clear that Irena is stalking Alice in conscious reprisal rather than through the compulsion of heredity. This manifestation of violence can be read as an impugnment of female desire, a release of libidinal energy that seeks not to annihilate itself or its erotic object in an act of pure, convulsive excess but to destroy its rival. This, at last, is the evil woman recognizable from the misogynist canon. It is precisely at this juncture that Irena becomes perfectly legible, the inscrutability of her animality replaced by a human, identifiably "female," pattern of behavior.

When at last husband Oliver admits his love for Alice and his wish for a divorce, Irena begins to murmur inaudibly, her fingers/claws slashing the couch. The response, while uncontrollable, can be read as issuing not from the prefigurement of her genealogy (the inexorable destruction of the love partner) but from "female" nature run rampant (the exteriorizing of "cattiness"). When, shortly afterward, Oliver brandishes a T-square against the panther in his and Alice's defense, it is transformed in chiaroscuro into a cross. Now, at last, the shift of terms from doomed to evil woman, from compulsion to vengefulness, is complete. Oliver, in battling to protect the "true couple," invokes divine protection ("In the name of God, leave us in peace"). Irena, no longer unknowable, stands in contradiction to Dyer's equation of evil/unknowable, for she is only now unequivocally evil. Her ravaging of the psychiatrist soon after is a return to a defensible, preordained bestiality, her death taking on a tragic tone in its echo of her initial sketch of the impaled leopard. But it is the appellation "jealous woman" that crowns the constellation of semic connotations attached to Irena in the film and it is this representation that transforms *Cat People* from fairy tale to modern morality tale. This vision of excess female libido and its potential for destruction of both subject and object shifts to a struggle of good and evil only upon the appearance of an identifiably human/female emotion, sexual jealousy. This final move attaches a moral judgment to the narrative which functions as a warning to real women to curb the excesses of their own passions. Yet it is only through the loss of inscrutability that this shift of levels can occur.

The historical distribution of films in "The Inscrutable Female" category suggests a moderate rather than dramatic incidence of this ideological substream during the war years. It is only when the shape of the category's distribution is appended to that of the "Evil Woman" category (see appendix C) that a sense of the historical determinacy of this component of female representation becomes discernible. While the "inscrutable" variant peaks in 1942, declining to a lower level for the remainder of the war years, dropping off altogether afterwards, the "evil" woman rises precipitously in 1946 during the time of the backlash against the emergent female whose double duties as wife/mother and well-paid worker were effectively ended. The statistical evidence here is scant, but there is the suggestion of continuity with a shift of inflection between the "inscrutable" and "evil" woman.

The Evil Woman

Son of Fury (1941)
Orchestra Wives (1942)
In This Our Life (1942)
Notorious (1946)
The Dark Mirror (1946)

The female personae of this category are linked to those of the "inscrutable" rubric through a shared exteriority to the generative centers of knowledge and structuration. They too are constructed through an alterity from the male subjectivity which, with few exceptions, organizes discourse. In this grouping, however, while female motives are apt to be veiled in mystery, as in the previous one, the actions of the female protagonists are characteristically malevolent. In contrast to the conventionalized notion of woman as nurturer (see the discussion of the concept of an idealized "mother class" by early American feminists in chapter four), these women are the destroyers. They violate male trust (*Manpower*, 1941; *Son of Fury; The Woman in the Window*, 1944; *Scarlet Street*, 1945; *Notorious; The Killers*, 1946), wreak their vengeance upon family members (*In This Our Life; The Dark Mirror; Leave Her to Heaven*, 1946), and are often themselves in torment (*Possessed*, 1947). As has been noted, a marked frequency of such representations occurred at the end of the war, although the "faithless woman" archetype is as old as narrative. Nevertheless, some degree of historical determinancy can be attributed to the films of this category, not only through their high incidence during the backlash of the immediate post-war era (six of nineteen films sampled from 1946 were classifiable here), but through a progressive transformation within the grouping.

In the earliest variants, the "Evil Woman" is quite likely to be balanced by one or more "good" female characters. This process is exemplified in *Son of Fury*, in which two characters named Isabel assume polar functions and characteristics. One (Frances Farmer) is a temptress-cousin who goads the Tyrone Power character into regaining his birthright through a kind of sexual taunt ("When you find a way to become master of Bretholm, you'll find a way to make me your wife") while the other is a lowly barmaid (Elsa Lanchester) who becomes his willing benefactress by helping him escape from the authorities. The two Isabels are opposed in class (gentlewoman versus serving woman), physical appearance (beautiful versus plain), and character (betrayer versus donor). Despite the fact that Farmer's faithlessness is realized by the hero only after many years of exile and self-deception, the balancing effected by the second Isabel mitigates against the severity of the evil woman as ideological form. It is worth noting, however, that it is the beautiful Isabel who is venomous, since an unattractive woman would be afforded no functional stake in the Oedipal itinerary underlying the diegetic movement of the Hollywood mainstream; hence she would have no power to destroy or to trigger the narrative flux through a deferral of male gratification. (An exception might be an evil aunt or mother figure, usually hideously ugly, whose access to the hero is based on consanguinity. There are no such figures in *Son of Fury*.)

An even less thorough-going critique of female malfeasance occurs in *Orchestra Wives* (1942), a tale of life and love among Glenn Miller Band members and their wives. The female group in this film is roughly equivalent to the assortment of types in George Cukor's *The Women,* with its share of catty remarks traded among bored wives (Lynn Bari, Carole Landis, Virginia Gilmore, and Mary Beth Hughes). When the Ann Rutherford character (this film's juvenile-equivalent of the Joan Fontaine character in *The Women*) joins the caravan as the wife of the very handsome trumpet player (George Montgomery), the ineffectual bantering becomes more serious. Bari, the band's female vocalist, is the real culprit, for she is the only unattached woman and is determined to have Montgomery for her own. Up until this point, female improprieties have been limited to casual affairs and hard-boiled one-liners (as Rutherford bids a tearful goodbye to her hometown cronies, one orchestra wife remarks, "If there's anything I hate, it's a leaky dame"). Bari's machinations pay off in the form of a three-way cat-fight, Rutherford's departure and the band's break-up. The breach is at last healed when band and couple are reunited with all members, save Bari, intact. In this instance, an array of female stereotypes are depicted, ranging from homewrecker to goody-goody. The evildoing committed is distinguishable as slightly aberrant female behavior and is capable of being absorbed and expelled by the group.

The pairing of opposed moral valences occurs once again in John Huston's *In This Our Life* (1942) but, in this case, the paired women are sisters who constitute the dramatic focus of the film. Curiously, the sisters both have men's names. Roy (Olivia de Havilland) is the even-tempered, unassuming daughter of a crumbling southern family while Stanley (Bette Davis) is the hellion who steals her sister's husband and tries to pin her own hit-and-run accident on a young black man (to name but two of her many offenses). Stanley maintains a distasteful relationship with her autocratic uncle from whom she has received indulgences in exchange for her more-than-daughterly attentions. The attachment is the more reprehensible in that Uncle William has just squeezed Stanley's honorable but passive father out of business. Instead of marrying her fiancé, an upstanding local attorney ("You're much too sweet," she tells him), Stanley leaves town with her brother-in-law Peter who earlier has spoken these identical words to Roy. Racked with guilt, Peter commits suicide and Stanley returns home, thereupon determining to regain her old beau, Craig, now engaged to Roy.

Roy's character is constructed in clear opposition to the destructive force that is her sister. When told by Craig that she has intelligence, she replies, "That's a trait every man admires . . . in another man." She is a rational being whose scrupulous manner is far less exciting than the impulsiveness of sister Stanley (of her torturing Peter to his suicide: "I couldn't help it . . . I never could help anything"). The irresistible impulse is the province of the female, for it lies at the root of her appeal to men who have yoked their own desires to the performance principle (Stanley's three pursuers are a doctor, a lawyer, and an industrialist). Stanley functions as the very antithesis of sublimation, the principle which Freud deemed the foundation of the (patriarchal) culture.

Stanley is the daughter whose desires have been indulged; she has been free to pursue her fancies at will and, as in previous Davis roles such as *Jezebel* and *Dark Victory*, the spectacle of female gratification is both sexually appealing to men and necessarily to be punished. This response (markedly sado-masochistic) is expressed early on by the leering Uncle William who ends up begging Stanley for her affections: "What Stanley needs is a firm hand . . . somebody with gumption enough to make her tow the line." The Davis character's untrammelled appetites are the object of male fascination, the enactment of inadequately repressed eroticism. When asked to accompany Roy and Craig to the opera, she replies: "I'd have to keep still at the opera . . . and I'd rather do anything than keep still." Stanley's kinetic sexuality is incapable of being balanced by Roy's demure presence. When at last Davis' hit-and-run and cover up attempt are realized by the attorney Craig, he summons up the afflatus of his law-giving function while concurrently repressing his erotic attraction (becomes the phallus rather than possesses it) in order to telephone the police. In panic, Stanley flees her retribution and conveniently destroys herself in a speeding automobile. While the pairing in *In This Our Life* appears at first glance to be in terms of good/bad woman, it is the compulsive attraction/repulsion between the female libido-figure Stanley and three different men (Uncle William, Peter and Craig) which fuels the narrative apparatus. Stanley is the site of much projection for this trio, whose sublimation of sexual energy is incomplete (all are professionally accomplished but desirous), but whose dedication to the pleasure principle is likewise imperfect (Peter commits suicide in a fit of remorse, Craig calls the police). Stanley's punishment is less a chastisement for crimes committed than an act of disavowal of man's own polymorphous perversity.

The pairing of sisterly antipodes reaches a psychological peak in Robert Siodmak's *The Dark Mirror* (1946) in which Olivia de Havilland plays identical twins, Ruth and Terry Collins, one of whom has committed a murder. It is the task of a psychologist specializing in twins, Dr. Scott Elliot, to determine which sister is guilty and, of course, to fall in love with the innocent one. Based on a Rorschach test, Elliot is immediately able to tell the police that "one of our young ladies is insane . . . very clever, very intelligent, but insane."

As the film progresses, Ruth (the good twin) and Terry (the evil one) begin to wear different colors and thus become increasingly distinguishable; Terry, whose wardrobe fades to black, is often framed in shadows. In fact, when Elliott gives Terry a polygraph test, the word "Ruth" causes the needle to jump sharply. In a scene toward the end of the film, the twins are composed in a succession of two-shots using the bedroom mirror, with Ruth dressed in white, Terry in black. Yet only one or the other of the sisters is ever fully imaged within the frame; the reflective surface splits and opposes the pair whose onetime consubstantiality is now replaced by an unbridgeable moral divide made visible.

On a formal level, then, the film systematically effects a division of the paired women, shaping the moral landscape into a neatly symmetrical field in which opprobrium can be fairly cast. Meanwhile, the psychologist in the film provides the theoretical basis for Terry's compulsive pathology:

> All women are rivals fundamentally but it never bothers them because they automatically discount the successes of others and alibi their own failures on the grounds of circumstances . . . luck, they say . . . (but not sisters, presumably, who are raised in similar circumstances). That's why sisters can hate each other with such terrifying intensity.

As was the case in *Cat People,* it is sexual jealousy that is shown to fuel Terry's hatred. We learn that during their disadvantaged childhood, Ruth, not Terry, had been wanted for adoption; on several occasions, young men had shown a romantic preference for Ruth. When a doctor in the medical building where Terry runs a magazine stand falls in love with Ruth on the basis of a day or two's substitution behind the counter, this is more than Terry can bear—she murders the doctor. When at last Scott reveals his full knowledge of Terry's design upon her alter ego by producing a live Ruth (Terry thinks she has successfully poisoned her), the black twin, her face contorted with hatred and rage, smashes the mirror containing Ruth's angelic image. This is the closest approximation to Ruth's destruction that Terry can manage.

The process of moral bifurcation undertaken in *The Dark Mirror* provides a means of inculpating the female persona under the guise of simple justice. In this instance, the fundamental sense of rivalry attributed to all women is merely intensified in one-half of these female siblings. Terry exhibits a purified strain

The Dark Mirror (Universal, 1946)
Olivia de Havilland's portrayal of twin sisters—one good, one evil—posits a familiar bifurcation of female behavior. More than that, the film externalizes schizophrenia as sisterly competition, suggesting the psychosis as the natural condition of women.

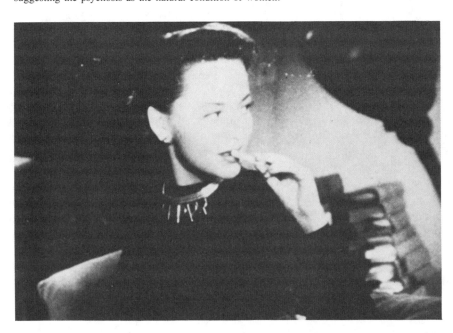

of that character trait (a combination of sexual jealousy and simmering ambition) which the patriarchal domain assigns to all women—the female version of the totemic myth in which Cronos dared to monopolize all women and was therefore devoured by his sons who then shared the women. Ruth is very much an idealized ego for Terry, one which she is driven to destroy in order to overcome her sense of inadequacy. By splitting the female persona in half, by isolating the intrinsic impulses of sexual jealousy and rivalry in one twin, the film can safely explore the limits of female turpitude and destroy it, knowing that a blameless alter ego remains to receive the reward of a wise and handsome man. Yet the film posits a fundamental animosity among women, a limiting condition for sisterhood, that should be distinguishable in any individual. The harshness of this vision is vastly ameliorated by the creation of a simple moral duality between identical twins. Yet, clearly, it is the female qua female that is found blameworthy.

A final exemplum of the "Evil Woman" category, Alfred Hitchcock's *Notorious* (1946), involves a far more complex and systematized structuring of the female persona. Unlike the majority of the films of this category, the male subject-center in *Notorious* is significantly undermined by a distinct bifurcation of male identification. (In *Son of Fury,* the Tyrone Power figure is a swashbuckling hero; *Orchestra Wives* are subservient to, even nameable by, their respective husbands; in *In This Our Life,* the ultimate law-giving function resides with the male despite the sensationalized focus on the Davis character; likewise, in *The Dark Mirror* the psychologist becomes the subjective center of the discourse through whom we observe the curious patterns of female behavior.) A viewing of *Notorious* suggests that the Ingrid Bergman character, Alicia Huberman, is indeed the perceptual and enunciative fulcrum of the film owing to the number and intensity of closeups (which encourage identification), point-of-view shots (which overlay our scopic drive with hers) and subjective point-of-view shots (in which we identify less with *what* she sees than *how* she sees it, as when Alicia realizes she is being poisoned). Despite the atypicality of this profusion of signifying elements which produce a significant and female domain of subjectivity, *Notorious* constructs a gridwork of male identification whose function it is to situate Alicia Huberman within an ideological field which renders her culpable, blameworthy, in effect, "notorious." Although the mildness of the moral indictment here, as compared to those against the "homewreckers" and homicidal sisters previously discussed, is undeniable, it must be recalled that Alicia appears to be the true heroine of *Notorious,* a woman who undertakes a dangerous mission for the United States government. It is the subtlety of the textual shifts, imbedded within the transparency of patriarchal ideology, which inculpates Alicia and which demands a closer examination.

The unified male subject that normally underlies the conditions for discourse within classical American cinema is fractured in *Notorious* by a process of parallel identification attached to the Cary Grant and Claude Rains characters, the agents of the law in its twin visages, Good and Bad. What might at first glance appear a subversion of phallocentrism emerges instead as the very basis for the subjugation and oppression of the female category in the film. From the first introduction to Dev (Cary Grant)—in which he is seated in the left foreground with his back turned to the camera, silent and in silhouette, a kind of "master spectator"—a strong sense of identification is mobilized that is significantly "male." Alicia is the object of Dev's lingering gaze here and elsewhere, a pattern inaugurated in the second shot of the film in which the camera peers through a crack in the courtroom door to steal a look at the mysterious beauty whose father is being sentenced for treason. The participants in the grouping termed the Good Law (Dev, his superior Captain Prescott, the motorcycle cop who interrogates Alicia during a drunken, late night drive) are, in relation to Alicia, the functional equivalents of the minions of the Bad Law (Alex Sebastian—Rains—and his Nazi cohorts) despite their nominal opposition. Both factions seek to control her as a figure within their particular erotic or political scenarios.

Sebastian is linked to Dev in their shared romantic attachment to Alicia and through visually potent compositions of object exchange. Dev forces Alicia to drink a "healing" potion to ease her hangover early in the film, a scene containing one of Alicia's previously mentioned "subjective" point-of-view shots, while Sebastian's poisoned coffee cup elicits yet another such moment towards the film's end. Both men bear a relationship to a key icon within the romantic discourse (a champagne bottle) which becomes a crucial element within the espionage subplot. The bottle which Dev intends as a spur to love in an early scene is transformed into the receptacle for the much sought-for uranium ore, the film's McGuffin. Another strong connection between the two men operates through a shared epistemology. When Alicia comes to tell Captain Prescott and the others of Sebastian's marriage offer, she submits to Dev's double-edged questioning. "May I ask what inspired Alexander Sebastian to go this far?" Alicia answers, "He's in love with me." "And he thinks you're in love with him?" asks Dev. After a dramatic pause, "Yes, that's what he thinks." This formulation applies equally to Dev and to Sebastian since the crucial knowledge factor, Alicia's true feelings, is withheld. As the text yields itself, the two men are clearly conjoined. Dev and Sebastian are, simply stated, functionally equal and thematically opposite.

Within the realm of the Good Law, Alicia's fondness for drink, seemingly no greater than that of Dev or Prescott, when coupled with her willingness to seduce and even marry a man who is repugnant to her to garner valuable intelligence for the American government, renders her "notorious": "I don't think there can be any illusions as to what kind of woman we're dealing with," says Prescott. She is different from the wives in Washington "who sit around and play cards," yet she is also different from Dev, Prescott and the rest whose names and reputations can never be impugned; she is a woman. And when, after the sham marriage to Sebastian, she visits Prescott for advice, he addresses her as

Mrs. Sebastian; her submission to the male nomenclature is accepted by the very instigator of the false union. Here the potency of sexual difference outweighs the concerns of geo-politics and international intrigue.

Concurrently, a significant degree of identification is encouraged with the apparent villain, Alex Sebastian, a figure of dual castration, leaderless and dominated by an overpowering mother, whose worst fears are realized. Sebastian's romantic insecurity, strong from the outset, is shared by every man less dashing than Cary Grant ("You made a pretty couple," says the diminutive Rains). He is given a plethora of point-of-view shots during his visual interrogation of the Grant-Bergman liaison during the ballroom sequence. If the spectator is motivated by a desire to see and know, it is Sebastian who most clearly embodies the crisis of those desires. Alicia has stolen Sebastian's love and his secrets, indeed his life, and she has feigned her love "with those clinging kisses" while lusting for another. If it is every man's suspicion that his mother is right—that she is the only woman he can trust—that suspicion is borne out by Alicia and by the film.

When Alicia is spirited away by Dev at the end of the film, it is Sebastian who remains behind, his fate sealed, and it is with him that the camera lingers. He dominates the closing images of the film; while subjective music accompanies his heavy steps, the thud of the sepulchral door signals the final fade-out. If it has been the work of the film to establish Alicia's "notoriety," it is through Sebastian that this semic ensemble is fully realized. "Once a thief, always a thief; once a tramp, always a tramp"; "first, last, and always not a lady"; a "marked woman" as Alicia calls herself in an opening scene—these verbally articulated components of the semic ensemble established throughout the film resonate with the experience of Sebastian, whose wife has betrayed, deserted and executed him. Sexual difference is energetically reinforced, displacing the clash of political or moral positions which appears to be the film's battleground. Despite the heroic dimensions of the female protagonist's exploits, the power of patriarchal ideology exacts a price for Alicia's transgressions, the sign of which is the very title of the film: *Notorious.*

In each of the films of the "Evil Woman" category discussed here, the female personae were positioned within a moral/ideological domain based upon the presence or absence of particular "female" traits. The intransigence of the presumption of the "essential female"—despite the alterations of lived experience and the fluctuations of public imagery linked to women—has been discussed at some length in chapters two and four. If the domain of the "eternal female" was found to be a place of nascent contradiction even resistance during the war years, this instability could itself be recuperated as the caprice native to women. Even so, a degree of variability, an expansion of typologies within the hegemonic, becomes discernible during the early forties.

In *Son of Fury,* as in several other pre-war instances, feminine perfidy was rooted in false seductiveness, yet the faithless woman was apt to be balanced by an equally trustworthy female character. This balancing grew more pronounced in *In This Our Life* and *The Dark Mirror* in which sisters, and then twins, were counterposed with the darker half exhibiting unrestrained willfulness, in the first case, and homicidal fury born of jealousy in the latter. In both films, the excesses of the evil sisters are the bases of the diegetic spectacle and of the narrative drive, excesses which are viewed as the result of inadequately internalized female instincts. Stanley in *Life* lacked a strong man to place her in tow, while *The Dark Mirror*'s Terry was the possessor of an inordinate share of sisterly rivalry. Neither woman was represented as deviant, but rather as the embodiment of womanhood run wild. While these women were punished for the rampancy of their desires, Alicia Huberman was rendered "notorious" even though the circuit of her own desire was subordinated to duty until the end. Her actions, although rendered in the name of the Law, are transgressions against a patriarchal order and must be punished.

Woman: Object of the Look

You'll Never Get Rich (1941)
Roxie Hart (1942)
The Heavenly Body (1943)
Coney Island (1943)

The third of the three categories constructed through a radical alterity from the male subject-center is that of "Woman: Object of the Look." A psychoanalytic term essential to an understanding of this grouping is "fetishism," a psychic process by which the (traditionally) male unconscious objectifies the female body in disavowal of the castration anxiety evoked by woman (through the visibly absent penis). This process necessitates an act of separation, a placing at a distance, in order to specularize the body, although, in cinema, the close-up of the female body part appears to contradict this theorem. In fact, the separation is one of subject and object whereby the male viewing subject is afforded the luxury of his gaze, simultaneously enforcing visual pleasure and blocking psychic unpleasure. In terms of the cinema, the fixing of the objectified form constitutes a blockage within the narrative economy, a stasis which threatens the metonymic flow of sounds and images. This contravention of narrative is exemplified by the performance sequences in most musicals as well as by the frozen imagery of the pin-up or fold-out which effaces the conditions for narration.

In "Visual Pleasure and Narrative Cinema," Laura Mulvey claimed that the preponderance of female personae in mainstream cinema are relegated to object-status through the structuring of the male gaze and that this gendered division of subject and object is the founding principle of the conventional narrative. In a formulation that has become canonical, woman becomes the signifier for the male other, the bearer rather than the maker of meaning.[7] Kaja Silverman has argued the case even more categorically: "It is . . . axiomatic that the female subject as she has been constructed by Hollywood cinema is denied any active role in discourse."[8] The premise of this study has been, on the contrary, that the positioning of the female within the filmic system is complex, variable and, in some measure, historically determinate. The power and modality (even the possibility) of female enunciation within filmic discourse is totally excluded in Mulvey's and Silverman's formulations, while a range of wartime films examined in chapter seven are concerned with precisely these questions. The present set of texts, placed within the rubric "Woman: Object of the Look," is the grouping most consistent with the traditional feminist critique, for it is the realm of the fetishized form, the beautiful object intended for the contemplation of men. Analysis of such texts, placed within the larger social field, intends to yield a more thorough-going understanding of what Peter Wollen has termed "the production of woman as fetish in a particular conjunction of capitalism and patriarchy."[9]

If, in fact, the damming of the circulation of meaning within the filmic system is produced through specularization, one can posit an isomorphic linkage to the blockage of libidinal energy resulting from fetishization as classically formulated. In Lacanian terms, the fetish signifies the lack—the absent penis of the mother— supplementing it by a "fullness" which simultaneously reaffirms the void. Implicit to this notion are the structures of disavowal and multiple belief. The true fetishist is thus barred from orgasm except through a rechanneling of desire through the fetish object. The libidinal flow, whose integrity is essential to the circuitry of reproductive sexuality, is thus transfixed at some anterior site. In like manner, the flow of the narrative economy is short-circuited through spectacle and the fetishizing process. In opposition to the classical Freudian model, however, the fetishizing impulse in cinema is capable of crossing lines of gender and sexual preference. The fascination with the beauty of movement and form projected in larger-than-life dimensions occurs for men and for women, for heterosexual and homosexual alike. Neither is it defensible to construct a reified notion of the fetishizing impulse or of an idealized domain of fetishized objects within cinema, for all moving images of all sorts offer the potential for an over-favoring within the scopic regime, particularly when encouraged by the agency of secondary identification.

If any film can engender the fetishizing impulse, it is necessary to theorize a principle of intermittency whereby a spectator's attention to diegetic concerns fades in and out in accordance with the level of his/her fascination with the imagery or even the sounds connected to that imagery (the ties between aural cues and erotic response have been well documented). The singularity of this process and its relations to the contours of individual psychic composition have been too little remarked upon. The weakness of Mulvey's argument lies precisely in its rigidity of gender specification and its hardened polemics which overlook the subtlety and polysemy of the fetishizing principle. If, after these qualifications, it seems contradictory to establish a special category for the fetishized female, the reader is encouraged to approach this taxonomical fixity as an unfortunate by-product of "laboratory conditions." These are the limit-texts of the fetishizing impulse grouped together for methodological convenience. In a more dramatic way than most, this category is placed "under erasure"—necessary but inaccurate.

The graphed distribution of the films of this category evidences a compressed periodicity coupled with a relatively flat amplitude. The peak year for this grouping is 1943, while the absence of films before 1941 or after 1944 makes this the only category existing entirely within the war years. Given the popularity of related cultural forms during the period, notably the pin-up, the lasciviously rendered women of Milt Caniff and other contemporary cartoonists, and the frequently displayed female form in the photojournalism of the day, this ascendancy is not at all surprising. These were the years during which Betty Grable ruled the lot at Twentieth Century-Fox and was chosen by the nation's exhibitors as the number one box office attraction.

Grable's stardom was, in terms of Laura Mulvey's dichotomous formulation, a product of spectacle rather than narrative. She was less identifiable with her wartime roles than as an emblem of healthy American womanhood—well-scrubbed, full-bodied, beyond suspicion. The sexual appeal of her well-traveled image (she was the uncontested pin-up queen with GIs around the world) could be the subject of a full-length study in itself. She lacked the cachet of a Veronica Lake (peek-a-boo hairstyle), a Dorothy Lamour (exotic sarong) or an Ann Sheridan (the "oomph" girl). She was neither vamp nor languorous seductress (Rita Hayworth), yet the grip of her eroticism remained undiminished by her chaste image (cf. Jeanne Crain, June Allyson) or by a surfeit of aggressive intelligence (Rosalind Russell, Katharine Hepburn, Claudette Colbert). Perhaps the plumpness of Grable's open face and form, the wide-eyed expression betraying neither judgment nor substantive intent, offered an unthreatening version of female sexuality for the fighting man. Stateside, the power of her appeal was sufficient to raise a $40,000 war donation in exchange for a single pair of her nylons in 1943.

The fetishizing impulse which has insured the primacy of the star system in Hollywood cinema (and such specialized forms as the "starlet," the "pin-up queen," and the "poster girl") is further attested to by the American mania for statistics. Whether in the form of batting averages, all-time high temperatures or minutely differentiated Nielson ratings, the American viewing public exhibits an obsessive fascination for the exactitude of facts and figures which, like the body part, represent a site of incomplete libidinal cathexis. The phenomenon of eroticized statistics becomes a metonymic inevitability typified by the notion of "vital statistics," that all-important recitation of a woman's bust, waist and hip measurements used as a gauge for corporeal perfection. (A breathy female voice promotes one San Francisco television station as "the perfect 36"—a broadcast ordination eroticized.) A curious case study of this phenomenon occurs in a *Life* magazine article entitled "The Girls of Hollywood" (August 3, 1942) which is a "limb-by-limb report" of the weights and measurements of ten of filmdom's favorite actresses. This inventory of nearly identical numbers (the range of "foot sizes," for example, is 5A to 6-1/2B) is intended as a "portfolio of pulchritude" and "an indication of current taste in American womanhood." These listings constitute an instance of product differentiation with a sexualized veneer. Nor is it surprising that the ten women can be broken down in pairs, each attached to one of five major studios (Paramount: Veronica Lake and Rosalind Russell; Warners: Ann Sheridan and Alexis Smith; Columbia: Rita Hayworth and Brenda Marshall; Fox: Gene Tierney and Carole Landis; MGM: Lana Turner and Hedy Lamarr).

In comparing this bevy of beauties to previous ideal types, the article concludes that "today there is a trend towards more purely female allure, because men at war want women to be attractive . . . they also want them to be sympathetic and companionable." These traits are somehow projected through the litany of statistics which follows, including age, number of marriages, height, weight, bust, hip, waist, leg length and foot size. As indicated earlier, the marvel of this exercise is the absence of significant variation, for product differentiation can only be understood within the context of another industrial maxim: the standardization of parts.

Important for the understanding of fetishism is an awareness of the internal contradiction which sustains it. Because the fetishized female is a figure of disavowal—a locus of male recognition of castration and its simultaneous denial—the fetish itself is treated with affection and hostility. The fetish is thus constituted as an over-valuation, a surplus attached to one part of the body, an intensification of the scopic drive overlaid with sadism (the result of the obsessive, pulverizing gaze of the subject). The women of this category are, among other things, scrutinized by a neurotic astronomer through his telescope (*The Heavenly Body*), ogled by judge, jury and counsel in a burlesque of American jurisprudence (*Roxie Hart*), made to sing and dance in a grass skirt (*Song of the Islands*), even tied up and publicly flogged (*Hitler's Children*). In all cases, the condition of spectacle momentarily retards diegetic activity; in all cases, the woman is established as the focus of three overlapping gazes—of the camera, of the characters within the diegesis, and of the spectator.

A particularly illuminating instance of the fetishized female occurs in the Betty Grable vehicle *Coney Island* (1943) in which Grable plays Kate Farley, a singer on the stages of old New York, a prized object contested by rival club owners, George Montgomery and Cesar Romero. Montgomery decides at one point to alter the style of her performance, which is up-tempo and highly mobile, by handcuffing her to a piece of the scenery moments before the curtain is raised and by stripping her of the flounces and feathers bedecking her costume. By forcefully immobilizing her, he is able to transform a dance hall chanteuse into the first torch singer wearing the first sheathed evening gown (while also stealing a kiss from her). Despite her fury, Kate realizes that the male audience is rapturous in its response to the tableaued form now offered up to its steady gaze. The process thus narrativized *is* the process of fetishization which established Grable as a box office topper who for years was rarely asked to act, but rather to be looked upon.

The strict characterization of the woman as the object of the gaze is severely challenged in a Fred Astaire film such as *You'll Never Get Rich* (1941). Paired with Rita Hayworth (as they were the following year in *You Were Never Lovelier*), Astaire is, as always, the "performer" par excellence and in that role commands the focus of attention throughout much of the film. Indeed, the film can be viewed as an ongoing struggle between two appropriations of the gaze—one, which encourages the spectator's attention to Hayworth through a heavily encoded display of "glamour," the other based upon Astaire's unparalleled virtuosity of movement and his centrality within the choreography of the mise-en-scene. Hayworth's glamour potential is exploited in *You'll Never Get Rich,* but not without contradiction, for she plays an aristocratic Sheila Winthrop who happens to dance in Astaire's chorus line. The eye is mechanically drawn to her during an early rehearsal sequence (the camera individuates her through a tracking movement), because Hayworth's dancing prowess will not suffice to do so (or at least such a display is suppressed). The question of individuation is essential to the romantic discourse, since Sheila is unable to attract the attention of Robert/Astaire (here, our gaze and that of the camera does not coincide with the inscribed onlooker). Sheila's task is, precisely, to capture Robert's gaze and then his heart, a matter complicated by the bevy of chorines surrounding her ("To a hungry man, a leg of lamb is a great dish, but to the butcher it's just another piece of meat," she says). Robert is the *metteur-en-gaze* whose visual attention and subsequent erotic interest by film's end fully authorize Sheila's centrality, so artificially imposed in the early scene.

Conversely, Astaire's appropriation of the look is based upon an irrepressible kinaesthetic potency achieved through the coupling of meticulous precision and "effortless" grace. When Robert is drafted into the Army, his entire chorus line comes to the station to bid him farewell with a routine entitled "The Boss Has Joined the Army." Again, Astaire is centrally framed among these marching beauties and remains so through a dissolve to a marching company of selectees. Yet, the eye is drawn to Astaire's famous feet even in their submission to the military cadence, perhaps to catch the subtlest syncopation of step, the sign of a joyful expressiveness undaunted by repression. The narrative calls for a reversal of pursuer/pursued, so that it is Astaire who furnishes the impetus towards resolution, male desire supplanting that of female. Curiously, the final scene of the film succeeds in collapsing the spectacle/narrative schism when Robert plants a real justice of the peace on stage during a wedding routine that constitutes a brief respite from military service. The performance is delayed for the duration of the hasty ''I do's,'' after which the duo share center stage and screen as they dance atop a tank-turned-wedding-cake. In effect, the struggle for control of the gaze is settled by a marriage of the twin currents of fascination—those attached to the glamorized female form and to the energized male body. Furthermore, this union is effected through a replacement of the female as agent of desire by the male, an accession to ''normalcy.''

The fetishizing impulse is played for laughs in Twentieth Century-Fox's 1942 release *Roxie Hart,* starring a leggy Ginger Rogers as a brash, gum-chewing showgirl who becomes fond of the criminal limelight when she is charged with the murder of an admirer. (The film announces its dedication to ''all the beauties who have filled their men full of holes out of pique.'') The key visual motif is signaled in Rogers' initial on-screen moment—a close-up of a pair of net-stockinged legs hastily climbing down a fire escape. Roxie is caught soon thereafter by a street-wise reporter with an angle to sell who locks her in a closet for safekeeping. When she kicks one shapely leg through the door, the reporter advises her: ''Take it easy will you, honey, you'll ruin your defense.'' Sensationalized newspaper coverage follows, the reporter counseling his protegee throughout the photo sessions with the imprecation, ''the knees, Roxie, the knees.'' When, at long last, Hart is brought to trial, the all-male jury is mesmerized by the sight of her well-publicized limbs—the proceedings actually grind to a halt as she recrosses her legs. For much of this scene, Rogers is placed dead center within the frame, facing the camera, with the jury positioned over her shoulder: the spectator fully replaces the jury as the source of the gaze.

The film's narration is enunciated through an exchange of flashbacks by two reporters sharing drinks and memories in a shabby bar. With the courtroom spectacle fully narrated, Roxie can no longer command the limelight of her privileged objecthood. In the final scene, Roxie arrives at the local tavern to pick up the George Montgomery character, having married him and given birth to six children. The trial's culmination has put an end to her public access as fascinating, specularized object and instead the drab narrative of a woman's everyday life has been free to unfold. Beneath the surface of jibes and snickers (at one point, Roxie's wrestling match with another inmate is overlaid with the sound of cats fighting), *Roxie Hart* offers a rather sobering view of female possibilities in a man's world.

A final instance of the category ''Woman: Object of the Look'' is the 1943 MGM release *The Heavenly Body,* a film whose title invokes the twin compulsions of the male protagonist, William Powell. For, as Professor Bill Whitley, Powell is troubled by a clearcut split between his eroticized and sublimated selves. On the one hand, he is married to a wide-eyed innocent of a wife played by Hedy

Roxie Hart (Twentieth Century-Fox, 1942)
In this film the spectacle of the female form interrupts the flow of narrative and or jurisprudence itself: the spectator is made to replace the jury as the source of the gaze.

Lamarr; on the other, he is a renowned astronomer and the director of a major observatory. Naturally, both facets of his life demand his constant nighttime attention and therein lies the basis of the dramatic conflict. Whitley, for his part, attempts to bridge the gap between his domestic and professional responsibilities through various ritual observances, chief among them, the appropriation of a telescopic lens at 11:00 each night for the observation of wife Vickie who stands waving good night to him from her bedroom balcony miles away. This male gaze is paradigmatically linked to cinema spectatorship itself in the radical scissure of a voyeurist-exhibitionist structure, a structure which is, once again, organized by the binary oppositions of active/passive, subject/object relations. For, as Metz and others have pointed out, cinema, unlike the performing arts, denies the reciprocity of the gaze, enforcing instead "the absence of the object seen."[10] The pro-filmic performance and the viewing audience are ineradicably separated by time and space. So too are the participants in this curious ritual.

The wave of Vickie's hand is, precisely, a ruse, a gesture for the benefit of the sighted male. Furthermore, the metonymic power of this fetishizing "scene" is produced through the location of the miming female form (miming communicative exchange)—she stands at her bedroom balcony in a negligee, a doubly eroticized contiguity articulated through the "bodies" of the home and the wife. These conditions, so favorable to the fetishizing impulse, are reinforced by the autocracy of Powell's gaze; since he alone controls the apparatus, he alone is privy to this eroticized representation. In much the same way, one can talk about the enforced sado-masochism of filmic and theatrical representation in which the costumed female form is made to parade before the camera or the footlights, offering stiff smiles and gestural flourishes to the inanimate male spectator whose center of erogeny is displaced from penis to eye. The theatrical performance is staged within a nexus of capitalist exchange: the female performer receives a small percentage of the generated capital, for she is subjected to and controlled by both the gaze of the consumer and the profit incentive of the entrepreneur. Vickie, for her part, receives no outright payment from the professor who functions both as procurer and audience, for the nexus of this negotiation is marriage, and requires no apparent payment for services rendered.

There is some corrective to Whitley's perversely scientized gaze offered by the film. For, in fact, Whitley (as the name implies) is something of a screwball at heart, who becomes greatly agitated when Vickie, believing the prognostications of her astrologer, falls in love with another man. The crisis of the professor's anxieties is also a moment of contrived metaphoricity, for just as Whitley is preparing to present a newly discovered comet to a colloquy of renowned colleagues he learns that Vickie is en route to a liaison with her intended lover. Whitley has hoped to prove the inevitability of a collision of heavenly bodies—his comet and a planet—based upon his calculations. Instead, he rushes off to forestall a different kind of collision of bodies scheduled to occur at his mountain-top cabin.

(It is noteworthy that the scientist's territorial claims are attached to both classes of "heavenly bodies.") The tryst is subverted, Whitley reclaims his wife and the proprietary nature of his attachment remains unchallenged. Earlier, he has referred to Vickie's "silly little head" while scorning her interest in astrology ("The nonsense that grown women can be taken in by!"). Now he tells her, "You deserve a good beating . . . and so do I, for not knowing how much I needed you." This is the full extent of Whitley's admission; he affirms some level of emotional dependency. This admission is, of course, related to the fetishist ritual of the 11:00 P.M. telescopic sightings. So long as Whitley exercised control over the sighted apparatus and was able to orchestrate the exact timing and content of the performance while maintaining a position of pure voyeurism (seeing but not being seen), he was assured of a disconnected arousal that admitted no "need." Instead, in a manner analogous to the institutionalized cinema, Whitley obtained pleasure through a mechanized structuring of the gaze, made possible by the complicitous masquerading of the female as object. The admission of the male protagonist reduces the degree of perversity of the film's sexual discourse through its reluctant acknowledgment of the interpersonal character of male pleasure. Vickie is but nominally de-objectified, however, while remaining entrapped and rigorously controlled within her home and within the patriarchal domain that authorizes the narrative.

The films of this category, as manifestations of the fetishizing impulse, evidence little historical specificity. Unlike the "inscrutable" and "evil" women of previous groupings, the female objectified through the gaze is a figure whose ideological positioning replies in a very limited way to contextual currents. This assertion appears at first glance to be in contradiction to the concentration of these films in the war years 1941–44 (see appendix C). For, in fact, the objectification of the woman and the prizing of female beauty, held up for the contemplation of men, was strongly encouraged by the exigencies of the war crisis, combat conditions, the self-described "maleness" of the period, and so on. Yet, once the fetishizing dynamic is evoked within cinema, there appears to be little concern or even potential for representational variation. This invariancy is consistent with the character of specularization previously described, as blockage in both the libidinal and narrative economies.

The most historically explicit example within this grouping is *Hitler's Children,* which includes a rather sensationalized sequence during which Bonita Granville is partially stripped and flogged in high Nazi fashion. Yet the mode of narrativization of the fetishizing impulse in any specific instance remains largely irrelevant. In *Hitler's Children,* a vicious and de-humanizing brand of sadism is imputed to the enemy, but it is the representation and consumption of the savagery within the filmic format that is at stake. The fascination of this scene (which unquestionably constitutes the film's claim to fame in the public memory) is produced for the spectator at the expense of the villainous Nazis—the viewer is spared any moral ambiguity the better to focus on the pro-filmic event. Such a strategy was recognized and widely exploited by C. B. De Mille and others in the biblical epics of an earlier era. The visualization of the lascivious or evil within a comforting framework which offers a complete displacement of moral responsibility produces an ideal setting for the fetishizing process. In sum, the films of this grouping, ''Woman: Object of the Look,'' are historically determinant in the frequency of their appearance but not markedly so in the mode and variation of their signification.

7

Figures in/of Enunciation

Finally we take up the examination of woman-centered films whose protagonists constitute the focus and chief support of the narrative. While the films considered in this chapter are characterized by a centrality for the female within the diegesis as was the case in the films discussed in chapter 6, the key distinction to be made among them pertains to the discursive functions accorded the female protagonists. The concern for characterization and emplotment (the domain of diegesis) is here replaced by the structuration of the specific speech act (the discursive) and the precise methods by which utterance is generated (enunciation). At stake in the emphasis upon enunciation is the question of the subject's place in language. Derived originally from Emile Benveniste's distinction between the statement (énoncé) and the speech act (énonciation), theories of enunciation in cinema have linked the attribution of discursive authority (the ability to initiate and control sound and image) within a text to questions of socially inscribed power and sexual difference.[1]

Although discursive function becomes the primary object of the analysis that follows, this is not to say that all the films of the final two categories offer instances of "women's speech." If this work challenges the presumption of Hollywood cinema as an exclusively male domain at the level of enunciation, it does so in a qualified and historically specific way. Indeed, the films of the "Thematic Presence/Enunciative Absence" category are noteworthy for the extent to which they suggest the necessity of gender-specific speech through their concentration on fictive females extraordinary for their courage and durability— without delivering on that promise. The realm of female subjectivity is displayed, discussed and rendered enigmatic, but never explored from within through the delegation of enunciative authority. It remains for the texts of the final category, "Enunciation against the Grain," to develop this notion of female potency understood at the level of cultural representation, an idea which takes as its necessary precondition a set of material conditions to which such aesthetic developments correspond. Such instances, representing as they do a limited and provisional play of resistance within patriarchy-as-the-hegemonic, offer testimony to the greater elasticity of classical Hollywood cinema, the more expansive field of difference or heterogeneity it is capable of mobilizing. Yet even such a modest claim as this becomes noteworthy in the face of certain pronouncements within feminist criticism far too programmatic and totalizing, that "the participation of the female subject in the production of discourse is nonexistent."[2]

Thematic Presence/Enunciative Absence

Take a Letter, Darling (1942)
Ladies Courageous (1944)
Spellbound (1945)
The Shocking Miss Pilgrim (1946)

The films of this category present fictionalized women noteworthy for their vitality, strength of purpose and, in several instances, the durability of their sisterly ties. The affirmative character of these personae places these films beyond the pale of conventional female representation during any period of Hollywood production. Here one encounters pilots (*Ladies Courageous*), executives (*Take a Letter, Darling*), street-smart journalists and photographers (*No Time for Love*, 1943), secretaries (*Dixie Dugan*, 1942), nurses (*Sister Kenny*, 1946), doctors (*Spellbound; You Belong to Me*, 1941), outlaws (*Belle Starr*, 1941; *Women Without Names*, 1940; *Allotment Wives*, 1945) and labor activists (*The Shocking Miss Pilgrim*)— all women, all treated with some degree of integrity. These female protagonists are the fictive constructs responsive to the burgeoning possibilities of the American wartime woman (extensively documented in chapter 2). As characters, however, they remain disenfranchised from the source of discursive authority, for although they constitute the object-centers of audience interest and of narrative elaboration, they are denied any originary power over the production of sounds and images or the unravelling of the hermeneutic structure. Indeed, it is noteworthy that only three of the sixteen films of this grouping (*Belle Starr, Sister Kenny* and *Spellbound*) offer a strongly encoded hermeneutic patterning (see appendix A). In each of the three cases, the enigma (*Spellbound*'s cure, *Sister Kenny* and *Belle Starr*'s fictional/biographical teleology) is evinced and resolved through diegeticized male figures or through a retrospective, more or less omniscient voice that is identifiably male. The remainder of the films of this sub-category are, with few exceptions, light comedy/romances which effectively undercut the potency of female characterization. The films of this category appear to reinforce the position developed by Kaja Silverman ("Not only does the male subject occupy positions of authority within the diegesis, but occasionally he also speaks extra-diegetically from the privileged place of the Other"[3]) and others, that there exists a pronounced asymmetry of male and female subjectivity in mainstream narrative cinema.

An analysis of the titles alone bears witness to the pivotal status of the female personae, a condition clearly endorsed by the active participation and high visibility of their flesh-and-blood referents. Ten of sixteen film titles are purely nominative, either proper names or their slightly sensationalized equivalents; for example, *The Shocking Miss Pilgrim, Ladies Courageous, The Flame of New Orleans, Dough Girls*. The most striking title of all is *Take a Letter, Darling*, in which not only is the enunciative source female but the imperative mood is utilized. (One senses that the subversive character of such a title is easily overestimated given that the film's "hook" is constituted through simple role reversal, never in itself a revolutionary strategy.)

There is no numerically dramatic occurrence of these films; in contrast to the sharp rise and fall of the distribution of particular blocs of texts from among all films sampled, this sub-category appears with a measured regularity from 1940 through 1946. Since no single year produced more than three films of this category, with only sixteen films overall, it would be ill-advised to speculate on the specifically historical character of this version of female representation, at least in global terms, except to note that there was a consistent interest in the woman-centered narrative for the duration of the war years and into the post-war melodramas (*Daisy Kenyon, Ruby Gentry*). Part of the flatness of this grouping's curve of distribution can be accounted for by recalling that a number of contextually explicit films closely related to this category are placed elsewhere (see "Woman: The Helper" and "Woman: The Martyr or Source of Inspiration").

It is worth returning to the notion of the expropriation of the woman's discursive voice occurring within the texts under consideration, for herein lies the key to the containment of the emergent female within one representational system. Rarely if at all is the spectator allowed access to the subjective world of these women; they are narrative objects within a third-person rhetorical scheme that precludes the organization of discourse through the female. The marks of extra-diegetic enunciation (voice-over narration, framing expository material, the voice of Law discernible in the didactic roll-ups of *Allotment Wives* or *Ladies Courageous*) are the determinate traces of patriarchal hegemony. These female protagonists are neither imbricated within point-of-view structures nor endowed with the power to generate subjective music. For although they are not fetishized objects—they are often fully characterized, even glorified—these personae remain locked within the narrative system, unable to elude or even comment upon the discursive framework which names, elaborates and controls them.

A limited counterexample is offered by *Spellbound* in which the Ingrid Bergman character is, among other things, the prime mover within the hermeneutic encodement of the first portion of the film. As in many Hitchcock films, the woman is significantly subjectivized through the play of point-of-view, radical close-ups and non-diegetic music. Bergman's Dr. Constance Peterson is marked by a progressive tension between her rational/scientific/male and intuitive/emotional/female selves. The more developed her "female" component becomes, the less control she exercises over the hermeneutic elaboration. The visual ingredients of the doctorly Constance Peterson (or Miss Frozenpuss, as one male colleague calls her), are familiar enough: the rimless glasses, the cigarette holder, the joyless countenance. Her work is accused of being "brilliant but lifeless . . . no intuition in it," while holding her is "rather like embracing a textbook." The thaw occurs with the appearance of a very needy Dr. Edwards (Gregory Peck). As their eyes meet, two major codes of romantic representation intervene: a swirl of strings in Miklos Rozsa's most extravagant style occurs on the sound track (the first such break with fully diegetic sound) while both characters are carefully eye-lit to underscore the shared intensity of the interlude. Immediately, Peterson begins to develop nurturing instincts towards Edwards, as during the latter's sudden swoon at the institute's communal dining table resulting from the tracing of a pattern on the tablecloth with a fork. If the signs of Peterson's "womanization" and growing vulnerability are not unequivocal, the blatancy of the "unlocking" metaphor that accompanies the first kiss insures that reading. As Edwards approaches and embraces her, we see images of door after door opening—an instance of extra-diegetic enunciation originating with the female, but one that serves a pointedly male position in its evocation of repression's end, a female "coming-into-being" through a long-overdue submission to the male embrace. The example illustrates a crucial point, that an unexamined cataloguing of the instances of "female" enunciation is of little value without the analysis of its function within the filmic system and, beyond that, within ideology, the site of the inscription of social meanings. In this case, female subjectivity is invoked and represented in order to mythologize that subject with heightened effect. Herein lies the implicit danger of the taxonomic impulse and the erection of discrete groupings based on the internal evidence of the text, for without an unremitting attention to the position and function of a given figure, such an enterprise lapses into a kind of reification that offers few rewards.

But if romance is the cure for Dr. Peterson ("the human glacier and the custodian of truth"), Edwards' cure is only effected through the agency of the fatherly mentor Professor Fleece. It is he who voices that most devastating of one-liners: "Women make the best psychoanalysts . . . until they fall in love. Then they make the best patients." While Peterson succumbs to a growing list of lovesick female symptoms (she is willing to sacrifice her career for the man she loves; she can't eat out of love and anxiety for the patient-turned-lover), Professor Fleece takes over the curative function. By the narrative's end, Peterson's own pathology, that of gender confusion, has been reversed, the transition from male to female evidenced by her pronouncement that "the mind isn't everything . . . the heart can see deeper sometimes." As for Edwards, he is encouraged by Fleece (a homonymic nod to Freud's own Fliess) to recall his own "primal scene"—his inadvertent role in the impalement of a brother in early childhood—and then to recall the details of a murder he observed but did not commit. The Professor, having announced with absolute certainty that "a woman in love is operating on the lowest level of the intellect," usurps the therapeutic role, reconstituting Peterson as a defrosted specimen of nurturing femininity. What enunciative authority is given the Bergman character is articulated as revelation of her concealed female self while her duties as knowledge-seeker and mainspring of the hermeneutic system, regarded as incompatible with her emergent love-struck persona, are placed in the hands of the paternal figure Fleece. As was the case in Hitchcock's *Notorious,* the centrism of the Bergman figure, an amalgam of sturdy beauty, rich inner resources and incipient vulnerability, is undercut by a restructuring of female self-sufficiency in favor of an idealized romantic union necessitating the woman's abdication of authority—over her fictional self and over the discursive regime.

In opposition to *Spellbound,* the films of this category are, for the most part, devoid of any traces of "female" enunciation. Instead, the fictionalized women contained within these texts are fully narrativized, placed within the constraints of formal conventions and of the "vraisemblable." Yet, there is a tension within many of these films, related perhaps to the relative instability within the social formation (confusion of sex roles, the speed and intransigence of social/familial displacement), which sustains a subversive element, at least within the context of female representation in the Hollywood film. In fact, the notion of subversion of or by a text is a problematic one (subversive to whom and under what conditions of spectatorship?), yet there is no denying the historical eccentricity of a film like *The Shocking Miss Pilgrim,* a Betty Grable film released in 1946 which celebrates female emancipation in the workplace within a nineteenth century setting. Why, at a time when American culture was energetically relocating its working women, would such a topic be deemed appropriate by Twentieth Century-Fox? The built-in "lag time" between story development and final release (often as much as twelve to eighteen months) might begin to explain the anomaly. The film was certainly an "A" production with Grable, a George Seaton script and direction, and music by the Gershwins. The appearance of *Pilgrim* in 1946, rather than 1944, no doubt bears witness to the oft-noted caution of studio decision-makers in matters of contemporary values—their dedication to hindsight over sponsorship. A brief analysis of the film suggests that whatever subversive elements may be deduced are aimed at the subtextual construction of an emergent woman. The marvel of such films as these lies precisely in the dexterity of their sleight-of-hand which first posits then deconstructs the self-sustaining female persona.

The Shocking Miss Pilgrim begins on a precise day (June 10, 1874) with a specific historical reference to 1874 as the year "women became free." This alleged freedom is connected to the invention of the typewriter, a machine which created new opportunities for female entry into the all-male preserve of business. June 10, 1874, is the first graduation day at Packard Business School and Miss Cynthia Pilgrim (Grable) is class valedictorian. Pilgrim has been placed with the Boston-based Pritchard Shipping Company, but, upon her arrival and the speedy realization of her womanhood by young John Pritchard (Dick Haymes), she is summarily dismissed. Pritchard is moved neither by Pilgrim's protestations of injustice nor by her pseudo-feminist ideals: "I don't care about the money . . . I just want a chance to prove to you that women are just as efficient as men." It is only when Aunt Alice, suffragette and company president, arrives on the scene that Cynthia is rehired.

Pilgrim is forced to confront, if only for a moment, one of the real problems of the forties working woman, that of housing. She finds a room among a Hollywood-perfect assortment of social misfits (a poet, a painter and a musician) who are alleged to survive by praising and purchasing each other's work. Meanwhile, Pilgrim attends her first suffrage meeting with Aunt Alice during which she takes part in an animated rendition of "Women Are People Too." The lyrics are a pointed reminder, if one should be tempted to forget, that the historical referents for the film are of World War II America, not Boston, 1874. While posing as an inspirational tune for the "right to vote" movement that was only just beginning to gain widespread support in the 1870s, the song clearly addresses the larger question of gender division and work roles, the quintessential World War II woman's topic. Note, in particular, the final verse:

"Women Are People Too"

Stand up and fight, we're in the right.
March out of the darkness, into the light.
We've been fed too long on sugar coating,
There's no reason why we can't be voting.

Land of the free, you've got to see
We're only requesting equality.
Like it or not men have got to take the view
That women are people too.

Why can't we be judges judging evildoers?
Why can't we be engineers and book reviewers?
Why can't we be chief commissioners of sewers?
Butchers, bakers, undertakers, next November
      Cabinet members . . .
Aren't women human beings?

The narrative winds down into matrimony, but not before Cynthia is presented to John's mother who, it so happens, is learning to type in her spare time. The women get along famously. Pritchard demands that Pilgrim quit work and the suffrage movement in order to become a true wife, whereupon she lustily demurs, leaving the company to organize Boston's first typing school for women. Sensing defeat, Pritchard agrees to moderate his old-fashioned ways so that, as the film concludes, male capitulation nominally replaces the submission of the woman to the marital bond (this despite Pilgrim's earlier declaration, "I have no intention of becoming anyone's chattel!").

With the narrative scheme thus elucidated, the film's "subversive" character can be evaluated for what it is—a sop, a masquerade in the grand tradition, enticing in order to retrench. By placing the conflict of work and romance at a safe historical remove, the film hedges its bets from the beginning. The ideologically loaded snares and half-truths that follow are familiar but they have a cutting edge: viz., the beautiful valedictorian is not interested in money, but in proving female efficiency; the all-male crew of artistic but non-productive housemates supports itself by exchanging capital; the Boston matron is oblivious to class difference, is, in fact, a closet secretary; and John Pritchard is willing to recant on all substantive issues in exchange for Cynthia's hand.

Pilgrim's statement, "I don't care about the money," is the expression of a brand of liberalism that applauds equality as an abstraction rather than as a struggle for "equal pay for work of equal value," a goal that eluded the wartime woman and continues to do so. The "proof of efficiency" stance can be seen as an early stage in the working woman's struggle and is certainly palatable in the 1874 context, but by 1946 such proofs were superfluous (and it is the 1946 woman who is being addressed). The artistic menagerie is an ideal foil for the productive aspirations of the working woman. People who choose to express themselves outside the mainstream bear an extrinsic relationship to the production of capital; this private circuit of exchange is an easy target, one that underscores the primacy of the industrial workplace and conventional productive relations. Given the film's simplistic choice of social categories, and the wartime mania for universal participation in the interest of full productivity, there is little doubt that Cynthia's "outsider" status (which is linked to self-sufficiency through the reductio ad absurdum of the household's autonomous economic cycle) is a brief and light-hearted one. Only delightful screwballs can afford to waste their productive capacities, while Pilgrim's pursuit of work and social integration (ultimately marriage) is depicted as a common-sensical response to her circumstances. Then, too, the aristocrat who recognizes no barriers of class background, status or aesthetic tastes is a fairy tale inversion of the Bostonian prototype that supports the "marry-the-boss" fiction which was, ironically, a frequent ingredient in the early woman-power campaigns. In this instance, the liaison between boss and typist is encouraged by a militantly feminist aunt and a sympathetic mother. The film's resolution fuses its idealized pretensions by offering Cynthia a rich husband, a pioneering position in the workplace and a support system of right-minded women. How can such a scenario have been received in 1946 by women whose labor rights had been so thoroughly and peremptorily abrogated? Even within a technicolor musical format, the shock of *The Shocking Miss Pilgrim* was reserved for those disillusioned Rosies whose own dreams of meaningful, well-paid work had been so recently shattered.

Quite an alternate elaboration of the "marry-the-boss" theme occurs in *Take a Letter, Darling* (1942) in which Rosalind Russell plays an advertising executive who requires the services of a male secretary. In a comic shift of terms, Russell's Ms. MacGregor (called "Mac" by her friends and business associates) is soliciting a particular kind of man for the job, one who can act as her after-hours escort ("Are you married . . . can you dance . . . how do you look in decent clothes—tails?") Indeed, the film plays upon the reversal of gendered polarities at a number of levels concurrently through a reshaping of the roles attached to the workplace, to the romantic discourse, even the regime of the look. Fred MacMurray is slightly miscast as Tom Verney, a rambling man in the Jack London tradition, who, having squandered his inherited income, has worked on a freighter, as a banker's bodyguard and as a professional football player. His appearance at the offices of Atwater and MacGregor Advertising Company creates quite a stir among the women workers. They unabashedly ogle the puzzled Verney, reversing the dynamic of gaze/object relations as conventionally depicted. When he hesitates at handing over his letter of introduction to Russell ("Wait a minute, this is for MacGregor, personally"), he is met with a curt reply: "I am MacGregor, personally." This initial scene between Russell and MacMurray is played for all its "squirm" value, as Verney is made to feel the object of a physical and impersonal appraisal of the type usually reserved for women ("Sit down, Bernie"—"That's Verney.") Although Verney passes the test, Mac makes the terms of employment very clear, the fundamental condition being the maintenance of employer/employee relations despite the personal nature of the job: "Four of your predecessors went out of here on their ears because their unusual duties gave them illusions of irresistibility." Whereupon Mac sends Verney off to buy a full suit of dress clothes at the finest men's store, an act that establishes a recurrent semic element attached to Verney. On a number of occasions, various characters assume that Verney is a "kept man," a presumption of female sexual dominion rooted in the material dependency of the male. At this point, it is clear that Mac is intent upon insuring her absolute authority over her hired man in every way. The slight hermeneutic development begun here is derived from the tension aroused in the spectator between the stipulated working relations and its reversed gender dynamic on the one hand, and our experience of male/female behavioral patterns (particularly within the Hollywood format) on the other.

In the early portion of the film, neither of the two characters occupies an unequivocal dominance within the narrative system (despite Mac's domination within the discourse of social power, it is unclear as to "whose film" this will be). Mac commandeers the narrative focus in the following segment of the film as she enters her partner Atwater's office wearing fur-lined bedroom slippers (a negation of dress codes forced upon working women and the reverse of her wardrobe demands towards Verney). We learn that eight years before she had been "the best secretary a guy ever had" and through her wits and charm had risen to the top—a female Horatio Alger. A particularly pertinent point of language is raised when, in response to Mac's frustration at the male hostility she inevitably encounters, Atwater explains that "they just don't know the difference between a woman and . . . ," to which hesitation, Mac replies, "What am I?" "I don't know," says Atwater, "they don't have a name for you yet." This is the moment of the film's richest polysemy, the point at which it attempts to represent the unrepresentable. Russell's character, already given the most masculine of names—Mac—is the site of a catachrestic failure of language. In fact, Mac, as here depicted, bore a concrete historical relationship to a small band of women executives whose lives and images were seldom represented within popular culture. What coverage they received was likely to focus on the loss of family and romance which, it was assumed, accompanied a high-level, man-threatening career. The inadequacy of language alluded to in this scene is best comprehended as a plumbing of the limits of the vraisemblable.

While Atwater has regressed to the level of a bored child in his partnership with MacGregor (he is forever tossing rings over stakes or playing with mechanized toys during work hours), Mac's take-charge attitude threatens to emasculate her "man Friday": "I don't feel honest; I don't even feel like a man," says Verney. (Interestingly, Mac's long-standing rejection of Atwater's romantic proposals and her assumption of the decision-making authority within the company produces a kind of infantilism. The woman's power to castrate is also the power to engender regression.) When Mac and Verney share a working weekend together at Mac's lakeside retreat, the local grocer remarks to his helper, "What kind of a man is that?" Verney's identity, his ability to be placed within the vernacular, is, like Mac's, rendered problematic by the reversal of conventional power relations. At last, Tom reveals a facet of himself, withheld until this point, that utterly restructures the interpersonal dynamic through his revelation that "I'm an artist, but I paint what I like." Moreover, he suggests to Mac that, although she doesn't know it, they are really very similar. Like her, he does as he pleases; unlike her, his satisfaction is not defined by the marketplace. He intends to head for Mexico to paint "soon as I get enough money for a jalopy."

At this point, the balance of power has begun to swing toward Verney, the creative, self-motivated loner who is only biding his time in a job which is no part of his true identity. Mac's reply verifies Verney's claim of kindred nature, for she reveals that she writes poetry. (Here again, a reversal occurs as the man elicits self-disclosure from the woman, inspiring the acknowledgment of the character's inner life.) The formula which dictates that the romantic couple share an unspoken linkage is thus fulfilled while the "unnatural" dominance of the female is effectively negated. The hermeneutic configuration, which is at this moment essentially resolved, has yet to run its course since Verney is not yet sufficiently assured of his status within the relationship. In his insecurity, he calls her "a beautiful brain in beautiful clothes . . . no temperature, no pulse"—a near equivalent to one male description of *Spellbound*'s Constance Peterson. Mac responds that she is every bit the romantic that he is, and if ever she falls in love, "it'll be the sea crashing against the rocks." The metaphor expresses the equilibrium sought throughout the film—the irresistible force and the immovable object—the collision of two equals. But it will become clear that the union of equals is itself unrepresentable in the idiom of forties Hollywood romance.[4]

The following portion of the film involves an alternation of induced jealousies with a gradual position of dominance developing for Verney. Despite the attentions of a wealthy and handsome client, Mac yearns for her secretary who has begun to avoid her with conspicuous regularity. One image neatly encapsulates the trajectory of the gender conflict: Verney asks Mac to pull off his boots with which she complies by straddling his leg for proper leverage. Verney places his other boot against her posterior and gives her a more-than-helpful shove. In a visual composition soon afterward, Mac is imaged between twin cupid statues, pinioned between marriage to Caldwell, an adoring millionaire who recognizes her autonomy, and an entanglement with a penniless artist who will have her only on his terms. In the final shot of the film, Verney is on his way south in the jalopy purchased with a portion of his bonus from the Caldwell deal (Bohemian accoutrements abound, including a weather-beaten guitar strewn across the back seat). Standing at the road's edge is Mac who has decided against marriage, wealth and the timid respect of an outclassed male in favor of the very outcast existence rejected by Cynthia Pilgrim (only here the spheres of artistic self-definition and romance are made to coincide). Thus, the role reversal is unhinged, the exnomination of the female terminated, through an idealized escape into uncharted terrain— foreign, capitally non-productive, beyond the confines of institutional life, even, perhaps, beyond marriage. But the concomitant of this escape is a return . . . to the standard position of female submission figured in the boot scene and by Mac's passive stance along the roadside. She is allowed to join Verney in *his* jalopy and *his* fantasy on *his* terms. The film certainly posits a trajectory of desire whose complexities and reversals are uniquely convoluted, but its ultimate destination is all too familiar: a reinscription of the status quo ante of gender relations.

As noted at the outset, the films of this grouping abound with female personae occupying positions outside the mainstream of life. Often they are renegades; more often, they are eccentric because of their work roles—as a taxi driver, a doctor, or a member of the military. The burgeoning of job opportunities, beyond the teacher/nurse/secretary cachet of the white collar sector or the textile/electrical/garment syndrome of the industrial workplace, is undeniably figured by the rainbow of female characterizations within this category of films.

The military women are particularly noteworthy because of the requisite militancy of their profession. Although service and self-sacrifice are the hallmarks of the female, collective action, rather than personal involvement, is scarcely a part of traditional female representations in American cinema. Groups of women, from D. W. Griffith on, were likely to be bands of censorious do-gooders or town gossips (*The New York Hat, Intolerance*). Male combat films have long heralded the melting-pot myth of American culture through a "one of each" method of casting—one Italian; one Jew (usually from Brooklyn); one farmboy; one college man; eventually, one racial minority. But the heterogeneity in *Ladies Courageous* is, for the most part, far outweighed by a homogeneity encouraged by the war crisis. These women are ex-stunt pilots, flying instructors and aerial performers who have joined the Women's Auxiliary Ferrying Squad to perform the mundane duties of domestic air transport so that men can be released for active duty. (Note that, even in active participation, female achievement is defined as ancillary to the male, the "woman behind the man behind the gun.")

What little variation is manifested within the female group in *Ladies Courageous* is related to personal motivation rather than external differences of ethnicity or mannerism. In this regard, *Courageous* offers an internalized view of a working unit that is also, in terms of the prevailing aesthetic ideology, a "feminized" one. The film includes its share of character demarcation through behavioral traits (one pilot is a dangerous show-off, another is vain, yet another suspects her husband's infidelity), but it is a series of flashbacks that most convincingly defines several of these women. The flashbacks are personalized versions of the *Why We Fight* theme so common to wartime culture. One woman is fighting for a young GI of her acquaintance who was traumatized during his months on Guadalcanal. Another reminisces in a more general way as she flies over her home town, contemplating, in the tradition of Capra's *War Comes to America,* the humble virtues of Americana worth dying for. The emotionalizing tactic of the film's narrative is thus overdetermined, connected both to conventions of female representation (subjectivized and personal) and to the cultural practices of patriotic sponsorship both documentary and fictional (cf. the serial structure of *Gangway for Tomorrow* whose successive flashbacks of male and female war workers en route to the factory constitute the entirety of the film).

The dramaturgical tension in *Ladies Courageous,* expressed in the minor flourishes of individual struggles, is a by-product of the defining conditions of military service. In the words of the Lt. Colonel (Loretta Young), "We all have to take a rain-check on the future." Each woman who climbs aboard her aircraft (whose names—"The Dutchess," "Classy Lassie"—speak to female wish-fulfillment rather than to the eroticized projections of the male pilot) is forced to subordinate personal dramas to the larger struggle. The real question posed by the film is whether or not women can be soldiers; if, in fact, they are capable of performing under pressure in a disciplined and controlled manner. In narrative terms, this conflict is problematized by a suspended question as to whether or not the women will be allowed to take part in the "Big Push" by delivering aircraft to a beleaguered overseas installation. The decision is to be issued by male command personnel and is complicated by such cogent asides as "Women who went flying around two hundred years ago were called witches." While an immediate obstacle arises in the person of a self-destructive pilot whose crash-landing calls the abilities of all into question, the problematic is a larger historical one. The ultimate accession to a greater role for these women is also a fictional recreation of the birth of the Women's Air Force service wing, a major breakthrough in the history of the American military and of the working woman. The final scene of the film is a documentary-looking montage of aircraft taking off, intercut with the proud, upturned faces of Loretta Young and Geraldine Fitzgerald. The knowledge that women are the unimaged pilots of these flying machines (produced through a kind of intellectual montage) renders this film a tribute to the small victories achieved by the American wartime woman.

Enunciation against the Grain

Dance, Girl, Dance (1940)
Star Spangled Rhythm (1942)
Priorities on Parade (1942)
Tender Comrade (1943)
Since You Went Away (1944)
Lifeboat (1944)

If the films of the previous category exhibit a subversive element, that element can best be understood as the capacity to challenge the hegemonic (that always contested terrain of dominant social beliefs) through limited representational assaults. But the implicit threat of these texts exists at the level of the signified, as representations straining against the dominant; the challenges posed are recuperable within the confines of the filmic system. For, given the fundamental resilience of the vraisemblable, the textual system establishes its discursive limits within an ideal domain which it marks off from the social field and whose effects it attempts to control. If Dr. Constance Peterson is characterized as a brilliant and beautiful woman who chooses to ignore the awkward advances of her male colleagues, her aloofness can be peremptorily shattered by a violent attraction to a man who needs her. The pattern by which she comes to offer her emotional rather than professional self (with the therapeutic function shifting to a fatherly mentor) is the result of careful craftsmanship which convinces as fiction. This patterning functions concurrently at the level of ideological discourse, overturning the resistance of one self-sustaining woman to the roles of support—as wife, mother and helper.

In like manner, each of the films of the ''Presence/Absence'' category proposes some variation of the female—as a site of meaning-production somewhere on the frontiers of female representation (woman as boss, woman as outlaw), and as a shaper of her environment rather than as an ornament within it. Yet these forays to the edges of the representable are cast in an arc of return—expanding, renaming, but at last fortifying the borders of the vraisemblable. These films are triumphs of "histoire" over "discours"—the tangible traces of female enunciation effaced in the service of the recuperative act.

The question then arises as to the distinction between the paired categories of this chapter: what precisely is at stake in the attribution of enunciative power to the female persona? And in what way does this limited discursive function affect the articulation of the film's ideological trajectory? In an essay entitled "The discursive and the ideological in film: Notes on the conditions of political intervention," Colin MacCabe examines the way in which discourses both produce and are produced from subject positions: "It is necessary to elaborate a non-subjective theory of enunciation able to grasp the institutional site of a particular set of articulations which produce specific subject-positions."[5] For MacCabe, it becomes crucial to analyze the specific effectivity of the discursive and its position in the elaborate play of imaginary and real forces which constitute any form of ideological practice. In this context, MacCabe cites the work of Michel Pecheux for whom the analysis of discourse is, precisely, an attempt to understand language and its organization into discursive formations in relation to the production of particular subject positions, while retaining a sense of the imbrication of these formations with political and ideological struggles. Given this usage of discourse, the claim that the female personae of these films wield a degree of enunciative power means that these characters, functioning as sites of coherence and identification for the spectator, particularly the female spectator, evidence a potency of affect which can only be comprehended through a concrete analysis of their constitution and position within the textual system. This, then, is the final level of analysis—the discursive, occurring within the textual system which is, in turn, inscribed within the larger spheres of history and ideology.

The link between enunciative power and subject-positioning is crucial for the present enterprise. Indeed, the scrupulous excavation of texts containing instances of woman-as-enunciator becomes a hollow exercise unless the spectator-connection is retained within the analytic process. Particularly at a time of destabilized self-concept within the women's community, it is important to examine the instances of textualized interpellation (the Althusserian term for the "hailing" function constitutive of all ideological practices, the movement through which ideology embroils the concrete individual within its domain, transforming individual into "subject"). The instances of female enunciation are privileged nodes of contact between text-as-ideology and woman-as-subject, for it is at these points that the text offers maximal entry via projection/identification to the female spectator. It is unclear at what level these bridges of connection were recognized or invoked. But if the degree of conscious intent is of little relevance to the present enterprise, the degree of control of the interpellative figure *is* a matter of critical concern.

Certainly, there is no intention of attaching an a priori meaning to these atypical elements of gender-specific signification. In one sense, discursive authority linked to the fictional female is simply a by-product of heightened interest in "women's issues" and a recognition within the film industry of a significantly female audience to be addressed. Yet these instances of specifically female address, isolated and sporadic as they may be, occasion considerable critical interest, even fascination, for the cogency of their appeal to the spectator.

The films under consideration most often exhibit extremely limited instances of female enunciation connected to the powers of imaging and address of a specific female character. This notion of discrete units of filmic articulation as site of spectator entry (gender-specific address to a female audience) is far removed from any version of the "woman's film" as a generic or global entity. Yet, these units are only discrete for purposes of identification. Forms of direct address to the female audience cannot be adequately assessed outside the play of signifying elements which traverse the specific text; such instances are, nevertheless, constituted by a materiality which survives the overarching play of recuperation achieved through the totality of the work. Despite the terms of narrative resolution and recovery, the marks of the enunciative process remain. That women were, in limited cases, endowed with the powers of speech indicates an enfranchisement within the institutionalized and patriarchal domain of the Hollywood cinema. That real women were, in fact, acknowledged as subjects of address within filmic discourse is an equally trenchant sign of the vigorous presence established by women during the war years.

A very conditional form of female enunciation occurs in Alfred Hitchcock's *Lifeboat,* linked primarily to the Tallulah Bankhead character's identity as a photographer and journalist. Although her Constance Porter character is directly involved in the tangle of events and inter-personal conflicts which transpire aboard the lifeboat, it is she who assumes the most externalized vision of the proceedings. At the very beginning of the film, her camera surveys the watery surroundings, establishing the locus of the drama within a space defined through its substantial absence. The male figure played by John Hodiak the ur-man, accidentally knocks her camera overboard, but it is clear that Connie Porter's power to frame space is also a power to analyze and to narrate, all of which threatens the elemental man.

It is Connie who keeps a log, who assumes the function of popular memory when visual recording is no longer possible. As a character, Connie is contoured along both traditional and "new woman" lines. She has been ambitious and single-minded in her climb from the "southside" to the top of the heap, yet she is vain and is angered by the loss of her cosmetics, and she is a romantic who passionately kisses a fellow traveler when the end seems near. But it is as the ironic narrator of the internecine struggles aboard ship, the metaphorized conflict between male types which figures the world conflict, that Connie's identity as Greek chorus and as woman become enmeshed. "And what now, little men," she says. Porter observes and is allowed to comment upon a process whereby rampant nationalism becomes linked to a more elemental conflict: that of the Nietzschean will-to-power definable in its male aggressivity.

Porter's responses to rescue contradict the potency of her enunciative function: first she cries, then she rushes to put on her make-up. Nevertheless, this female character is constructed through a play of countervailing positions, the bulk of which are recognizably typed, the "womanly" shifts from active to passive, for example. But Porter's occasionally external voice and eye offer the female spectator a unique if temporary point from which to survey the dramaturgy. The power of this position, although fleetingly experienced, is worthy of note as an embryonic instance of female enunciation.

A different sort of enunciative scheme is evidenced in *Star Spangled Rhythm*, a Paramount musical which showcases many of that studio's major talents. Although protagonist Betty Hutton is the unstoppable force behind the narrative flux, the real enunciative breakthroughs occur in two musical numbers, one performed by Hutton, the other by an all-female chorus. In the former number "Doin' It for Defense," Hutton addresses a jeepload of soldiers to whom her sexuality is proffered as patriotic gesture:

> Mr. Bones, get this right,
> I'm your date for tonight.
> For when I hold you tight,
> I'm doin' it for defense.
>
> Months and months, you've been drilled,
> Now it's time you were thrilled.
> Start from here, then we build,
> I'm doin' it for defense.
>
> If you touch my lips and you feel me respond
> It's just 'cause I can't afford a bond.
> If you think you're Cary Grant, brother relax,
> You're just a rebate on my income tax.
>
> Don't get hurt, don't get sore,
> I'm a pal, nothing more.
> This ain't love, this is war.
> I'm doin' it for defense.
>
> Once I start, I can't quit,
> I said I'd do my bit.
> So if I thought you're it,
> I'm doin' it for defense.
>
> Orders are for today,
> Just relax, come what may.
> Duty calls, I obey.
> I'm doin' it for defense.

Your morale needs building up
You must agree,
Your morale stays built
When it's built by me.

Put your face to starboard
And give us a kiss.
Heaven help a sailor
On a night like this.

Let's pretend how it tacks
Your defense mustn't crack.
This ain't war, it's murder, Jack.
I'm doin' it for defense.

The song is not directly pitched toward the female spectator. While its "I/you" syntax is intensified by the imperative mood ("Put your face to starboard and give us a kiss"), the orders are directed at the soldiers within the diegesis and in the audience (the film was a huge success among service audiences). Nevertheless, a determinate female subjectivity is established within the song which encourages a modicum of identification in the mass female audience ("If you think you're Cary Grant, brother relax; You're just a rebate on my income tax"). Interpellation, insofar as it exists here, operates through the beckoning power of shared experience; the first-person singular implies a plurality of voice. The fundamental drive of the song as ideological expression is toward the fusion of the twin thematics, war and sexuality, resulting in the representation of female sexual response as patriotic duty. The song is an extended double entendre which connects the much-promoted theme, the sacrifice of the American woman, to the servicing of the hard-working GI. The song is also a tongue-in-cheek disclaimer of emotional involvement or moral turpitude ("Duty calls, I obey").

The imagery which accompanies "Doin' It for Defense" underscores the sexual reading—Hutton is bumped and bounced about within the careening jeep, forcibly thrown from one lap to another in a parody of gang rape. At one point, she is ejected from the jeep altogether and gives chase on foot, while the vehicle itself repeatedly enters tunnels and swerves between the wheels of larger military vehicles. As the song builds its momentum, a succession of eccentric visual motifs are introduced. There are a myriad of oddly shaped wipes, fast motion photography and diagonal framing canted from both left and right. "Doin' It for Defense" is a song characterized by compression in which are fused a comic version of the female protagonist's motivation; the personalizing and sexualizing rationale for womanly patriotism; a declaration, at least implicitly, of the film industry's intentions to do what it can do best for the war effort (which is presumably to make films like *Star Spangled Rhythm*); and finally, this particular film's willingness to illustrate the extremes of a wartime "crisis" mentality through an eccentric alteration in its visual style—all in the name of defense, the war effort, the crisis moment.

This musical sequence makes it very clear that an enunciative function tied to a female voice, occurring at the level of the signifiers, does not insure a progressive or even "female" signified. It can be argued from the outset that "Doin' It for Defense" does not in fact constitute a bona fide case of female enunciation, that it only appears to assume a meta-discursive function external to the narrative but is essentially a catchy Tin Pan Alley tune mouthed by the female lead. On the other hand, analyses of relatively autonomous song lyrics have, on occasion, suggested the ways in which such extra-diegetic instances serve to narrate, even deconstruct, the ideological conflict center of the film, e.g., Charles Eckert's "Anatomy of a Proletarian Film."[6] The key to understanding the limitations of this particular song as enunciative figure lies in its rhetorical structure. By addressing itself not to the female but to the male audience, and by encouraging a rather mild form of gender identification among women, "Defense" fails to negotiate a female subjective position of significant durability or coherence in the manner discussed by MacCabe and Pecheux. The song's interpellative powers are insufficiently generated or expressed. Such is not the case in another of *Star Spangled Rhythm*'s tunes.

"On the Swing Shift," another of the Harold Arlen-Johnny Mercer collaborations, offers a far more complex study of the hailing authority embedded within the least assuming musical sequences. The entire lyric, with the notable exception of the last line, assumes a first person-autobiographical shape which conceals the urgency of the rhetorical appeal:

> Like some old tabbie who sleeps in the sun,
> I dream all day of the night that is done.
> Not that we frequent the same habitats . . .
> But in a way . . . I'm a cat.
>
> Life is fine with my baby on the swing shift,
> On the line, with my baby on the swing shift.
> Oh, it's the nuts, here among the nuts and bolts,
> Plus a hundred thousand volts shining from his eyes . . .
>   He's an interceptor.
>
> What care I if they put me on the wing shift,
> He's nearby in the fusilage.
> Overtime, here's why I'm doing it free,
> Baby's with me on the swing shift jamboree.
>
> Life is fine with my baby on the swing shift,
> On the line, with my baby on the swing shift.
> He's for me, he's the whole darn factory,
> He gets the love machinery working in my heart . . .
>   He's the beautiful bomber.
>
> What care I if they put me on the wing shift,
> He's nearby painting camouflage.

> Overtime, here's why I'm doing it free,
> Baby's with me on the swing shift jamboree.
>
> (*Repeat Chorus*)—*ADD:*
>
> Join us on the swing shift jamboree.

The interpellative energy of the number is produced in large measure through the seductiveness of the mise-en-scène. Glamour, romance and high-spirited camaraderie are all communicated through the choreography of high-kicking ingenues within a fluid performance space. The scene vigorously invites female projection through its blend of real and fantastic elements; the fictional workplace is recognizably endowed—with a space ("Eagle Aircraft Co"), tools (the chorus members wear screwdrivers and hammers at their belts), and the language of production ("nuts and bolts," "swing shift," "fusilage")—but transformed into an imaginary site through a structuring aesthetic. The symmetry of bodies and of objects, the kinetic appeal of choreographed movement (both of actors and of camera), the driving rhythms of the big band accompaniment: these are the seductive ingredients of the mise-en-scène. The invitation of the lyrical text offers further evidence of a constructed subjective position for the female spectator.

The song is performed by a succession of Paramount ingenues (including such starlets as Marjorie Reynolds and Betty Jane Rhodes). The first of these actresses, clad in satiny, two-piece pseudo-overalls, initiates a key strategy of the sequence—the displacement or shifting of terms from the natural sphere to the cultural. She sings, "but in a way . . . I'm a cat." This is doubly meaningful in that it explains her feline willingness to submit to the nocturnal rhythm of the swing shift while introducing the motif of the replacement of slang terms for "straight" ones. "Cat" becomes "(hep) cat," just as the "swing" of the square dance caller later in the sequence becomes the "swing" of the jitterbugging dancers. This new meaning of "swing" becomes attached to the term "swing shift," transforming that most unpopular eight-hour workshift into a sexualized and appealing "jamboree."

The square dance segment, which occurs near the mid-point of the number, is itself a conspicuous anomaly, with the sudden appearance of its participants utterly unmotivated. The men and women of this grouping are the human equivalents of the old tabbie cat from the first line of the song. They are the "natural" antecedents of the swinging workers, and are clad in the work clothes of pre-war occupations: denim overalls, the leather apron of the craftsman, the visored and gartered costumes of cashier and clerk, and, most significantly for the female spectator, the uniforms of the waitress and domestic servant. The rhythm of banjo and fiddle has homespun appeal, but when the square dance segues into energetic swing, there can be little doubt as to the intended sense of the sequence. The unrestrained movement of the jitterbugging workers is analogous to the new tempo of industrial production into which women entered. The pressures of wartime production quotas and the demanding work of the assembly line are meant to be counterbalanced by the elation of the new status and higher pay scales of the working woman. The rhythm of the musical routine is the new rhythm of life and *Star Spangled Rhythm* is the perfect appellation for a style of salesman-ship that is quintessentially Hollywood. A patriotic appeal becomes connected to foot-tapping, finger-snapping tunes that can perform a miraculous transmutation—from the stress of working and fighting rhythms to the celebra-tion of rhythm itself.

A temporary removal from the relentless energetics of "On the Swing Shift" allows several historical observations to be drawn. First, the call for women to the aircraft industry was necessitated by the loss of young, draftable manpower, the husbands and boyfriends who, in the song, are "nearby, painting camouflage." In fact, the eligible young men were more likely to be wearing camouflage. Second, employers preferred hiring women from twenty-five to forty who had dependents and were "stabilized" on that account.[7] Third, many factories discouraged the hiring of married couples for fear of diminished productivity, quite in contrast to the wholesale pairing in the sequence. Fourth, women were commonly rotated from night shift work every two to three months to avoid over-fatigue, since many women had daytime child care responsibilities and all did housework.[8] Indeed, recent government-sponsored research on the health con-sequences of shift work indicates that working unconventional hours presents "a distinct health hazard," causing a higher incidence of industrial accidents, clinic visits, alcohol use, digestive and sleep problems, as well as significant disturb-ances of mood and personality.[9] During the World War II years, the swing shift was the bane of the female workers' existence. Finally, and this was never ap-parent in the popular imagery of the day, many women workers were motivated by the need for wages as well as by patriotism. Even during the thirties, when women were castigated for stealing men's jobs, a sizeable percentage of the female work force was the primary source of family income.[10] The profile of the war-time woman worker that emerges from such statistics, when compared to the Para-mount imagery, begins to reveal the gap between fact and glamorized fiction.

With respect to visual style, the "Swing Shift" sequence may be said to resem-ble the mass formations of the Busby Berkeley musicals and, in a limited way, Fritz Lang's *Metropolis*. Several differences of mise-en-scène in connection with ideological function help to explain the divergent effects of *Star Spangled Rhythm*. In the case of the Berkeley films, the use of overhead camera angles, extreme long shots and sculptured lighting tended to emphasize formal aspects over mat-ters of literary content—pure shape, color or movement over the lyrics of the song. "On the Swing Shift" uses a majority of medium-long to full shots, with an emphasis on individual performers and the words they sing. A further distinc-tion results from posing the Berkeley visual strategy, characterized by an em-phasis on mass formations and kaleidoscopic effects, with that of the MGM musicals of the Arthur Freed unit. There, the camera rarely recedes beyond medium-long shot range, constantly reinforcing the relationship between the performers (Astaire, Charisse, Kelly) and their environment. The comparable proximity of camera to performer in *Star Spangled Rhythm* occurs for very different reasons. The performers in the sequence are largely of the anonymous Berkeley variety and the sequence is narratively autonomous so the camera is not drawn in out of deference to star power or for purposes of intensifying character identification. It is the primacy of the lyrics that controls camera placement in the sequence, for as each chorine takes a verse of the song, the camera moves in attentively. Here the ideological agenda overpowers formal or stylistic conventions so that the look of the sequence is dependent upon the posed content of the lyrics and its interpellative function.

As for the *Metropolis* connection, the ominous imagery of deadened workers changing shifts in the German film is apotheosized through the introduction of rhythmic movement and the highlighting of emotive faces. In brief, "Swing Shift" is an upbeat *Metropolis* whose infectious rhythms effectively contradict the vision of alienated labor that might otherwise be suggested. *Star Spangled Rhythm* combines a message-orientation with a rhythmic, promotional appeal for its audience. It glamorizes, modernizes, and legitimates a kind of work for women that had been virtually nonexistent only the year before. While it recasts the economic needs of black or minority, working class or middle-aged women into youthful, high-kicking frivolity, the film is effective popular culture in that it promptly responded to a radical alteration of American life, albeit in a characteristically undigested manner.

In terms of interpellative rhetoric, "On the Swing Shift" makes a direct appeal to the female viewer; the familiar strategy of the Hollywood product (entertain in order to inveigle) is accompanied by a far less common advocacy engendered by wartime priorities. The final line of the song ("Join us on the swing shift jamboree") constitutes the convergence of all preceding elements. "Join us, recognize us as yourselves"—this is the vital linkage of real and imaginary forces engaged in the process of subject positioning, a process which characterizes discursive formations in the manner defined previously. Here, female enunciation is appropriated in the service of the state. As we have already seen, the materiality of the female enunciative instance, while obviating the complete expropriation of the woman as presence or as voice, in no way insures against the recuperative powers of the ideological process. The power of enunciation *in* a text is radically distinct from the power to control the enonces *of* a text. And that power resides outside the textual system in the mode of aesthetic production itself and is hence a question of social power, a question to be broached elsewhere.

Priorities on Parade, another 1942 Paramount musical, narrates the shifting valence of wartime female identity by counterposing paradigms of female behavior and attitudes in the persons of the two female leads. The story of a swing combo that goes to work in a defense plant in order to entertain the workers but stays on instead to become workers, *Priorities* is a parable of the triumph of productive over non-productive forces during wartime. The band in question, the all-male Dixie Pixies, features a female vocalist-dancer (Ann Miller) who refuses to take employment in the factory under any circumstances. The anodyne bandleader Johnny Draper (Johnny Johnston), having more than a professional interest in D'Arcey, points out to Miller that "they've got a lot of useful jobs in there for women." But Donna D'Arcey (a name whose Gallic inflection connotes artistry and, by extension, nonproductive labor) is horrified that the band is willing to work on the assembly line and entertain the workers during their breaks. A hard-nosed professional whose jive language separates her from the industrial workplace while aligning her with the Hollywood showgirl tradition, D'Arcey splits from the band with the succinct reminder, "I coo for moo, remember?"

The other half of the film's female polarity is the androgynously labeled Lee Davis (Betty Rhodes) who is Draper's boss in the welding booth. Indeed, in his first outing as apprentice welder, the inept Draper endures considerable humiliation at the hands of his supervisor while remaining unaware of her womanhood. Davis refuses to allow her gender to subvert her authority: "In this welding booth, I happen to be the boss . . . *your* boss . . . and the boss of any other manpower mental midget they send in here. . . . As far as you're concerned, I'm *Mr.* Davis." Draper's first response is to impugn his new boss's femininity to his buddies: "To me, she's Biceps Bessy, Gargantua's sister, Minnie the Muscle, two yards wide and built like a barbeque pit."

But Lee's position is both diegetically and historically reinforced. Everywhere in the film are signs of production fever (a poster reads "Be a Worker"); in fact, 40 percent of the aircraft industry was female by 1944. Popular culture of the war years, as surveyed earlier, celebrated the oxymoronic shock of the female factory worker in such song titles as "The Lady at Lockheed," "We're the Janes Who Make the Planes," and "Rosie the Riveter" as well as in book titles such as *Wenches with Wrenches* and *Hit the Rivet, Sister*. Despite the range of difference of character and ideological perspective evinced within the film, Davis and Donna D'Arcey share a level of assertiveness and confidence in their work roles. At one point, Lee assails Draper with a rapid-fire manifesto: "Let me tell you something, all you men are alike . . . it frightens you to think that women have something on the ball besides an out curve . . . well, you better get over the notion that the hand that rocks the cradle can only knit a typewriter!" On various occasions during the course of the film, Davis shoves Draper, punches him in the face (three times) and breaks a vase over his head. The bandleader's romantic response is strong as he falls in love with this iconoclastic female: "You hit me over the head with a bowl and make me like it."

Donna D'Arcey's attitude toward her work is not automatically recognizable as an incorrect one since her narcissism and ambition conform to the canons of show business lore. Women with a drive to succeed, however, are far less likely to be glamorized than their male counterparts (e.g., *The Hard Way, Old Acquaintance, Mildred Pierce*), especially when they lay aside romantic concerns for those of a career, as in D'Arcey's admonition: ''You know me, Johnny . . . I want to go places, with you if you're around. I've just gotta climb.'' Extrapolating from the ideological domain of the period, one can surmise that the hard edge of D'Arcey's statement serves to discourage strong identification for the female spectator. That process is reinforced by D'Arcey's cruel treatment of Davis when she unexpectedly introduces the latter in the midst of her cabaret act. ''I'd like you to meet a person who illustrates what can happen if you eat all your vitamins and spinach,'' says D'Arcey, while proclaiming Lee ''Club Martel's Freak of the Week'' to the strains of ''For He's A Jolly Good Fellow.'' Davis has already proved her mettle in word and deed; she can sing like a nightingale and talk like a hipster (''Yeah, sound homicide, right from the jive hive. Say, what did you think I was, a square from Delaware?''). She is called upon to justify herself and her less than familiar identity once again.

It is at this point in the film that the interpellative energetics commence in earnest. Up to this point, two attractive women have been presented who share an interest in a man and a strength of purpose in their metiers, but who are distinguishable by the degree of social connectedness of their work. D'Arcey is cynical and self-motivated, while Davis emerges as an enthusiastic booster for a unified war effort in the manner of government promotionals. The film's intent at this key juncture is to underscore the correctness of Lee's social stance, to vindicate her womanhood and to encourage active identification in the female spectator. Refusing to allow D'Arcey's comments to place her on the defensive, Davis promptly accedes to Donna's description of her working identity, adding: ''As a matter of fact, there are quite a lot of us and there's gonna be a lot more.'' In a forceful speech shot in medium close-up, Davis takes the offensive: ''Of course, if one of my brothers wasn't in the Air Corps and another in the Navy, why they might be doing this welding job instead of me . . . I know it sounds funny . . . women riveters, women welders, women metal stampers, women ambulance drivers and, believe it or not, we even have women mothers . . . we can do everything.''

At this point, a significant rupture of the visual codes of classical cinema occurs. The fiction film is identifiable as a discourse which effaces the marks of its enunciation so that it seems to be a story with no perceivable source of elaboration. One strongly encoded element of the classical cinema thus concerns the denial of the apparatus. But the Lee Davis character, in a gesture which is both diegetic and metadiscursive (her address is directed both to the inscribed audience and the spectator), delivers a one-sentence message directly to the camera: ''But it's getting to be the smart thing to do for girls to get in there and pitch too, whatever way they can.'' During the remainder of the shot, both before and after this statement, Davis speaks with her face at an acute angle to the camera. The turn of her head and the frontal gaze thus produced establishes the urgency of the rhetorical position while fracturing a standard rule of Hollywood film practice. The ideological domain, produced within the context of social crisis, intrudes upon and radically alters the formal structure of the film. What is at stake is the active recruitment of the female spectator and a reinforcement of that spectator's social investment in the spectacle unfolding before her. This visual and rhetorical figure can thus be considered as an intervention, a moment of female enunciation which seeks to restructure the relationship of spectator to text and to the social system represented by the text. The urgency of the interpellative gesture risks shattering the delicate balance of real and imaginary forces which support the concurrent belief and disbelief in the fictional construct. For the pitch is only as effective as the projection/introjection complex which ties the audience to the protagonist and the maintenance of that preconscious state is threatened by the isolated moment of didacticism. Such a risk is rarely undertaken in Hollywood cinema; historical conditions overruled the usual caution. This segment of the film, then, brief and anomalous though it may be, is the visible manifestation of Paramount's wartime agenda, its own priorities on parade.

A considerable amount of critical attention has been given to the direct address of female characters in Hollywood cinema.[11] One dramatic and theoretically engaging instance occurs toward the end of Dorothy Arzner's *Dance, Girl, Dance* when the Maureen O'Hara character, fed up with playing a vaudevillian stooge for the titillation of a jeering male audience, comes out from behind the curtain to make reply and to redirect the camera's gaze (the scene includes both a slow pan from the protagonist's point-of-view across the now silent audience and a frontally composed medium close-up of the impassioned O'Hara as she berates her audience):

> I know you want me to tear my clothes off so's you can look your 50 cents worth . . . 50 cents for the privilege of staring at a girl the way your wives won't let you. . . . what's it for . . . so's you can go home when the show's over and strut before your wives and sweethearts and play at being the stronger sex for a minute. I'm sure they see through you just like we do.

The speech is startling in its direct address to the inchoate voyeurism and fetishization of the female body inscribed in spectacle and performance, applicable both to theater and film. The wonder of the scene is that an assault on film spectatorship can at once be so smoothly narrativized and so boldly figured. Of course, much of the attention given this scene relates to the recent theoretical work done on visual pleasure, the scopic drive as related to cinema, and the complex structuring of the gaze as an organizing principle of film texts.

There are, however, important distinctions related to the ideological effects of female enunciation which ought to be made between the instances of direct address in *Dance, Girl, Dance* and *Priorities on Parade* and among similar figures occurring elsewhere. In *Dance*, a *female* enunciator (Arzner) produces a moment of specifically female enunciation through direct address aimed at a *male* audience. The return of the gaze is defiant, oppositional, consciously alienating. The concurrent dialogue reinforces the sense of power reversal; the frontal composition of the direct address demands its opposite visual figure—the point-of-view pan of the theater audience. In *Priorities*, a *male* enunciator (Albert S. Rogell/Paramount) produces an instance of direct female address aimed at the *female* audience. As an interpellative trope, it is conciliatory, invitational, an attempt to bridge the subject/object gap rather than expose or critique it. In contrast to the standard accounts of direct address in the fiction film as innately self-referential and distancing, here the return of the gaze produces an increased urgency of communication closely aligned with the non-fictional film of persuasion. There is no point-of-view shot to heighten the subjectivity attributed to the speaker, for the emphasis is being thrown back upon the viewer; introjection forcefully displaces projection.

Female enunciation occurs in a variety of modes in the 1943 RKO release *Tender Comrade,* a consciously progressive dramatization of the plight of the "lonely wife," the woman left alone to fight the war on the home front, a film whose social advocacy is attributable in part to the left-of-center politics of director Edward Dmytryk and screenwriter Dalton Trumbo. A dedicational verse by Robert Louis Stevenson opens the film:

"To My Wife"

Teacher, Tender Comrade, Wife,
A fellow-farer true through life,
Heart-whole and soul-free
The August Father
Gave to me.

These lines introduce a regime of intersubjective address based upon a play of absence and presence which is a crucial component of the film's narrative structure. Although all human exchanges, including speech, gesture and writing, are constituted through an elaboration of auditory, tactile and visual cues or traces of always already absent referents of thought or emotion and all representational forms are, in an absolute sense, defined through the absence of that which is represented, an unusually high proportion of the key enunciative instances in *Tender Comrade* are, like the Stevenson verse, addressed to an absent party. This condition of enunciation is certainly consistent with the prevailing circumstances of a 1943 America in which absences and separations were being felt most keenly. The flashback, for example, a formal device quite in evidence in wartime films, can be seen as a kind of spatio-temporal recovery which is often an involuntary communication between the present-tense subject and his/her past-tense

Since You Went Away (Selznick/United Artists, 1944)
Ann Hilton (Claudette Colbert) communes with her absent husband Tim through the smell and feel of the garment left behind. Here, as in many wartime melodramas, the male structures discourse even in his absence.

self—a form of internal address. Another variant of absent address is the letter or telegram either read aloud, narrated on the soundtrack or graphically displayed. Yet another instance is the address of one person to another who is the substitute for a third, a process in which paired participants are but nominally present; the true recipient of the address is absent.

A film such as *Since You Went Away,* a 1944 Selznick production, is a notable example of this absent-address format. in its representational strategy, it remains surprisingly faithful to the Margaret Buell Wilder book which is a succession of letters to an absent husband. Much of the book's formal allure, as with other such epistolary works since Samuel Richardson's *Clarissa,* arises from the readerly interpolation required to compensate for the inequality of knowledge between reader and writer. For although the actual letters of reply never appear, each successive inscription incorporates and alludes to the unseen responses. A filmic flashback would violate such a unidirectional flow and elliptical strategy. *Since You Went Away* offers a panoply of instances of absent address via telegrams, the imaging of significant objects (photographs, a garment, a treasured pipe or chair) through which communion is achieved with their absent owner, and the anthropomorphizing of and direct address to the bulldog Soda, the remaining male presence in the female household. The intermittent voice-over narration by the female protagonist controls and modulates the narrative, addressing itself to the absent husband while in fact addressing the audience (which becomes a kind of surrogate narratee, to use the term adopted by Seymour Chatman in *Story and Discourse).* [12]

Many of the forms of enunciation-in-absence surveyed here occur in *Tender Comrade;* all are connected to the female protagonist Jo, played by Ginger Rogers. Indeed, the film is one of the richest of wartime texts in its elaboration both of left-liberal social values (for which its makers suffered a short time later) and of strategies for recasting monologue into a myriad of narrative shapes. For these exchanges-in-absence are, in the final analysis, monologues: internalized communications that resist the cinematic verities of a proairetic, action-oriented format.

The notion of communication-in-absence is inaugurated in an opening scene by Jo's husband Chris (Robert Ryan). With only a few hours remaining before he is to be shipped overseas, Chris tells his wife: "No matter how tough things are . . . no matter how bad they seem, all I'll have to do is think of you and I'll come through." This scene establishes the potency attributed even to the most intransitive mode of connection between the romantic couple, that which is constructed entirely within the mind. This interlude occurs in present time and, with a single brief exception, is the last such encounter between them; their microcosm is destroyed by the conditions of war. From this point on, the hermetic domain of the couple can only be reconstructed through memory or projected in absence. This physical restriction, in turn, allows for the creation of a unique reformulation of the microcosm within Hollywood terms, as Jo turns to other women for the support of a family structure. Moreover, the communal arrangement formed among five GI wives serves to mediate between the usually distinct levels of private and public (both in terms of spatial orientation and thematic concerns). For here the conflicts of the individual become collectivized so that personal dramas are placed within a social/historical frame. Jo jokingly refers to the all-female household as a union local, "War Widows #37." In terms of the conventions of the Hollywood romance, *Tender Comrade* is a rare species indeed, a nonhermetic melodrama in which the interactions of the romantic couple are structured in absence.

Dramaturgically, the film can be termed nonhermetic because of the parity of the group dynamic with that of the couple, the equal weight given to shared experience and internalized emotion (a household discussion may occur in contiguity with one of Jo's flashbacks), and the recasting of privatized space (characteristically, the house as refuge from external forces) into collective space (again, a house, but one in which five overlapping dramatic perspectives coexist). *Tender Comrade* offers a rare spectacle—five women engaged in an experiment in collective living. In an early scene, Jo and three of her co-workers at the Douglas Aircraft factory decide to rent a big house and share one car instead of each having a little "rabbit hutch" and wearing out separate sets of tires. They place an ad for a fifth woman:

WANTED—Woman to cook and keep house
for four women employed in war plant until
husbands' return from the service. Apply
957 W. Adams after 4:30 p.m.

The woman who responds to the ad—of German extraction whose husband is
also in the service—performs all household chores while sharing equally in the
pooled surplus produced by the other four (that which remains after the rent,
food costs, and general expenses are met). The system they create for themselves
is extrinsic to the categories of capital; within the household, value is determined
by human labor power rather than through its rate of exchange in the money form.
(This is a collectivist rather than a utopian counter-economy of the sort mock-
ingly portrayed in *The Shocking Miss Pilgrim*.) The house becomes a space whose
character is generated and defined through a process which is both collective and
female and is thus an amalgam of micro- and macrocosms (a *social* space defined through its *autonomy* from the dominant mode), offering a workable lifestyle
alternative while adhering to the realities of wartime service. That these women
are "war widows," factory workers, solid citizens who grapple over the problems of rationing and conservation confers upon them the requisite validation
to counterbalance the naively oppositional social system they create. This cautious
approach to a socialist practice was in keeping with the strategies of the left in
Hollywood and elsewhere throughout the war years. Superpatriotism and staunch
Americanism were the safeguards of the left which were to prove woefully inadequate protection during the purges which lay ahead.

If the house is a collective space, it is also a specifically female one. In the
discussion of house rules that occurs, the suggestion is made to avoid old patterns of behavior, "like having a bunch of smelly old men around the house."
Of course, there is a degree of equivocation on this point, evidenced by the exchange between Jo and Doris (Kim Hunter). "Gee, aren't men fools?" says Jo.
"Um hmm," replies Doris dreamily. "But aren't they sweet?" adds Doris. "Um
hmm," replies Jo with an equally far-away look in her eyes. But the real intrusion of the male occurs in two ways linked to Jo's imaginary processes—through
flashbacks to important moments in her life with Chris, and through her interactions with her newborn son, Christopher Latham Jones, Jr., who becomes the
husband surrogate. With regard to the structuring of the discursive regime, both
forms of male intrusion in the house are constituted through a play of
presence-in-absence.

Jo's first flashback occurs as she prepares for bed in the new house for the
very first time. Embarking as she is on a new lifestyle, Jo returns to a prior moment of redirected choices (Chris' marriage proposal and the discussion that accompanied her acceptance). In fact, each flashback is built around an issue held
in conflict between the romantic couple. When in the first memory sequence Chris
pops the question, Jo makes it clear that certain of Chris' prototypical male traits,

such as his identity as a "strong, silent type," endanger the relationship by forcing her to emote for both of them: "With a tight-mouthed clam like you, (a woman's) never safe." Chris predictably tells Jo to shut up and give a one-word reply, the implication being that her substantive criticism is nervous female chatter.

The next flashback is triggered by a radio report listing one of the other husbands missing in action during the Battle of Midway. As in each memory sequence, the flashback is introduced by a long shot of Jo and Chris in partial silhouette approaching each other on a hilltop with most of the frame occupied by sky and clouds; the music is ethereal. Jo recalls a confrontation with Chris, whose apparent banality during this moment of emotional distress in present time is belied by the seriousness of the sexual-political critique it suggests. Chris has just complained of no buttons on his shirt and Jo's frustrations with the thanklessness of female domestic labor boil over: "Now I know what you wanted me for in the first place," says Jo. "Me, I'm just a cheap substitute for a housekeeper. All you want is someone to work and slave and scrub and cook and clean the house and dust the furniture and lay out your clothes and scrub the bathtub . . . and then sit with her hands folded in the evening and watch you read." When Chris justifies his irritability by the overtime he's working to help provide for Jo after he ships out, as though she is incapable of taking care of herself, Jo's reply is terse: "Don't give me that Horatio Alger 'woman-on-a-pedestal' baloney." Her demand is clear: either he spends the evenings with her so that she can enjoy his companionship while she can or she gets a job herself to make the money he wants for her. Again, the memory sequence bridges the gap between private experience, the realm of melodrama enacted through personal dramas, and the larger social fabric by raising questions of shared experience whose historical referents must have been clear for a contemporary audience. Certainly, open discussions of sex roles, of employment options for women or of male behavioral traits—all initiated by women—were encouraged by the enhanced economic power and social status of the American wartime woman. *Tender Comrade*'s uncharacteristic recourse to collective experience over private passions marks it as a film produced within a specific conjuncture, the "popular front" period of the American left during the years of the Soviet-American wartime alliance.

The notion of communication-in-absence between Jo and her absent husband is closely tied to the birth of Chris Jr. with whom Jo carries on continuing conversations. The child's position within the discourse of the family is twofold; he both holds the place of the father *for* the father—through his name and his physicality (Jo's maternal embrace is overdetermined by the blurred father-son distinction)—and holds the place of the father *for himself.* In the final moments of the film, Jo speaks to her child of his Dad: "He never made speeches . . . but he went out and died so that you could have a better break than he had when you grow up. . . . He died for a good thing . . . don't let them swindle you out of the world your Dad bought for you with his life.'' Here, Jo speaks to the man-her-son-will-be. Once again, the address is constructed in absence but with a future temporality replacing the more common past time frame. For, unlike flashbacks or the imaging of objects which retain past significance (as in *Since You Went Away*), the rhetoric of this address structure is future conditional.

It is absolutely crucial that Jo's offspring be male rather than female for a variety of reasons whose ideological resonance extends well beyond the film text to the culture at large. Intratextually, the birth of a son ruptures the exclusively female space of the house, proposing a resolution to the threat of the autonomous, co-equal female which is, literally, an imminent one; the process whereby the male is resurrected from the body of the female re-establishes the figure of woman-as-nurturer, the female yoked in biological service to the male. Chris Jr.'s birth constitutes a regeneration which is both material and spiritual—the replication of the species as work force, military supply, erotic object and mate. The male principle interposes itself within *Tender Comrade*'s female domain in other ways as well.

The mother/son configuration of the film's conclusion is also a formal one whose power is derived from its liturgical iconographic antecedents as well as from contemporary public imagery. The graphics of a United States Rubber Company ad appearing in *Life* magazine on 21 December 1942, bear a striking resemblance to the *Tender Comrade* composition, while the verse accompanying the ad features a similar rhetorical and ideological structure. The advertising image bespeaks the absent address mode in its pairing of a contemporarily coiffed mother, her eyes gazing up and out of frame right, her perfect lips set in resolution, one foreshortened hand securing the baby's blankets, and an androgynous infant, well-swaddled, gazing out of frame left, its face and head bathed in ethereal light. The verse, though nominally addressed to the child, begins with the bold-faced words YOUR FATHER—the invocation to the male who controls the female and her discourse through his absence.

> YOUR FATHER will not be here for this, your first
> Christmas.
> The war has taken him far away from us, but his love warms
>   our family hearth.
> You are the son of a man whose principles are his strength.
> He has gone to war for those principles. He has taken up
>   arms against evil.
> His faith is our faith. His strength is our strength.
>
> When he went away, I thought I should not survive. I have
>   survived and grown strong.
> The long months of not knowing where he was, were the
>   months of my greatest trial.
> New strength came to me.

Tender Comrade (RKO, 1943)
The male principle intrudes even within *Tender Comrade*'s female domain. The photographed image of the absent husband splits the spatial continuity of the two women.

The war drove us from our first home. I found strength in
   that small hardship.
I have tended you through all the hours of your days. I
   have grown strong with the tending.
I have scrubbed for you all the weeks of your life as I
   had never thought to scrub for a mortal soul.
I have scrimped and saved so that each day's pennies could
   add their might to winning the war.

Now we two are about to celebrate our first family Christmas
   though your father will not be here.
We have loaned him to America.
We have loaned him to the America you, too, will grow up
   to love.
We have loaned him, so that in the years to come, young
   mothers everywhere, on Christmas day, shall be
   able to say "Merry Christmas" to their sons.

The absent father is defined by unassailable abstractions—love, warmth, strength,
and faith—which the woman borrows for the duration. For her part, the mother
offers hours of personal service, tending, scrubbing, scrimping and saving. Sexual difference is here an outright distinction of class based on opposing forms
of labor: moral/spiritual for men, servile for women.

Unquestionably, the wartime experience produced conditions which rendered
the American woman a far more vocal and visible participant in the social affairs
of the nation. It is important, however, when assessing the character and potency
of female enunciation in the Hollywood film, to recognize the limits of authority
available to the woman within the dominant forms of culture. Even in a film such
as *Tender Comrade,* which became a cause celebre for its celebration of collective female values, self-expression and autonomy for the woman are contained
and recuperated. As in the United States Rubber ad, the woman as centrally framed
representational form and as enunciative source can be dispossessed by recourse
to the intransigent values of the patriarchal domain. The woman's presence, boldly
and brightly figured as it may be, can be displaced even by the male's absence.

Conclusion

I have attempted in these pages to propose a critical itinerary for the study of a group of Hollywood films, one which combines historical inquiry with textual analysis. I have viewed this joining of critical discourses as a methodological necessity insofar as a study of historical/ideological determinancy within a text demands both historiographical and analytical expertise; one must have both a theory of history and of the text before their interplay can be understood. Moreover, these two areas of critical focus seem to me to be inseparable, the historical approach restoring the dimension of process and dynamic to the estimable advances of semiotic and deconstructionist inquiry.

As for my own claims in the present instance, I would suggest a two-fold contribution. I have, on the one hand, constructed a sound framework for the analysis of female representation in Hollywood's World War II cinema. I speak of a "framework" in the sense of a theoretical model for continuing analysis. I have argued for the necessity of a particular critical agenda for the study of popular culture, one which recognizes the levels of mediation between human experience and cultural product. As a result, the regions of history and ideology have been surveyed here in some detail as a prerequisite for the study of a body of films. Rather than claiming to have produced the definitive readings of specific films of the war years or to have erected the most unassailable categories for grouping these films, I have offered the reading and the groupings *most consistent* with the historical and ideological material and with the categories of critical thought constructed over the past fifteen or so years of feminist film criticism.

My intent has been to mobilize readings in which more or less self-contained processes of meaning are placed in a significantly elaborated social context. In his widely influential study of textuality and narrative, *S/Z,* Roland Barthes chose to isolate the Referential Code as one source of meaning in all fictions. I have attempted to enliven and expand this regime of social reference which, in fact, intervenes at every level of critical inquiry. I suggest that each of Barthes' master codes (the five interwoven voices of the text that produce the fabric of narrative) contains an explicitly historical dimension. The Hermeneutic Code, for instance, devoted to the elaboration and resolution of enigmas which drive the narrative forward, is in part determined by the kinds of questions which *can* be asked within a culture at a particular historical juncture. As for the cinema, formal elements—conventions of acting and expression, lighting codes, fashion—which are the plastic materials used by the filmmaker, demand their own historical placement. I have therefore attempted to open up the very notion of context to account for the richness and complexity of historical determinancy.

The work contained herein has done more than carry out the claims of its theoretical assumptions, however, for along the way a number of quite specific areas of historical and theoretical interest have been illuminated. These more specific findings constitute the second aspect of this study's yield. The very structure of the three specifically historical chapters and the sharpening of focus from the general to the particular has enabled the reader to place the film industry within a larger framework—as a major employer and a vital industry, as the object of concerted government interest, as the source of promotional and morale-building entertainment, as a key outlet and site of identification for working women. The charting of the many-faceted character of Hollywood as social institution provides the material basis for determining the range of social meanings generated in any given text produced within that institution.

Another historical note of some interest has been the discovery of contradictions and inconsistencies in the literature covering the period (here, I refer to secondary as well as primary sources). How many women entered the work force during World War II?; what percentage of female war workers were employed prior to Pearl Harbor?; was independent film production encouraged or savaged by war conditions?; did "B" film production increase?; what, in fact, constitutes a "B" film during the war years? These and other enigmas serve notice that history resists pat formulations and that historical discourse is ever in need of concerted self-examination.

The chapter on ideology and propaganda aimed at an intervention of a specific kind: to come to grips with the defining conditions for both terms and to examine the heightened intensity of persuasion of the wartime Hollywood film. The term "interpellative urgency" was coined as a key to the analysis of the persuasive component of any social message. The greater the urgency, the more energetically "hailed" the recipient, the more likely the appellation "propaganda," even for entertainment forms. The degree of interpellative urgency is ascertainable through reference both to its historical grounding and its mode of expression—the formal conditions of its presentation. Once again, the regions of historical and textual analysis coincide.

As for the films themselves and the analyses undertaken in the final section, I have, in a number of cases, avoided extended examination of the best known, previously analyzed texts. Or, if the much-discussed film has been examined, I have attempted to shed new light on it by foregrounding its relations to particular ideological currents or to other, less available films which rework the problematics of the original text. The textual category which produces the most speculative analysis, appearing in chapter seven ("Enunciation Against the Grain"), examines the linkage between woman as thematic focus and woman as source of enunciation. But for each of the groupings, the analysis attains its specificity and clarity only through reference to the historical/ideological ground-work assembled in previous sections.

My general approach to grouping the texts has stressed the multiplicity and variety of the films and their implications. Although I have been concerned to uncover the didacticism and sponsorship of war aims that motivated so many of these films, I have been equally intent on the level of resistance evidenced within them, resistance to unified or coherent social messages for or about women. The categories, in their variation, examine the levels of conflict and contradiction within a body of Hollywood films even in the most univocal historical moment, two years of war mobilization. The contradictions are evidenced among films (the categories are themselves specific sites of contradiction); likewise, the individual text has been seen as a ground of warring messages.

Certain of the films, particularly those of the "Family Melodrama" and "Moral Tales" categories continue the investigation of ideological directives begun in chapter four. The seductions and proscriptions evidenced in these films are played out in moral terms in the tradition of the melodrama with its insistence on charged emotion and intense dramatic reversals. The ethical judgments of these films, placed in an intertextual frame, are rendered historically explicit. The fairy tale of a European monarch's romantic entanglements in *The Princess O'Rourke* thus emerges as a parable rooted both in myth and in a quite specific 1943 world, while *Meet Me in St. Louis* speaks both to the conflicts of modernity for a turn-of-the-century midwest family and to the desire of a 1944 audience to re-experience the relative stability of the family-based conflict amidst the entropy of war.

Certain categories aim at cross-referencing a particular, thematized "female" characteristic, such as the "Inscrutable Female." Here, the range of inscrutability attached to the female persona becomes a measure of the bewilderment registered by the predominantly male culture in the face of the visible, participating woman. "Woman: Object of the Look" is more directly addressed to a single theoretical question raised by feminist critics, that of the fetishization of the female form. The films of this grouping provide visually explicit instances of the female as externalized and unknowable, the status of all the personae of the categories comprising chapter 6. The pin-up presents the female-as-spectacle in purest form, as "instant furlough" for the embattled soldier class.

Representational as well as enunciative modalities of female personae have been examined in some detail. Disc jockeys and welders, journalists and combat nurses, long-suffering mothers and martyrs have been found to be the diegetic focus and, less frequently, the discursive mainspring of the text. I have attempted to assess the breadth and tenor of female potential which entered into the cultural vernacular through these films while suggesting areas of continuity and discontinuity both with contemporary public imagery and with lived experience. Such an undertaking attempts to gauge the effects of these films, effects judged to be textual (i.e., instances of direct address) as well as socially experienced (the latter responses ranging from hairstyles and fashion trends to the more hypothetical and internalized reaction formations which may help us to understand the postwar female psyche).

I emerge from this work with no unyielding truisms about the character of wartime Hollywood. I have resisted seizing upon the war years as a moment of outright discontinuity, although the exceptional conditions of the period tempt one to do so. I have insisted instead upon a theory of variable relations between the industry and state power and on a mutual interpenetration and determinacy of cultural expression and milieu. What limited observations I have made with regard to the period have been carefully considered; for example, the location of the roots of film noir's "evil woman" in the crisis of female self-image produced by sudden adulation and its reversal at war's end.

My hope is that the work begun here can be used as a basis for further study by those who share my theoretical assumptions and scholarly concerns. I have come to the World War II years with an interest in understanding contemporary events and, in particular, the unsteady course of self-fulfillment achieved by the American woman. I emerge from this work with a fuller comprehension of how cultural expressions borrow shape and substance from human experience and of how, unfairly or not, they come to bear the stamp of history. At the same time, I have discovered how arduous can be the task of recovering a more complete range of meaning than that stamp of history would seem to bear.

It would, however, be disingenuous to suggest that this book was motivated only or even primarily by the desire to understand in more detail the relationship between cultural production and its conditions of existence in any abstract way. If the choice of the war years was intended as a way to examine that moment when relative autonomy for the cultural sphere was most challenged, the focus on female representation was an equally calculated strategy. As Patricia Mellencamp avers in a recent essay on video artist Cecelia Condit, "feminism is . . . in this dazed silence of 1986 . . . the only political, theoretically lively game in town."[1] The decision to cast the textual categories in the shape of prevailing feminist critical models—to attempt to offer support and challenge to particular theoretical premises through reference to a broad range of often lesser-known film works—results from my perception that these debates, far from being moribund, remain crucial for theories of culture.

I am somewhat less reassured as to the place of the male critic in this context of feminism. Stephen Heath begins his reflections on "Male Feminism" with a daunting pronouncement: "Men's relation to feminism is an impossible one."[2] If Heath is right, if the male desire to be a subject "in feminism" is "only the last feint in the long history of (woman's) colonization," the only appropriate response is silence. The book that precedes these reflections retains a strong and abiding relationship to feminist scholarship while choosing not to occupy a position squarely within feminist discourse. Rather, this is a work of cultural theory and criticism that presents concrete historical inquiry and a range of textual analyses that may be of use in the ongoing project of feminist scholarship.

Perhaps the most optimistic—and sensible—position that can be adopted in this regard is the one Heath borrows from Luce Irigaray to end his essay. Irigaray's answer to the problem of male/female coexistence under the shared tyranny of a patriarchal order is the cultivation of that which "has never existed between the sexes. Admiration keeping the two sexes unsubstitutable in the fact of their difference. Maintaining a free and engaging space between them, a possibility of separation and alliance."[3] It is in that sense of an allied but separable endeavor that this study of female representation in American popular culture is offered.

Appendixes

Appendix A

Categorical Breakdown of Films

I. **Woman: The Martyr or Source of Inspiration**

    The Mortal Storm (Metro-Goldwyn-Mayer, 1940)
    Caught in the Draft (Paramount, 1941)
    The Immortal Sergeant (Fox, 1942)
    Joan of Paris (RKO), 1942)
    Joe Smith, American (Metro-Goldwyn-Mayer, 1942)
    Journey for Margaret (Metro-Goldwyn-Mayer, 1942)
    Keeper of the Flame (Metro-Goldwyn-Mayer, 1942)
    Mrs. Miniver (Metro-Goldwyn-Mayer, 1942)
    Wake Island (Paramount, 1942)
    The Great Man's Lady (Paramount, 1942)
    Reveille with Beverly (Columbia, 1943)
    China (Paramount, 1943)
    Behind the Rising Sun (RKO, 1943)
    Five Graves to Cairo (Paramount, 1943)
    Flight for Freedom (Paramount, 1943)
    Gangway for Tomorrow (RKO, 1943)
    Mission to Moscow (Warner Brothers, 1943)
    The North Star (Goldwyn, 1943)
    Lassie Come Home (Metro-Goldwyn-Mayer, 1943)
    Cry Havoc! (Metro-Goldwyn-Mayer, 1943)
    So Proudly We Hail (Paramount, 1943)
    Here Come the Waves (Paramount, 1944)
    Roughly Speaking (Warner Brothers, 1945)

II. **Woman: The Helper**

    Juarez (Warner Brothers, 1939)
    Young Tom Edison (Metro-Goldwyn-Mayer, 1940)
    I Wake Up Screaming (Twentieth Century-Fox, 1941)
    Pacific Blackout (Paramount, 1941)

Sullivan's Travels (Paramount, 1941)
Flying Tigers (Republic, 1942)
The Glass Key (Paramount, 1942)
The Talk of the Town (Columbia, 1942)
Somewhere I'll Find You (Metro-Goldwyn-Mayer, 1942)
Government Girl (RKO, 1943)
Ministry of Fear (Paramount, 1943)
Watch on the Rhine (Warner Brothers, 1943)
To Have and Have Not (Warner Brothers, 1944)
Lost Weekend (Paramount, 1945)
Over 21 (Columbia, 1945)
Pride of the Marines (Warner Brothers, 1945)
Kiss of Death (Twentieth Century-Fox, 1947)

III.   Woman in the Family Melodrama

Dark Victory (Warner Brothers, 1939)
Shop around the Corner (Metro-Goldwyn-Mayer, 1940)
The Great Lie (Warner Brothers, 1941)
The Lady Eve (Paramount, 1941)
Penny Serenade (Columbia, 1941)
King's Row (Warner Brothers, 1941)
Always in My Heart (Warner Brothers, 1942)
Juke Girl (Warner Brothers, 1942)
The Major and the Minor (Paramount, 1942)
The Male Animal (Warner Brothers, 1942)
Now, Voyager (Warner Brothers, 1942)
The Palm Beach Story (Paramount, 1942)
You Were Never Lovelier (Columbia, 1942)
Seven Sweethearts (Metro-Goldwyn-Mayer, 1942)
The Lady Is Willing (Paramount, 1942)
I Walked with a Zombie (RKO, 1943)
A Lady Takes a Chance (RKO, 1943)
Miracle of Morgan's Creek (Paramount, 1943)
Heaven Can Wait (Twentieth Century-Fox, 1943)
The Human Comedy (Metro-Goldwyn-Mayer, 1943)
Meet Me in St. Louis (Metro-Goldwyn-Mayer, 1944)
The Clock (Metro-Goldwyn-Mayer, 1945)
My Name Is Julia Ross (Columbia, 1945)
Anchors Aweigh (Metro-Goldwyn-Mayer, 1945)
State Fair (Twentieth Century-Fox, 1945)
Janie Gets Married (Warner Brothers, 1946)
A Stolen Life (Warner Brothers, 1946)

From This Day Forward (RKO, 1946)
Duel in the Sun (Selznick, 1946)
Deadline at Dawn (RKO, 1946)
The Courage of Lassie (Metro-Goldwyn-Mayer, 1946)

IV.   **Moral Tales for Women**

Jezebel (Warner Brothers, 1938)
Wife, Husband and Friend (Twentieth Century-Fox, 1939)
Remember the Night (Paramount, 1939)
Waterloo Bridge (Metro-Goldwyn-Mayer, 1940)
Comrade X (Metro-Goldwyn-Mayer, 1940)
Kitty Foyle (RKO, 1940)
Two-Faced Woman (Metro-Goldwyn-Mayer, 1941)
Blood and Sand (Twentieth Century-Fox, 1941)
Sun Valley Serenade (Twentieth Century-Fox, 1941)
The Gay Sisters (Warner Brothers, 1942)
Shadow of a Doubt (Universal, 1942)
The War against Mrs. Hadley (Metro-Goldwyn-Mayer, 1942)
Woman of the Year (Metro-Goldwyn-Mayer, 1942)
The Black Swan (Twentieth Century-Fox, 1942)
Blondie for Victory (Columbia, 1942)
Gentleman Jim (Warner Brothers, 1942)
Rings on Her Fingers (Twentieth Century-Fox, 1942)
The Hard Way (Warner Brothers, 1943)
Stage Door Canteen (Lesser, 1943)
The Princess O'Rourke (Warner Brothers, 1943)
Old Acquaintance (Warner Brothers, 1943)
Slightly Dangerous (Metro-Goldwyn-Mayer, 1943)
I Love a Soldier (Paramount, 1944)
Two Girls and a Sailor (Metro-Goldwyn-Mayer, 1944)
Mr. Skeffington (Warner Brothers, 1944)
The Spiral Staircase (Selznick, 1945)
The Enchanted Cottage (RKO, 1945)
Mildred Pierce (Warner Brothers, 1945)
Bedlam (RKO, 1946)
Young Widow (United Artists, 1946)
To Each His Own (Paramount, 1946)
The Stranger (Universal, 1946)
Without Reservations (RKO, 1946)
The Ghost and Mrs. Muir (Twentieth Century-Fox, 1947)
Sorry, Wrong Number (Paramount, 1948)

V.   Woman: The Inscrutable Female

Ball of Fire (Goldwyn, 1941)
My Favorite Blonde (Paramount, 1942)
Across the Pacific (Warner Brothers, 1942)
Berlin Correspondent (Twentieth Century-Fox, 1942)
Cat People (RKO, 1942)
The Fleet's In (Paramount, 1942)
Claudia (Twentieth Century-Fox, 1943)
The Ox-Bow Incident (Twentieth Century-Fox, 1943)
Andy Hardy's Blonde Trouble (Metro-Goldwyn-Mayer, 1944)
Laura (Twentieth Century-Fox, 1944)
Gilda (Columbia, 1946)

VI.   The Evil Woman

Son of Fury (Twentieth Century-Fox, 1941)
Manpower (Warner Brothers, 1941)
Orchestra Wives (Twentieth Century-Fox, 1942)
In This Our Life (Warner Brothers, 1942)
The Woman in the Window (RKO, 1944)
Scarlet Street (Universal, 1945)
The Razor's Edge (Twentieth Century-Fox, 1946)
Notorious (Selznick/RKO, 1946)
The Killers (Universal, 1946)
The Dark Mirror (Universal, 1946)
Shock (Fox, 1946)
Leave Her to Heaven (Twentieth Century-Fox, 1946)
Possessed (Warner Brothers, 1947)

VII.   Woman: Object of the Look

You'll Never Get Rich (Columbia, 1941)
Sweater Girl (Paramount, 1941)
Kiss the Boys Good-Bye (Paramount, 1941)
Roxie Hart (Twentieth-Century Fox, 1942)
Holiday Inn (Paramount, 1942)
Song of the Islands (Twentieth Century-Fox, 1942)
The Gang's All Here (Twentieth Century-Fox, 1943)
The Heavenly Body (Metro-Goldwyn-Mayer, 1943)
Coney Island (Twentieth Century-Fox, 1943)
Lady of Burlesque (United Artists, 1943)
Hitler's Children (RKO, 1943)
Pin-Up Girl (Twentieth Century-Fox, 1944)
Hollywood Canteen (Warner Brothers, 1944)

VIII.   **Thematic Presence/Enunciative Absence**

Women without Names (Paramount, 1940)
You Belong to Me (Columbia, 1941)
The Flame of New Orleans (Universal, 1941)
Belle Starr (Twentieth Century-Fox, 1941)
Dixie Dugan (Twentieth Century-Fox, 1942)
She's in the Army (Monogram, 1942)
Take a Letter, Darling (Paramount, 1942)
The Heat's On (Columbia, 1943)
No Time for Love (Paramount, 1943)
Dough Girls (Warner Brothers, 1944)
Janie (Warner Brothers, 1944)
Ladies Courageous (Columbia, 1944)
Spellbound (Selznick, 1945)
Allotment Wives (Monogram, 1945)
The Shocking Miss Pilgrim (Twentieth Century-Fox, 1946)
Sister Kenny (RKO, 1946)

IX.   **Enunciation against the Grain**

Dance, Girl, Dance (RKO, 1940)
Star Spangled Rhythm (Paramount, 1942)
Priorities on Parade (Paramount, 1942)
Tender Comrade (RKO, 1943)
First Comes Courage (Columbia, 1943)
Since You Went Away (Selznick/United Artists, 1944)
Lifeboat (Twentieth Century-Fox, 1944)

Appendix B

Chronological Distribution of All Films Sampled (Total 167)

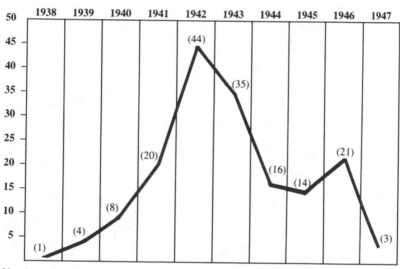

Appendix C

Chronological Distribution by Category

Category I: Woman: The Martyr or Source of Inspiration

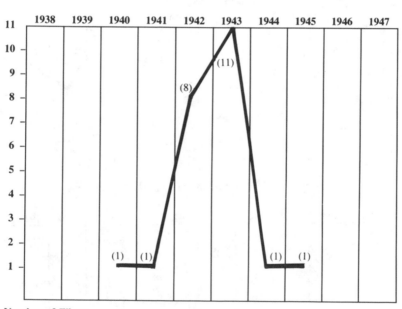

Number of Films

Category II: Woman: The Helper

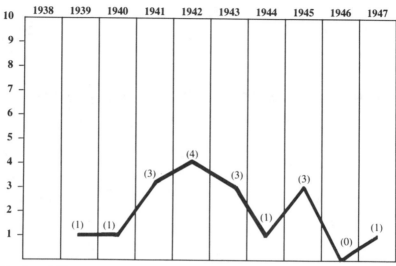

Number of Films

Category III: Woman in the Family Melodrama

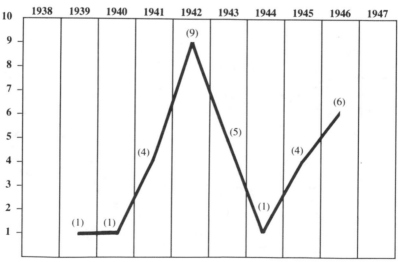

Number of Films

Category IV: Moral Tales for Women

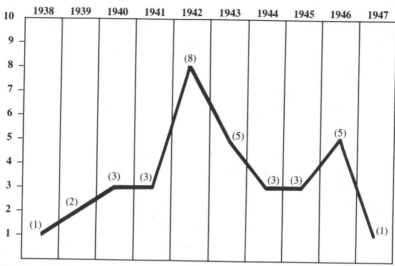

Number of Films

Category V: Woman: The Inscrutable Female

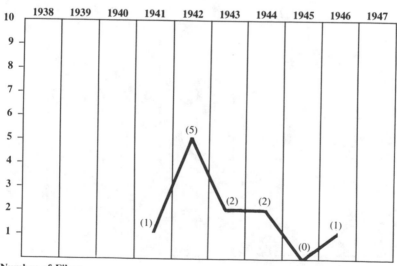

Number of Films

Category VI: The Evil Woman

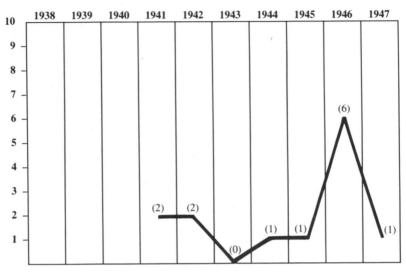

Number of Films

Category VII: Woman: Object of the Look

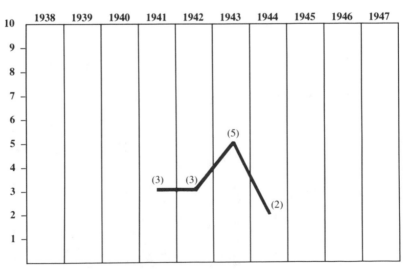

Number of Films

Category VIII: Thematic Presence/Enunciative Absence

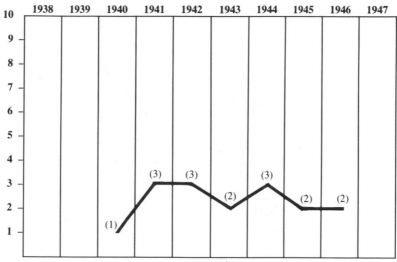

Category IX: Enunciation against the Grain

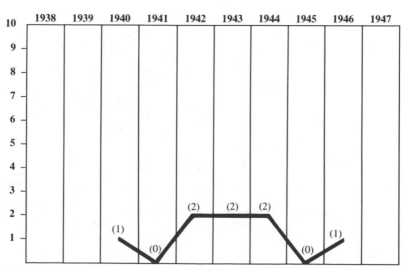

Appendix D

Distribution of Films by Studio

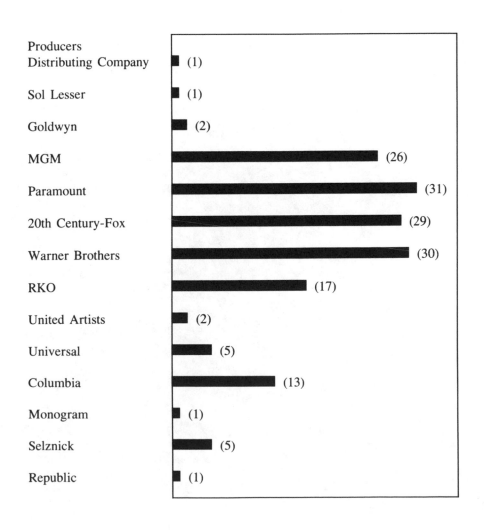

Notes

Introduction

1. Kevin McDonnell and Kevin Robins, "Marxist Cultural Theory: The Althusserian Smokescreen" in *One-Dimensional Marxism* (London: Allison & Busby, 1980), p, 176. While a very thorough critique of the *Screen* position (and secondarily of other critical stances including that of Hindess and Hirst as well as the *Working Papers in Cultural Studies* group), the essay seems to overstate its case. McDonnell and Robins take issue with the easy attribution of "materialist" to certain canonized aesthetic practices as well as to the theories that account for them ("Everyone today sees themselves as more or less a materialist"). The corrective offered to *Screen*'s version of Althusser's self-judged "theoreticism" is, in general, a useful one. The analysis is, however, endangered by the judgments offered on the various "avant-garde" philosophies seen as endangering the Marxist enterprise, principally Lacanian psychoanalysis and deconstruction of the *Tel Quel* variety. Notions such as "subject" (that of psychoanalysis rather than of class struggle) or "text" are meant to be too rarefied, the emptily idealist categories of those who only mime a concern for a Marxist practice. For an American reader, the essay offers the rare opportunity to become engaged in a polemics of Marxist orthodoxy.

Introduction to Part One

1. E. H. Carr, *What Is History?* (New York: Vintage Books, 1961), p. 22.

2. Louis Althusser, *For Marx* (New York: Vintage Books, 1969), pp. 255–56.

3. Norman Geras, "Althusser's Marxism: An Account and Assessment," *New Left Review*, No. 71 (January–February 1972), p. 80.

4. Louis Althusser, *Essays in Self-Criticism*, (London: New Left Books, 1976). See in particular "Elements of Self-Criticism" in which Althusser acknowledges the "theoreticist deviation" in his account of the "epistemological break" (from bourgeois ideology) in the work of Marx from 1845 onwards. One result of this error, according to Althusser, was the undervaluation of class struggle in the framing of this "rationalist-speculative drama"—for which Althusser was strenuously rebuked in many quarters. The de-emphasis on class struggle was seen as no mean omission, but rather as evidence of an elitism which elevated the role of the intellectual at the expense of his/her proper alliance with the revolutionary classes. One critic has gone so far as to characterize the key features of Althusserianism as the neutrality of science and the necessity of philosophy. A second effect, more pertinent to this discussion, was the explanation of the "break" in terms that contrasted "truth" and "error" in the "form of the speculative distinction between *science* and *ideology*, in the singular and in general. The contrast between

Marxism and bourgeois ideology thus became simply a special case of this distinction." (p. 106) Althusser's auto-critiques were the response to a series of attacks in France and Britain from the late sixties onward. See in this regard J. Ranciere, *La lecon d'Althusser* (Paris: Gallimard, 1974); A. Glucksmann, "A Ventriloquist Structuralism," *New Left Review*, no. 72 (March–April 1972); E. P. Thompson, *The Poverty of Theory* (London: Merlin, 1978); Paul Q. Hirst, "Althusser and the Theory of Ideology," *Economy and Society*, Vol. 5, no. 4 (1976), pp. 385–412. More recent re-evaluations include a noteworthy volume, *One-Dimensional Marxism: Althusser and the Politics of Culture* (London: Allison & Busby, 1980), containing four critical articles from rather different perspectives (McDonnell and Robins' "Marxist Cultural Theory: The Althusserian Smokescreen" offers a particularly useful tracing of Althusserianism in the pages of *Screen*), and Steven B. Smith's *Reading Althusser* (Ithaca: Cornell University Press, 1984) which eschews diatribe in favor of an attempt at placing Althusser in a tradition of European philosophy as well as Marxist orthodoxy. Not to be overlooked is a valuable Ph.D. dissertation by Philip Rosen featuring an assessment of "Althusser on Consciousness, Ideology, and Art" which steers a middle path between valorizing the Althusserian project and vilifying it (Philip Gershon Rosen, "The Concept of Ideology and Contemporary Film Criticism: A Study of the Position of the Journal *Screen* in the Context of the Marxist Theoretical Tradition," Ph.D. dissertation, University of Iowa, 1978). This rather overwhelming, frequently vitriolic body of criticism notwithstanding, it is unquestionable that, in the words of Kevin McDonnell and Kevin Robins, "Althusser's theory of ideology has undoubtedly been the principal inspiration behind the recent upsurge of cultural theory in Britain," and, we might add, in the U.S. as well.

5. Gregor McLennan, Victor Molina and Roy Peters, "Althusser's Theory of Ideology," *Working Papers in Cultural Studies 10—On Ideology*, No. 10 (1977), p. 87.

6. Ibid.

7. Ibid.

8. For a much more complete discussion of ideology and its founding in misrecognition, see chapter four. Certainly the Althusserian version of ideology, which has been particularly influential for Anglo-American as well as French studies of film and popular culture, has depended upon the Lacanian rereading of Freud which judges the human subject to be a de-centered one "constituted by a structure which has no 'center' . . . except in the imaginary misrecognition of the 'ego', i.e. in the ideological formations in which it 'recognizes' itself" (Louis Althusser, "Freud and Lacan" in *Lenin and Philosophy*, New York: Monthly Review Press, 1971, pp. 218–219). Tautological as this may sound, this version of ideology is an advance over previous notions of "false consciousness" in that it borrows from psychoanalysis in order to posit a "structure of misrecognition" at the very inception of subject formation. Rosalind Coward and John Ellis elucidate an Althusserian version of ideology in their *Language and Materialism* in a manner that recalls Lacan's theory of subject formation: "The imaginary identity of ideology closes off the movement of contradictions, calling upon the subject as consistent. It puts the subject in the position of a homogeneous subject in relation to meaning, a subject who thinks him/herself to be the point of origin of ideas and of actions" (Coward and Ellis, *Language and Materialism* [London: Routledge and Kegan Paul, 1977], p. 77). Language is the cultural apparatus or bridge that links misrecognition at the level of the subject (ego-formation) with the parallel phenomenon culture-wide (ideology). Althusser is thus notable for spanning the divide between the historical subject (the familiar terrain of Marxism) and the properly psychological subject.

9. Althusser, *For Marx*, p. 62.

10. Ibid.

11. Historians such as Hindess and Hirst would do well to consider the position developed by film-makers Jean-Marie Straub and Danielle Huillet whose work frequently offers reflection upon the material traces of an unknowable past. But it is a present-tense effect that is intended ("A film on the past which is lucid can contribute to helping the present more than a film on the present without any lucidity on this present"). The Straub/Huillet films "reflect concretely on a few things," layering text upon text, representing the past through documents narrated in a perceptual present. Such efforts offer a valuable political intervention in their testimony to history as a struggle to be waged at the level of representation.

12. Christian Metz, in his essay on "The Imaginary Signifier," uses the term "cinematic institution" to include the industrial mechanisms of the filmmaking business as well as the internalized processes within the spectator. More to the present point are the usages of John Ellis in "The Institution of Cinema" and of Geoffrey Nowell-Smith in "On the Writing of the History of the Cinema: Some Problems," both in *Edinburgh Magazine #2*. All such references to the institution of cinema may well derive from Althusser's essay "Ideology and the State," which specifies the distinct and specialized institutions which constitute the ideological state apparatuses, including the cultural ISA.

13. John Ellis, "The Institution of Cinema," *Edinburgh '77 Magazine—History/Production/Memory*, Number 2 (1977), p. 59.

Chapter 1

1. Thomas Parrish, ed., "Neutrality Acts," *The Simon and Schuster Encyclopedia of World War II* (New York: Simon and Schuster, 1978), p. 432.

2. Garth Jowett, Film: *The Democratic Art* (Boston: Little, Brown and Company, 1976), p. 303.

3. Richard Polenberg, *War and Society: The United States 1941–1945* (Philadelphia: J. B. Lippincott Company, 1972), p. 1.

4. Ibid., pp. 7–8.

5. Richard Polenberg, ed., *America at War: The Home Front 1941–1945* (Englewood Cliffs, N.J.: Prentice-Hall, Inc., 1968), p. 21.

6. Polenberg, *War and Society*, p. 240.

7. Richard R. Lingeman, *Don't You Know There's a War On?: The American Home Front, 1941–1945* (New York: G. P. Putnam's Sons, 1970), p. 127.

8. Ibid., p. 65.

9. John Morton Blum, *V Was for Victory: Politics and American Culture during World War II* (New York: Harcourt Brace Jovanovich, 1976), p. 122.

10. Polenberg, *America at War*, p. 26.

11. Ibid., pp. 52–53.

12. Polenberg, *War and Society*, p. 94.

13. Polenberg, *America at War*, p. 42.

14. Polenberg, *War and Society*, pp. 167–168.

15. Jack Goodman, ed., *While You Were Gone* (New York: Simon and Schuster, 1946), p. 200.

16. Ibid., p. 202.

17. Ibid., p. 212.

18. Ibid., p. 19.

19. Blum, p. 34.

20. Ibid., p. 94.

21. David Chierichetti, "Hollywood's Pomp Up Front Again," *Los Angeles Times,* January 4, 1980, "Fashion 80," p. 5, col. 1.

22. Blum, p. 227.

23. Polenberg, *War and Society,* p. 33.

24. Ibid., p. 21.

25. Blum, p. 233.

26. Goodman, p. 17.

27. Blum, p. 172.

28. Polenberg, *War and Society,* p. 65.

29. Ibid., pp. 62–63.

30. Blum, pp. 158–159.

31. *Los Angeles Times* (September 1, 1980), pp. 1, 12.

32. Blum, p. 185.

33. Ibid., p. 188.

34. Polenberg, *War and Society,* p. 128.

35. Blum, p. 204.

36. Goodman, p. 93.

37. Ibid., p. 94.

38. Lingeman, p. 334.

39. Ibid., p. 87.

40. Ibid., p. 93.

41. For a more extensive investigation of the relationship between film imagery and other related cultural forms during the war years, see my "Advertising/Photojournalism/Cinema: The Shifting Rhetoric of Forties Female Representation," in *Quarterly Review of Film Studies* 10, no. 4 (Fall 1985).

42. Lingeman, p. 210.

43. Ibid., p. 222.

44. Goodman, p. 364.

45. Ibid., p. 340.

46. Ibid., p. 493.

47. Ibid., p. 405.

48. Ibid., p. 377.

49. Ibid., p. 384.

50. Ibid., p. 386.

51. Ibid., p. 391.

52. Blum, p. 22.

53. Ibid., p. 26.

54. Goodman, p. 427.

55. Ibid., p. 431.

56. Polenberg, *War and Society,* p. 135.

Chapter 2

1. Eleanor F. Straub, "Government Policy toward Civilian Women during World War II," Ph.D. dissertation, Emory University, 1973, p. 317.

2. Ibid., p. 172.

3. Ibid., p. 5.

4. Ibid., p. 3.

5. Ibid., p. 21.

6. Margaret Mead, "The Women in the War," *While You Were Gone* (New York: Simon and Schuster, 1946), p. 280.

7. Leila J. Rupp, *Mobilizing Women for War* (Princeton: Princeton University Press, 1978), p. 52.

8. Ibid., p. 61.

9. Ibid., p. 64.

10. *Life Magazine* (22 September 1941), pp. 78–85.

11. Straub, p. 104.

12. Ibid., p. 108.

13. Ibid., p. 155.

14. Ibid., p. 63.

15. Rupp, p. 94.

16. Straub, p. 36.

17. Ibid., p. 10.

18. Rupp, p. 147.

19. Ibid., p. 150.

20. Straub, pp. 142–143.

21. Ibid., p. 323.

22. William H. Chafe, *The American Woman: Her Changing Social, Economic and Political Roles, 1920-1970* (London: Oxford University Press, 1972), p. 135. This particular statistic appears to contradict an earlier citation namely, that nearly two-thirds of the women working at the height of the war had been employed before Pearl Harbor. The 50 percent increase figure appears in William H. Chafe's *The American Woman* and is used to support his claim for World War II as a period of radical transformation for the economic outlook of the American woman. The point to make here is simply that these and other statistics regarding the woman worker vary from source to source and should be viewed with a critical eye. Often, the numbers used are the carefully selected supports for a polemical position and are subject to alternative interpretations.

23. Ibid., p. 144.

24. Ibid., p. 136.

25. Ibid., p. 140.

26. J. E. Trey, "Women in the War Economy—World War II," *The Review of Radical Political Economics* 4, no. 3 (Summer 1972), p. 44.

27. Chafe, p. 141.

28. Ibid., p. 138.

29. Robert James Havighurst and H. Gerthon Morgan, *The Social History of a War Boom Community* (New York: Longmans, Green, 1951), p. 51.

30. Straub, p. 193.

31. Ibid., p. 196.

32. Chafe, p. 158.

33. Ibid., p. 160.

34. Ibid., p. 162.

35. Straub, p. 263.

36. Ibid., p. 270.

37. Ibid., p. 282.

38. Ibid., p. 294.

39. Trey, p. 47.

40. Chafe, p. 138.

41. Straub, p. 86.

42. Ibid., pp. 83–84.

43. Ibid., p. 93.

44. Ibid., p. 98.

45. Ibid., p. 99.

46. Ibid., p. 100.

47. Ibid., p. 316.

48. Lingeman, pp. 82–87.

49. Straub, p. 322.

50. Lingeman, p. 151.

51. Trey, p. 48.

52. Sheila Tobias and Lisa Anderson, ''Whatever Happened to Rosie the Riveter?,'' *Ms.* 1, no. 12 (June 1973), p. 93.

53. Ibid., p. 94.

Chapter 3

 1. Lingeman, pp. 170–171.

 2. Ibid., p. 171.

 3. Ibid., p. 173.

 4. Jowett, p. 303.

 5. Ibid., pp. 304–305.

 6. Tino Balio, *United Artists: The Company Built by the Stars* (Madison: The University of Wisconsin Press, 1976), p. 171.

 7. Ibid., p. 164.

 8. Jowett, p. 299.

 9. Balio, p. 165.

10. Ibid., p. 202.

11. Jowett, p. 316.

12. Balio, p. 168.

13. Ibid., p. 169.

14. Ibid., p. 170.

15. Ibid.

16. Ibid.

17. Jowett, p. 310.

18. Balio, p. 189.

19. Ibid., p. 190.

20. Paul Kerr, ''Out of What Past? Notes on the B Film Noir,'' *Screen Education,* Numbers 32–33 (Autumn/Winter 1979/80), p. 57.

21. Leo A. Handel, *Hollywood Looks at Its Audience—A Report of Film Audience Research* (Urbana: The University of Illinois Press, 1950), p. 4.

22. Dorothy B. Jones, ''The Hollywood War Film: 1942-1944,'' *Hollywood Quarterly* 1, no. 1 (October 1945), p. 12.

23. Dorothy B. Jones, ''Tomorrow the Movies: III. Hollywood Goes To War,'' *Nation* 160, no. 4 (27 January 1945), p. 93.

24. Ibid., p. 94.

25. Ibid.

26. Jowett, p. 308.

27. Gregory D. Black and Clayton R. Koppes, "OWI Goes to the Movies: The Bureau of Intelligence's Criticism of Hollywood, 1942–1943," *Prologue* 6 (Spring 1974), p. 48.

28. Office of War Information, Bureau of Intelligence, "Introduction to Weekly Summary and Analysis of Feature Motion Pictures," Report No. 1, pp. 1–3, Box 1845, Records of the Bureau of Intelligence, Records of the Office of Government Reports, Record Group 44, Washington National Records Center, Suitland, Maryland (hereafter cited as RG____, WNRC).

29. Jones, *Hollywood Quarterly*, pp. 3–11.

30. OWI, Bureau of Intelligence, "Film Review of STAR SPANGLED RHYTHM," Report No. 10, p. 30, Box 1845, RG 44, WNRC.

31. OWI, Bureau of Intelligence, "Motion Pictures and the War Effort," Special Services, File No. 72, pp. 4–5, Box 1842, RG 44, WNRC.

32. Black and Koppes, p. 53.

33. Letter from Ray Bell to Arch Mercey, MGM File 320, pp. 1–2, Box 1514, RG 208, WNRC.

34. Jowett, p. 311.

35. Lingeman, p. 170.

36. Goodman, p. 526.

37. *Movie Lot to Beachhead* (Editors of *Look*), (New York: Doubleday, Doran and Co., 1945), p. 58.

38. Frank Capra, *Frank Capra—The Name above the Title* (New York: The Macmillan Company, 1971), p. 340.

39. Peter A. Soderbergh, "The Grand Illusion: Hollywood and World War II, 1930–1945," *The University of Dayton Review* 5, no. 3 (Winter 1968/69), p. 17.

40. Ibid.

41. *Movie Lot to Beachhead*, p. 40.

42. Report by War Activities Committee, "The Industry at War," *The Hollywood Reporter*, Twelfth Anniversary Issue.

43. *Movie Lot to Beachhead*, p. 41.

44. Ibid., p. 104.

45. Ibid., p. 205.

46. Soderbergh, p. 17.

47. Goodman, p. 529.

48. *Movie Lot to Beachhead*, p. 229.

49. Jowett, p. 309.

50. Lingeman, p. 174.

51. The Proceedings of the Writers' Congress, Los Angeles 1943 (Berkeley: University of California Press, 1944), p. 396.

52. Ibid., p. 410.

53. Lingeman, pp. 192–193.

54. Report by War Activities Committee, p. 2.

55. Ibid., p. 1.

56. Jowett, p. 322.

57. Jones, *Hollywood Quarterly,* p. 9.

58. Ken D. Jones and Arthur F. McClure, *Hollywood At War: The American Motion Picture and World War II* (South Brunswick: A. S. Barnes and Company, 1973), p. 16.

59. Floyd B. Odlum, "Financial Organization of the Motion Picture Industry," *The Annals of the American Academy of Political and Social Science* 254 (November 1947), p. 23.

Chapter 4

1. Gregor McLennan (for Editorial Group), "Introduction," *Working Papers in Cultural Studies: On Ideology,* No. 10 (1977), p. 5.

2. Terry Eagleton, *Criticism and Ideology* (London: Verso Editions, 1975), p. 70.

3. Douglas Kellner, "Ideology, Marxism, and Advanced Capitalism," *Socialism Review* 8, no. 6 (November–December 1979), p. 39.

4. Karl Marx, *A Contribution to the Critique of Political Economy* (Moscow: Progress Publishers, 1970), p. 21.

5. *Karl Marx and Frederick Engels, The German Ideology—Part One* (New York: International Publishers, 1970), pp. 64–66.

6. Roland Barthes, *Mythologies* (New York: Hill and Wang, 1972), p. 142.

7. Ibid., p. 146.

8. Louis Althusser, *Lenin and Philosophy and Other Essays* (New York: Monthly Review Press, 1971), p. 174.

9. Ibid., p. 159.

10. Ibid., p. 161.

11. Raymond Williams, *Marxism and Literature* (Oxford: Oxford University Press, 1977), pp. 61–62.

12. Cited in *Working Papers in Cultural Studies,* p. 49.

13. Kellner, p. 55.

14. *Writers' Congress,* p. 360.

15. Katherine Glover, *Women at Work in Wartime* (New York: Public Affairs Committee, Inc., 1943), p. 5.

16. Ibid., p. 28.

17. Ibid., p. 30.

18. *Writers' Congress,* pp. 22–23.

19. Memorandum from D. W. Smithburg to George Pettee, "Government Statements on Women," Office for Emergency Management, File 56, p. 1, Box 1849, RG 44, WNRC.

20. *Writers' Congress,* p. 380.

21. Memorandum from Meredith P. Gilpatrick and Robert Eisner to George S. Pettee, ''Statements of Private Thought Leaders On Women and the War,'' Office for Emergency Management, File 58, p. 3, Box 1849, RG 44, WNRC.

22. Interoffice memorandum on ''Womanpower Strategies'' from Mary Brewster White to Robert R. Ferry, pp. 1-3, Box 156, RG 208, WNRC.

23. Norbert Guterman, Review of books on propaganda analysis, *Studies in Philosophy and Social Science,* Vol. IX, no. 1, 1941, p. 161.

24. Axel Madson, *William Wyler* (New York: Thomas Y. Crowell Company, 1973), p. 214.

25. *Writers' Congress,* pp. 376-377.

26. Office of War Information, ''Womanpower Campaigns,'' p. 3. Box 156, RG 208, WNRC.

27. Ibid., p. 11.

28. Plan Book by the Information Service of the War Manpower Commission, ''America at War Needs Women at Work,'' p. 1, Box 156, RG 208, WNRC.

29. Ernesto Laclau, *Politics and Ideology in Marxist Theory* (London: Verso Editions, 1977), pp. 92-93.

30. Ibid., p. 107.

31. Pamphlet published by the War Advertising Council, Inc., ''How Industry Can Help the Government's Information Program on WOMANPOWER,'' p. 1, Box 156, RG 208, WNRC.

32. Ibid., p. 9.

33. Cited in Laclau, p. 93.

34. Advertising copy for Bell Telephone, *Time* 40, no. 9, (11 July 1942), p. 12.

35. Jacques Lacan, *Ecrits* (New York: W. W. Norton & Company, Inc., 1977), p. 2.

36. Lingeman, pp. 183-184.

37. Ibid., p. 184.

38. Jowett, p. 302.

39. Black and Koppes, p. 49.

40. Chafe, p. 146.

41. For further discussion of this problematic—the positioning of the woman within a narrative system on the basis of an imposed moral agenda—see my ''From Identification to Ideology: The Male System of Hitchcock's *Notorius,*'' *Wide Angle* 4, no. 1 (Summer 1980), pp. 30-37.

42. Lingeman, p. 89.

43. Chafe, p. 177.

44. Straub, pp. 183-184.

45. Ibid., p. 184.

46. Ibid., p. 185.

47. Ibid., p. 321.

48. Ibid., p. 351.

49. Ibid., p. 143.

50. Ibid., p. 182.

51. Glover, p. 1.

52. Rupp, p. 140.

53. Straub, p. 140.

54. Advertising copy for North American Aviation, *Life* 13 (19 October 1942), p. 56.

55. Straub, p. 127.

56. Ibid., p. 130.

57. Ibid., p. 137.

58. Rupp, p. 137.

59. Chafe, p. 152.

60. Ibid.

61. Straub, p. 182.

62. Polenberg, p. 10.

63. Lingeman, p. 92.

64. Rupp, p. 69.

65. Polenberg, pp. 2–3.

66. Jones, p. 174.

67. Chafe, p. 139.

68. Polenberg, *War and Society*, p. 149.

69. Straub, p. 18.

Introduction to Part Two

1. Christian Metz, "The Imaginary Signifier," *Screen* 16, no. 2 (Summer 1975), p. 21.

2. Ibid., p. 35.

3. Discussed in Teresa de Lauretis' *Alice Doesn't* (Bloomington: Indiana University Press, 1984), p. 48.

4. For second thoughts on the limits of her groundbreaking essay, see Laura Mulvey's "Afterthoughts on 'Visual Pleasure and Narrative Cinema' Inspired by *Duel in the Sun* (King Vidor, 1946)," *Framework*, Nos. 15/16/17 (1981).

Chapter 5

1. War Advertising Council in cooperation with the Office of War Information and Retraining and Reemployment Administration, "How Your Advertising Can Help the Veteran Readjust," miscellaneous, p. 2, Box 167, RG 208, WNRC.

2. For amplification on melodrama as a dramatic form with a precise, class-inflected history see Thomas Elsaesser, "Tales of Sound and Fury: Observations on the Family Melodrama," reprinted in *Movies and Methods, Volume II*, Bill Nichols, ed. (Berkeley: University of California Press, 1985), pp. 165–189.

3. The reference here is to Northrop Frye's influential formulation of fictional modes which attempted to situate aesthetic forms within large historical epochs. Fictions were classified within this system not on the basis of particular moral codes as they had tended to be previously, but on the hero's power of action in relation to normal human capacities. See Frye's "Historical Criticism: Theory of Modes," *Anatomy of Criticism* (Princeton: Princeton University Press, 1957), pp. 33–67.

4. Sigmund Freud, "Family Romances," *The Sexual Enlightenment of Children* (New York: Collier Books, 1963), pp. 41–45.

5. Stephen Heath, "Contexts," *Edinburgh Magazine,* No. 2 (1977), p. 40.

6. Freud, p. 41.

7. Christine Gledhill, "Developments in Feminist Film Criticism," *Re-Vision* (Frederick, MD: University Publications of America, Inc. and The American Film Institute, 1984), p. 18.

8. Julia Kristeva, "Woman Can Never Be Defined," trans. Marilyn A. August, in *New French Feminisms,* Isabelle de Courtivron and Elaine Marks, eds. (Amherst: University of Massachusetts Press, 1980), pp. 137–38.

9. For a provocative, in-depth examination of the twin sisters phenomenon during this period, see Lucy Fischer, "Two-Faced Women: The Double in Women's Melodrama of the 1940s," *Cinema Journal* 23, no. 1 (Fall 1983), pp. 24–43.

10. Serafina Bathrick discusses the depiction of stable family relations in *Meet Me in St. Louis* as an ideologically potent corrective to the crisis times of war in "The Past as Future: Family and the American Home in *Meet Me in St. Louis,*" *The Minnesota Review,* No. 6 (Spring 1976), pp. 132–39.

11. There is an inescapable similarity between the characters and structure of this film and the women's magazines and pulps which evolved into the romance comics of the fifties. There is an inexorability, a streamlined quality to the narrative which is linked to the melodramatic tradition of 18th and 19th century literature and to its precursor, the medieval morality play. But the dramatic contours and graphic simplicity of the film most suggest the romance comic format.

Chapter 6

1. Laura Mulvey, "Visual Pleasure and Narrative Cinema," *Screen* 16, no. 3 (Autumn 1975), p. 7.

2. Gledhill, p. 31.

3. Mulvey, p. 13.

4. Richard Dyer, "Resistance Through Charisma: Rita Hayworth and *Gilda,* " in *Women in Film Noir,* E. Ann Kaplan (ed.) (London: British Film Institute, 1978), pp. 91–99.

5. Pursuing the capacity of the represented male subject to be authoritative even in his absence, Kaja Silverman focuses on the dis-embodied voice-over which she judges to be "exemplary" for male subjectivity, "attesting to an achieved invisibility, omniscience and discursive power." In "Dis-Embodying the Female Voice," *Re-Vision,* p. 134.

6. The important distinction to be made here is between the twin notions of the Imaginary and the Symbolic in their relation to gendered difference. For Jacques Lacan, these two terms are, along with the Real, the essential orders of the psychoanalytic field with the Imaginary referring to subjective experience prior to the accession to language (the *sine qua non* of culture and of the Law). This is the terrain of desire, the primary process, and of the misrecognition which founds identity and ideology in the Althusserian usage. If, as is generally argued, the threshold to the Symbolic is patrolled by the Name-of-the-Father (culture as a formation constituted through the male agency), representations of the Imaginary are likewise held within the thrall of the patriarchal. That is, even the Imaginary-as-represented within the cinema is subject to male dominion. No better example could be offered than Budd Boetticher's infamous description of his own creative process from an interview with Bernard Tavernier: "What is important is what the heroine has caused to happen, or what she represents; what she inspires in the hero, whether love, or fear, or even indifference and how he behaves in consequence. She herself is of no importance." In *Budd Boetticher: The Western,* Jim Kitses (ed.), a BFI Education Department Dossier.

7. Mulvey, p. 7.

8. Silverman, p. 131.

9. The phrase occurs in the context of Wollen's analysis of Manet's "Olympia" in "Manet—Modernism and Avant-Garde," *Screen* 21, no. 2, p. 22. It is quoted in Teresa de Lauretis' *Alice Doesn't* as a notable instance of a strategy no longer judged central to feminist critical practice. De Lauretis wishes to move away from what she sees as the "pure, absolute negativity" of (presumably) Wollen's approach, claiming "this is no longer the task of feminist critical practice, though it may be crucial to men's work as they attempt to confront the structures of their sexuality, the blind spots of their desire and of their theories" (p. 77).

10. Metz, p. 62.

Chapter 7

1. See in particular Part V in Emile Benveniste, *Problems of General Linguistics* (Coral Gables, Florida: University of Miami Press, 1971). "In some way language puts forth 'empty' forms which each speaker, in the exercise of the discourse, appropriates to his 'person', at the same time defining himself (sic) as 'I' and a partner as 'you'. The instance of discourse is thus constitutive of all coordinates that define the subject . . . " (p. 227).

2. Silverman, p. 132.

3. Ibid.

4. One of the more resourceful efforts to achieve an equilibrium between the sexes at the level of representation occurs in *Woman of the Year* (1942). The attempt to strike a balance between the Spencer Tracy and Katherine Hepburn characters and thus to resolve the gendered tug-of-war familiar from other Tracy/Hepburn vehicles is signalled at the film's conclusion by a compromise appellation for the celebrated but loveless wife—she will now be called "Tess Harding-Craig." But of course the co-equality of the hyphen is overwhelmed by the larger claims for female submission urged through the film: Tess is visibly humiliated for her ignorance of domestic knowledge—attacked by coffee maker, toaster and waffle iron—and rendered unsympathetic for her indifference to children.

5. Colin MacCabe, "The discursive and the ideological in film: Notes on the conditions of political intervention," *Screen* 19, no. 4 (Winter 1978/79), p. 31.

6. Charles W. Eckert, "The Anatomy of a Proletarian Film: Warner's *Marked Woman*," *Film Quarterly* 17, no. 2 (Winter 1973/74), pp. 10–24.

7. Chester W. Gregory, *Women in Defense during World War II* (New York: Exposition Press, 1974), p. 78.

8. Ibid., p. 68.

9. C. M. Winget, "Telling Time By the Body Clock," *Runner's World* 14, no. 11 (November 1979), p. 64.

10. Chafe, p. 57.

11. See in particular Claire Johnston's discussion of *Dance, Girl, Dance* in "Dorothy Arzner: Critical Strategies" in *The Work of Dorothy Arzner* (London: British Film Institute, 1975), pp. 1–8.

12. Seymour Chatman, *Story and Discourse* (Ithaca: Cornell University Press, 1978), p. 253.

Conclusion

1. Patricia Mellencamp, " 'Uncanny' Feminism: The Exquisite Corpses of Cecelia Condit," *Afterimage* 14, no. 2 (September 1986), p. 13.

2. Stephen Heath, "Male Feminism," *Men in Feminism* (New York: Metheun, 1987), p. 1.

3. Ibid., pp. 29–30.

Bibliography

Sources on History

Allen, Robert C. and Douglas Gomery. *Film History: Theory and Practice.* New York: Alfred A. Knopf, 1985.

Balio, Tino. *United Artists: The Company Built by the Stars.* Madison: The University of Wisconsin Press, 1976.

Black, Gregory D. and Clayton R. Koppes. "OWI Goes to the Movies: The Bureau of Intelligence's Criticism of Hollywood, 1942–1943." *Prologue* (Spring 1974), pp. 46–52.

Blum, John Morton. *V Was for Victory: Politics and American Culture during World War II.* New York: Harcourt Brace Jovanovich, 1976.

Capra, Frank. *Frank Capra—The Name above the Title.* New York: The Macmillan Company, 1971.

Carr, E. H. *What Is History?* New York: Vintage Books, 1961.

Chafe, William H. *The American Woman: Her Changing Social, Economic and Political Roles, 1920–1970.* London: Oxford University Press, 1972.

_____. *Women and Equality: Changing Patterns in American Culture.* London: Oxford University Press, 1977.

Chierichetti, David. "Hollywood's Pomp Up Front Again." *Los Angeles Times* 4 January 1980, p. 5, column 1.

Goldfarb, Lyn. *Separated and Unequal.* Washington: Union for Radical Political Economics, 1975.

Goodman, Jack, ed. *While You Were Gone.* New York: Simon and Schuster, 1946.

Handel, Leo A. *Hollywood Looks at Its Audience—A Report of Film Audience Research.* Urbana: The University of Illinois Press, 1950.

Havighurst, Robert James and H. Gerthon Morgan. *The Social History of a War Boom Community.* New York: Longmans, Green, 1951.

Hindess, Barry and Paul Q. Hirst. *Pre-Capitalist Modes of Production.* London: Routledge & Kegan Paul, 1975.

_____. *Mode of Production and Social Formation.* London: The Macmillan Press, Ltd., 1977.

Hollywood Writers' Mobilization. *The Proceedings of the Writers' Congress, Los Angeles 1943.* Berkeley: University of California Press, 1944.

Honey, Maureen. *Creating Rosie the Riveter: Class, Gender and Propaganda during World War II.* Amherst: University of Massachusetts Press, 1984.

Huber, Joan, ed. *Changing Women in a Changing Society.* Chicago: University of Chicago Press, 1973.

Jones, Dorothy B. "The Hollywood War Film: 1942–1944." *Hollywood Quarterly* (October 1945), pp. 10–15.

_____. "Tomorrow the Movies: III. Hollywood Goes to War." *Nation* (27 January 1945), pp. 91–95.

Jones, James. *WWII: A Chronicle of Soldiering.* New York: Ballantine Books, 1975.

Jones, Ken D. and Arthur F. McClure. *Hollywood at War: The American Motion Picture and World War II.* South Brunswick: A. S. Barnes and Company, 1973.

Jowett, Garth. *Film: The Democratic Art.* Boston: Little, Brown and Company, 1976.

Kerr, Paul. "Out of What Past? Notes on the 'B' Film Noir." *Screen Education*, Nos. 32-33 (Autumn/Winter 1979/80), pp. 45-65.

Lingeman, Richard R. *Don't You Know There's a War On?: The American Home Front, 1941-1945.* New York: G. P. Putnam's Sons, 1970.

Look magazine editors. *Movie Lot to Beachhead.* New York: Doubleday, Doran and Co., 1945.

MGM File 320. Letter from Ray Bell to Arch Mercey. Box 1514, pp. 1-2, Record Group 208, Washington National Records Center, Suitland, Maryland. (Hereafter cited as RG____, WNRC.)

"Neutrality Acts." *The Simon and Schuster Encyclopedia of World War II*, 1978.

Office of War Information. Bureau of Intelligence. *Introduction to Weekly Summary and Analysis of Feature Motion Pictures.* Report No. 1, pp. 1-3, Box 1845, Records of the Bureau of Intelligence, Records of the Office of Government Reports, RG 44, WNRC.

_____. *Film Review of Star Spangled Rhythm.* Report No. 10, pp. 29-30, Box 1845, RG 44, WNRC.

_____. *Motion Pictures and the War Effort.* Special Services, File No. 72, pp. 4-5, Box 1842, RG 44, WNRC.

Polenberg, Richard, ed. *America at War: The Home Front 1941-1945.* Englewood Cliffs, N.J.: Prentice-Hall, Inc., 1968.

_____. *War and Society: The United States 1941-1945.* Philadelphia: J. B. Lippincott Company, 1972.

Rupp, Leila J. *Mobilizing Women for War.* Princeton: Princeton University Press, 1978.

Ryan, Mary P. *Womanhood in America: From Colonial Times to the Present.* New York: New Viewpoints, 1975.

Smuts, Robert W. *Women and Work in America.* New York: Schocken Books, 1971.

Soderbergh, Peter A. "The Grand Illusion: Hollywood and World War II, 1930-1945." *The University of Dayton Review* 5, no. 3 (Winter 1968-1969), pp. 14-20.

Straub, Eleanor F. "Government Policy toward Civlian Women during World War II." Dissertation, Emory University, 1973.

Tobias, Sheila and Lisa Anderson. "Whatever Happened to Rosie the Riveter?" *Ms.* (June 1973), pp. 92-95.

Trey, J. E. "Women in the War Economy—World War II." *The Review of Radical Political Economics* 4, no. 3 (Summer 1972), pp. 40-57.

War Activities Committee. "The Industry at War." *The Hollywood Reporter,* Twelfth Anniversary Issue.

White, Hayden V. *Metahistory.* Baltimore: Johns Hopkins University Press, 1973.

Women in Defense File. "Outstanding Women in Federal Government." Box 1690, pp. 1-3, RG 208, WNRC.

Sources on Ideology

Althusser, Louis. *Essays in Self-Criticism.* London: New Left Books, 1976.

_____. *For Marx.* New York: Vintage Books, 1970.

_____. *Lenin and Philosophy and Other Essays.* New York: Monthly Review Press, 1971.

Barthes, Roland. *Mythologies.* New York: Hill and Wang, 1972.

Bell Telephone advertising copy. *Time* 40, no. 9 (11 July 1942), p. 12.

Clarke, Simon, Terry Lovell, Kevin McDonnell, Kevin Robins and Victor Jeleniewski Seidler. *One-Dimensional Marxism.* London: Allison & Busby, 1980.

Eagleton, Terry. *Criticism and Ideology.* London: Verson Editions, 1976.

Filene, Peter Gabriel. *Him/Her/Self.* New York: Harcourt Brace Jovanovich, 1974.

Glover, Katherine. *Women at Work in Wartime.* New York: Public Affairs Committee, Inc., 1943.

Guterman, Norbert. [Review of books on propaganda analysis]. *Studies in Philosophy and Social Science* 9, no. 1 (1941), pp. 158–62.

Hirst, Paul. *On Law and Ideology.* Atlantic Highlands, New Jersey: Humanities Press, 1979.

Kellner, Douglas. "Ideology, Marxism, And Advanced Capitalism." *Socialist Review* 8, no. 6 (November/December 1979), pp. 37–65.

Lacan, Jacques. *Ecrits.* New York: W. W. Norton & Company, Inc., 1977.

Laclau, Ernesto. *Politics and Ideology in Marxist Theory.* London: Verso Editions, 1977.

MacCabe, Colin. "The discursive and the ideological in film: Notes on the conditions of political intervention." *Screen* 19, no. 4 (Winter 1978/79), pp. 29–44.

Marx, Karl. *Capital.* New York: International Publishers, 1967.

_____. *A Contribution to the Critique of Political Economy.* Moscow: Progress Publishers, 1970.

Marx, Karl and Frederick Engels. *The German Ideology—Part One.* New York: International Publishers, 1970.

Memorandum from Meredith P. Gilpatrick and Robert Eisner to George S. Pettee. *Statements of Private Thought Leaders on Women and the War.* Office for Emergency Management, File 58, Box 1849. RG 44, WNRC.

Memorandum from D. W. Smithburg to George Pettee. *Government Statements on Women.* Office for Emergency Management, File 56, Box 1849. RG 44, WNRC.

Memorandum from Mary Brewster White to Robert R. Ferry. *Womanpower Strategies.* Box 156. RG 208, WNRC.

North American Aviation advertising copy. *Life* 13 (19 October 1942), p. 56.

Office of War Information. *Womanpower Campaigns.* Box 156. RG 208, WNRC.

Rosen, Philip Gershon. "The Concept of Ideology and Contemporary Film Criticism: A Study of the Position of the Journal *Screen* in the Context of the Marxist Theoretical Tradition." Dissertation, University of Iowa, 1978.

Smith, Steven B. *Reading Althusser: An Essay on Structural Marxism.* Ithaca: Cornell University Press, 1984.

War Advertising Council, Inc. *How Industry Can Help the Government's Information Program on WOMANPOWER.* Box 156. RG 208, WNRC.

_____. *How Your Advertising Can Help the Veteran Readjust to Civilian Life.* Box 167. RG 208, WNRC.

War Manpower Commission, Information Service. *America at War Needs Women at Work.* Box 156. RG 208, WNRC.

Williams, Raymond. *Marxism and Literature.* Oxford: Oxford University Press, 1977.

Working Papers in Cultural Studies 10: On Ideology. No. 10. 1977.

Sources on Texts and Textuality

Balio, Tino, ed. *The American Film Industry.* Madison: University of Wisconsin Press, 1976.

Barthes, Roland. *S/Z.* New York: Hill & Wang, 1974.

Bathrick, Serafina. "The Past as Future: Family and the American Home in *Meet Me in St. Louis.*" *The Minnesota Review,* No. 6 (Spring 1976), pp. 132–39.

Bellour, Raymond. "Psychosis, Neurosis, Perversion." *Camera Obscura* 3-4 (Summer 1979), pp. 105–132.

_____. "Hitchcock, the Enunciator." *Camera Obscura* 2 (Fall 1977), pp. 69–94.

Benveniste, Emile. *Problems of General Linguistics.* Coral Gables, Florida: University of Miami Press, 1971.

Bergstrom, Janet. "Alternation, Segmentation, Hypnosis: Interview with Raymond Bellour." *Camera Obscura* 3-4 (Summer 1979), pp. 71–104.

_____. "Enunciation and Sexual Difference (Part I)." *Camera Obscura* 3-4 (Summer 1979), pp. 33–70.

Campbell, Joseph. *The Hero with a Thousand Faces.* Cleveland: The World Publishing Company, 1949.

Chatman, Seymour. *Story and Discourse.* Ithaca: Cornell University Press, 1978.

Coward, Rosalind and John Ellis. *Language and Materialism.* London: Routledge & Kegan Paul, 1977.

De Lauretis, Teresa. *Alice Doesn't.* Bloomington: Indiana University Press. 1984.

Derrida, Jacques. *Of Grammatology.* Baltimore: Johns Hopkins University Press, 1974.

Doane, Mary Ann. *The Desire to Desire.* Bloomington: Indiana University Press, 1987.

_____, Patricia Mellencamp and Linda Williams. *Re-Vision: Essays in Feminist Film Criticism.* Frederick, Md: University Publications of America, Inc. and the American Film Institute. 1984.

Dyer, Richard. *Stars.* London: British Film Institute, 1979.

Eckert, Charles W. "The Anatomy of a Proletarian Film: Warner's *Marked Woman.*" *Film Quarterly* 17, no. 2 (Winter 1973/74), pp. 10-24.

Edinburgh '77 Magazine: History/Production/Memory. No. 2. 1977.

Elsaesser, Thomas. "Tales of Sound and Fury: Observations on the Family Melodrama." *Movies and Methods, Volume II,* Bill Nichols, ed. Berkeley: University of California Press, 1985. pp. 165-189.

"Female Representation and Consumer Culture" (special issue). *Quarterly Review of Film Studies* 10, no. 4 (Fall 1985).

Fischer, Lucy. "Two-Faced Women: The Double in Women's Melodrama of the 1940s." *Cinema Journal* 23, no. 1 (Fall 1983), pp. 24-43.

Foucault, Michel. *The Archaeology of Knowledge and the Discourse on Language.* New York: Harper & Row, 1972.

Freud, Sigmund. "Family Romances." *The Sexual Enlightenment of Children.* New York: Collier Books, 1963; see pp. 41-45.

Frye, Northrop. *Anatomy of Criticism—Four Essays.* Princeton: Princeton University Press, 1957.

Haskell, Molly. *From Reverence to Rape: The Treatment of Women in the Movies.* New York: Penguin Books, 1973.

Heath, Stephen. "Contexts." *Edinburgh Magazine.* No. 2, 1977.

Higham, Charles and Joel Greenberg. *Hollywood in the Forties.* London: A. Zwemmer Limited, 1968.

Jardine, Alice and Paul Smith, eds. *Men in Feminism.* New York: Methuen, 1987.

Johnston, Claire, ed. *Notes on Women's Cinema.* London: SEFT, 1973.

_____. *The Work of Dorothy Arzner.* London: British Film Institute, 1975.

Kaplan, E. Ann. *Women and Film: Both Sides of the Camera.* New York: Methuen, 1983.

_____, ed. *Women in Film Noir.* London: British Film Institute, 1978.

Kuhn, Annette. *Women's Pictures: Feminism and Cinema.* London: Routledge & Kegan Paul, 1982.

Macherey, Pierre. *A Theory of Literary Production.* London: Routledge & Kegan Paul, 1978.

Manvell, Roger. *Films and the Second World War.* New York: Dell Publishing Co., Inc., 1974.

Marks, Elaine and Isabelle de Courtivron, eds. *New French Feminisms: An Anthology.* New York: Schocken Books, 1981.

Mellen, Joan. *Women and Their Sexuality in the New Film.* New York: Horizon Press, 1973.

Metz, Christian. *Film Language.* New York: Oxford University Press, 1974.

_____. "The Imaginary Signifier." *Screen* 16, no. 2 (Summer 1975), pp. 14-76.

Mitchell, Juliet. *Psychoanalysis and Feminism.* New York: Vintage Books, 1974.

Morella, Joe; Edward Z. Epstein and John Griggs. *The Films of World War II.* Seacaucus, New Jersey: The Citadel Press, 1973.

Mulvey, Laura. "Afterthoughts On 'Visual Pleasure and Narrative Cinema' Inspired by *Duel in the Sun* (King Vidor, 1946)." *Framework* 15/16/17 (Summer 1981), pp. 12-15.

_____. "Visual Pleasure and Narrative Cinema." *Screen* 16, no. 3 (Autumn 1975), pp. 6-18.

Polan, Dana. *History, Narrative, and the American Cinema, 1940-1950.* New York: Columbia University Press, 1986.

Propp, Vladimir. *Morphology of the Folktale.* Austin: University of Texas Press, 1968.

Radway, Janice. *Reading the Romance: Women, Patriarchy and Popular Literature*. Chapel Hill: University of North Carolina Press, 1984.

Renov, Michael. "Advertising/Photojournalism/Cinema: The Shifting Rhetoric of Forties Female Representation." *Quarterly Review of Film Studies* 10, no. 4 (Fall 1985).

_____. "From Fetish to Subject: The Containment of Sexual Difference in Hollywood's Wartime Cinema." *Wide Angle* 5, no. 1 (Winter 1982), pp. 16–27.

_____. "From Identification to Ideology: The Male System of Hitchcock's *Notorious*." *Wide Angle* 4, no. 1 (Summer 1980), pp. 30–37.

_____. "The Hollywood Film as Ideological State Apparatus." *Film Reader* 5 (Winter 1981–82), pp. 216–226.

_____. "*Leave Her to Heaven:* The Double Bind of the Post-War Woman." *Journal of the University Film and Video Association* 35, no. 1 (Winter 1983), pp. 28–36.

_____. "*Raw Deal:* The Woman in the Text." *Wide Angle* 6, no. 2 (Fall 1984), pp. 18–22.

Rosen, Marjorie. *Popcorn Venus*. New York: Avon Books, 1973.

Shindler, Colin. *Hollywood Goes to War: Films and American Society 1939-52*. London: Routledge & Kegan Paul, 1979.

Sklar, Robert. *Movie-Made America*. New York: Random House, 1975.

Suid, Lawrence H. *Guts and Glory—Great American War Movies*. Reading, Massachusetts: Addison-Wesley Publishing Company, 1978.

Waldman, Diane. "Horror and Domesticity: The Modern Gothic Romance Film of the 1940s." Dissertation, University of Wisconsin, Madison, 1981.

Walsh, Andrea S. *Women's Film and Female Experience: 1940-1950*. New York: Praeger, 1984.

Wolfenstein, Martha and Nathan Leites. *Movies: A Psychological Study*. New York: Atheneum, 1977.

Wood, Michael. *America in the Movies*. New York: Dell Publishing Co., Inc., 1975.

Index

9.27.88

9.27.88   pub $49.95   #37045